# COLORING
# THE NEWS

# COLORING
# THE NEWS

How Crusading for Diversity
Has Corrupted American Journalism

## William McGowan

ENCOUNTER BOOKS
SAN FRANCISCO

First edition published in 2001 by Encounter Books, an activity of Encounter for Culture and Education, Inc., a nonprofit tax exempt corporation.

Encounter Books website address: www.encounterbooks.com

Manufactured in the United States and printed on acid-free paper.

The paper used in this publication meets the minimum requirements of ANSI/NISOZ39.48-1992 (R 1997)(Permanence of Paper).

FIRST EDITION

Library of Congress Cataloging-in-Publication Data

McGowan, William, 1956-
   Coloring the news : how crusading for diversity has corrupted American
   journalism/William McGowan – 1st ed.
   p. cm.
   Includes index.
   ISBN 1-893554-28-7 (alk. paper)
1.   Journalism—Social aspects—United States. 2. Minorities—Press coverage—UnitedStates. I. Title.

   PN4888.M56 M39 2001
   070.4′493058′00973—dc21
   2001045125


10 9 8 7 6 5 4 3

*To the McGowans and the Lilienthals.*

# Contents

# Preface

With racial preferences under the first barrage of a populist attack that would continue for the rest of the decade, the *New York Times Magazine* in June 1995 ran a cover story headlined "What Happened to the Case for Affirmative Action?" Written by journalist Nicholas Lemann, author of an award-winning book on race called *The Promised Land*, the nine-thousand-word article stood out from most reportage devoted to this contentious issue in its detail and its depth of historical analysis.

Despite its attempts to summon a tone of scholarly detachment, however, Lemann's article was hardly neutral in its politics. Complaining that the case for affirmative action was not a simple one to make, the piece was clearly an attempt to rally the troops and to offer loyalists an ideological action plan. Explaining that affirmative action had become so vulnerable because a serious public debate about it had never taken place, Lemann wrote: "As far as the public discourse goes, the next move is affirmative action's supporters to make. They need to acknowledge and confront the other side's position and then explain why, nonetheless, America should still support affirmative action programs."

Lemann rested much of his case on an African-American doctor in southern California named Patrick Chavis, then forty-one. In 1975, Chavis had been one of five black students admitted to the University of California at Davis Medical School under a special minority preference program that would later be ruled unconstitutional by the Supreme Court's 1978 *Bakke* decision. Raised in poverty by a single mother, Chavis had returned to the ghetto after graduating to establish a thriving Ob-Gyn practice serving poor people in the blighted Los Angeles suburb of Compton.

To Lemann, Chavis was affirmative action personified—a living and breathing refutation of the conservative claim that racial preferences favored unqualified minorities over better-qualified whites. If

1

Chavis had not gotten into medical school, Lemann wrote, "his patients wouldn't be treated by some better qualified white obstetrician, they would have no doctor at all, and their babies would be delivered the way Chavis was, by whoever happened to be on duty at the emergency room of the county hospital."

By contrast there was Allan Bakke himself, the medical school applicant whose college grades and board scores made him the "better qualified" candidate whose place Chavis had taken. Bakke had eventually also gotten into the UC Davis medical school, courtesy of the 1977 Supreme Court ruling. But according to Lemann, he had not "set the world on fire as a doctor." After completing a residence in anesthesiology at the Mayo Clinic, Bakke, noted Lemann condescendingly, settled in Minnesota where "he had no private practice," and worked on an interim basis rather than as a staff physician at an obscure community college. To underscore the contrast to Chavis, who was photographed for the magazine's cover in hospital scrubs cradling a black baby he had just delivered, Bakke was photographed in shirtsleeves, carrying a briefcase as he walked across a parking lot.

Lemann used Chavis to illustrate one of his article's main points: that a meritocratic system based on measurements of aptitude like the SATs and medical boards is not just a denial of opportunity to individuals but a "denial of talent" to society. Unless "merit" systems like medical school admissions accommodated the diversity that an individual like Chavis represented, there was no other choice but to rely on preferences to provide minority communities with the professionals they would not otherwise have.

Chavis also provided Lemann with a means to boost affirmative action as a corrective to persistent white racism. Although conservatives liked to talk about a colorblind society, according to Lemann, "Chavis sees the old fashioned kind of racial discrimination everywhere": in the refusal of the Bank of America to give him a loan to build a house in Compton; in the decision of Long Beach Memorial Hospital to put him under professional review; in the fact that the IRS and state tax authorities had launched audits into his finances. These were not accidents, Chavis alleged, a charge that Lemann echoed.

After the beatification by the *New York Times Magazine*, Patrick Chavis became a symbol for supporters of affirmative action and was featured in a number of glowing media profiles during the bitter 1996 campaign for the California Civil Rights Initiative, or Proposition 209. According to *The Nation*, Chavis had an exemplary record in "providing primary care to poor women." Although Allan Bakke's scores were higher, the magazine asked, "Who made the most of his medical school education? From whom did California taxpayers benefit more?" Chavis also became the subject of partisan political rhetoric. According to Senator Ted Kennedy, who hailed him before the Senate Labor and Human Relations Subcommittee, he was the "perfect example" of affirmative action beneficiaries who later in life "are likely to benefit their professions and the communities in which they live."

Two years after Nicholas Lemann's piece first appeared, however, those portraying Patrick Chavis as a poster boy for racial preferences saw their efforts blow up in their faces. On June 19, 1997, the Medical Board of California suspended his license to practice medicine, citing his "inability to perform some of the most basic duties required of a physician." Finding him guilty of gross negligence and incompetence in the cases of three patients—one of whom had died—California administrative law judge Samuel Reyes said that letting Chavis "continue in the practice of organized medicine will endanger the public health, safety and welfare." Soon after, the Los Angeles district attorney announced that Chavis was the subject of a criminal investigation.

According to medical board investigators, Chavis had engaged in egregious malpractice while performing liposuction procedures on patients in a body-sculpting practice he had started as a side business after taking a cosmetic surgery seminar in Beverly Hills. For doctors looking for easy cash, liposuction had become a lucrative and largely unregulated business, and Chavis's New Attitude Body Sculpting had flourished, even in hard-bitten Compton. But the four-day short course Chavis had attended left him inadequately prepared to handle complications. Patients who lived told harrowing tales of Chavis's postoperative neglect when the procedures he had performed went bad.

After one botched procedure, Chavis stashed a patient in his home instead of admitting her to the hospital. Abandoning her for nearly forty hours, the doctor refused to return the frantic phone calls of the patient, who lost nearly 70 percent of her blood and was admitted to a hospital with a severe abdominal infection. A second patient told an almost identical story: a botched liposuction, massive internal bleeding, and Chavis's almost inhuman indifference to her suffering. A third patient was not as lucky. After another botched procedure, Chavis left her in his office for four and half hours, her blood pressure plummeting from severe abdominal hemorrhage, which left his clinic floor puddled with blood. By nightfall she was in cardiac arrest and died while her husband rushed her to the hospital.

Medical board investigators also heard from a doctor who had worked with Chavis. Citing "poor impulse control and sensitivity to patients' pain," the doctor gave investigators a tape recording of patients screaming horrifically, with Chavis responding, "Don't talk to the doctor while he is working," and, "Liar, liar, pants on fire." In addition, Chavis refused to take responsibility for anything that had happened to his patients. According to investigators, at one point Chavis said that it was the husband of the dead patient who should be brought up on charges, claiming that he had picked her up and put her into a wheelchair after surgery in violation of procedure. At another point he said he was the victim of a racist medical system that didn't like to see a black doctor do well.

Whether Chavis's egregious professional misconduct was an indictment of the affirmative action policies that launched him in his medical career more than twenty years before, or just the tragic meltdown of an individual with personal problems, was debatable. But fair-minded people should be able to agree on this much: After having set him up as such a model for "diversity" in university admissions, news organizations should at least have felt an obligation to report the sequel to the story. Indeed, as most journalists freely admitted when I spoke to them about the case, if it had been Allan Bakke who was caught in such flagrant malpractice, the press would have been all over the story without questioning the newsworthiness of such a development. But most of the media—print and broadcast, local and national—ducked the tragic denouement of the Patrick Chavis story.

The *Los Angeles Times,* which had profiled Chavis in glowing terms as a victim of white racism several years before, reported Chavis's suspension, as well as the gruesome details behind it when the story first broke. But it took more than two months for the paper to identify him as the same Dr. Patrick Chavis who allegedly made the case for affirmative action. And even when it did get around to tackling that angle of the story, the *Times* did so in the most anguished and ambiguous terms, giving space to defenders of affirmative action who rejected the notion that Chavis's downfall stood for anything larger than one man's weakness and allowing Chavis himself to call the official sanctions against him "a lynching." The same was true of the *Washington Post*, which ran nothing about the Chavis case in its national news pages, but did run a snide op-ed piece disparaging those who would make the Chavis case "a cautionary tale" about the danger of racial preference.

The *New York Times* itself, however, committed the most glaring journalistic malpractice. Of course the *Times Magazine*, which printed Nicholas Lemann's encomium about Chavis before the gruesome news about his liposuction patients, can be forgiven for not seeing into the future. One might wonder, though, whether Lemann, in setting Chavis up as a symbol, was overly credulous in evaluating the black doctor's Albert Schweitzer–like boasts, as well as in accepting the accusations of racism he made against loan officers and tax authorities. One might also ask whether a writer less openly sympathetic to affirmative action might have discovered Chavis's darker side as a result of more dogged and objective reporting. (A lot of the testimony considered at Chavis's license revocation hearing, for instance, involved a pattern of behavior that had occurred well before the *Times Magazine* piece was published.)

Should Lemann have informed the magazine of subsequent findings? More to the point, shouldn't he have published something to correct the impression his original piece had left with its readers? But even if it could be argued that such a follow-up was tactically impossible in a weekly insert, what of the daily *New York Times'* decision to ignore the Chavis malpractice story completely when it broke? Although Chavis had blood on his hands in a real sense, the *Times* ran nothing to amend its false portrait of an affirmative action hero, or to question the legitimacy of the race-conscious social policy that had made him a doctor. A riveting, nationally newsworthy story central to the country's discussion of racial preferences somehow ended up completely falling through the cracks.

In July 1999, several thousand minority journalists gathered in Seattle for a convention called UNITY '99. Jointly sponsored by the country's Black, Latino, Asian-American, and Native-American journalists' associations, UNITY '99 was underwritten with the generous assistance of the *New York Times*, the *Washington Post*, the major network news organizations, and other powers of American corporate journalism. For five days, the attendees participated in a series of plenary sessions and panel discussions on topics important to the cause of minority representation in the news business. The UNITY convention also doubled as a minority jobs fair, with news executives from around the country recruiting fresh new "faces of color" or poaching veterans from rivals. In fact, the minority jobs fair at UNITY was the biggest jobs fair of any kind in the history of American journalism, a sign of the importance that news organizations were attaching to the diversity movement.

UNITY '99 was the successor to an earlier minority journalists' gathering that took place five years before in Atlanta. Like its predecessor, the program of UNITY '99 boasted a variety of media luminaries such as Carole Simpson and Farai Chideya of ABC News, and Ray Suarez, then of NPR's *Talk of the Nation* and now at PBS's *Newshour with Jim Lehrer,* as well as some of the top print editors in the country, including Len Downie of the *Washington Post,* Mark Whittiker of *Newsweek,* Howell Raines of the *New York Times,* and Norman Pearlstine of Time-Warner. The parties and receptions too were lavish and glittering, with generous corporate benefactors—Knight-Ridder, Times-Mirror and Gannett, to name but a few of more than two hundred media corporations showing their flags—providing nothing but the best in the hospitality suites of Seattle's best hotels and restaurants.

As was done at the previous minority journalists' convention— and at nearly every other news industry gathering for most of the last decade—UNITY '99 convention participants loudly affirmed diversity as crucially important in bringing the news industry in line with the country's fast-changing racial and ethnic demographics, and in showing the proper sensitivity to minority communities often offended by organizations allegedly riddled with white majoritarian biases. They just as loudly scolded the news business, generally perceived as doing too little promote diversity, especially as the year 2000 loomed and long-states public promises of ethnic and racial proportionalism in newsrooms were falling far short of the participants' expectations.

In these professional gatherings, where the virtue of diversity is taken as dogma, people rarely stand up to challenge its driving assumptions or to question its journalistic impact. There may be a handful of dissenters here and there, but the criticisms they make are generally dismissed as reactionary grumbling from an old guard that needs to get out of the way; the facts they cite in their arguments just don't seem to be heard. Questions probing how the easy acceptance of the politics of diversity might be related to journalistic train wrecks like the Patrick Chavis story are unwelcome. A spirit of political advocacy and ethnic activism rules. As Kara Briggs, president of the Native American Journalists Association, insisted in one UNITY-related interview: "I was born into a tribe, not a newspaper."

Not that there was a shortage of opportunities to probe all sides of these complicated diversity-related issues. Times-Mirror, for example, sponsored a session called "Balance or Bias: Affirmative Action and the News Media." According to its promotional literature, the point of the panel was "to develop a report card" on the way affirmative action was being covered.

But the panel included nine supporters of affirmative action who easily overwhelmed the two opponents. One of the supporters was Farai Chideya, an ABC News correspondent who often reports on racial matters. Warning of incipient "de facto apartheid," she said that supporters of I-200, a 1998 Washington State ballot initiative that banned using race as a factor in public education admissions and public-sector hiring, had won a victory similar to that of Afrikaners in pre-Mandela South Africa. Instead of a detached inquiry into the professional quality of the coverage of affirmative action, the panel was almost wholly concerned with the politics of the issue, and roundly resisted unwelcome questions that might throw doubt on the issue itself and the way American journalism as a whole tends to report on it.

This book represents an effort on my part to pose unwelcome questions such as those dodged in the initial coverage of Patrick Chavis and at UNITY '99, and to raise intelligent dissent about the disturbing conformity that has spread over the journalistic community. For most of the 1990s I have been intrigued by journalism's attempts to deal with the issue of diversity and have followed efforts at major news organizations all around the country. While it has been interesting to see the effects on the internal workings of the newsroom itself, I have also been most curious about the impact that diversity is having on news coverage itself, particularly coverage of what might be called "diversity issues" of immigration, race, gay rights, feminism, and affirmative action. I think it is fair to say that these are the most important social issues facing the country—the core of what the pundits call "the culture wars." Has diversity helped or hindered American journalism's ability to make sense of them, and by extension, American society's ability to come to terms with them?

Given the industry's past sins of racial, ethnic and cultural exclusion, the steps it has taken to enhance minority representation in newsrooms and in news coverage represent a worthy, overdue, and historically necessary effort. But after nearly a decade of monitoring how the nation's most important news organizations cover these issues, I would say that the drive for greater diversity has failed to yield better journalism, and that this has negative implications for American society's growth as a multicultural society.

In a perverse Orwellian twist, instead of expanding the bandwidth of opinion, experience, and perspectives that are acknowledged in news coverage and commentary, diversity-oriented journalism has actually allowed a narrow multicultural orthodoxy to restrict debate just when the discourse about our changing national identity needs to be robust, well informed and honest. Instead of fostering detached, neutral reporting and analysis, the diversity mandate has given us advocacy. With the cultural topography of the country shifting beneath our feet, we need a press capable of framing essential questions and providing honest, candid and dependable answers. But the diversity-driven journalism we are getting has not done this, a failure that has consequences for our policy responses and our politics and our national conversation.

Most of those critical of the news industry's diversity effort have been conservatives offended by what they see as reporting skewed against their values. But liberals should also be dismayed. The identity politics that diversity journalism encourages is hardly the "progressive" force that its champions insist it is; for it runs at odds with the goal of assimilation and integration that progressives have historically championed. Liberals might also lament the way diversity journalism has contributed to liberalism's intellectual stagnation, as well as its debilitating self-righteousness, by depriving it of facts and insights that might encourage a re-thinking of dated positions..

Neither a conservative nor a liberal, I consider myself a pragmatist deeply committed to a frank and fair rendering of facts, to an intellectually honest, balanced debate about controversial diversity-related issues, and to the ideal of objectivity, which has come under fire in journalism and in the postmodern, multicultural university. Even if you are ideologically predisposed to pro-diversity political positions, I'd like to think that the facts I have marshaled will convince you that the journalism I have scrutinized has a slant to it, and that this slant may not be such a good thing for our country. I believe the public deserves unbiased information to help it through the democratic decisions it needs to make—and that journalism has an obligation to put aside its own political biases in the process of providing that information. Our press needs to rediscover a reverence for "armed neutrality in the face of doctrines," as Giovanni Papini, a disciple of the philosopher William James, once phrased it. To the extent that it has not done this, and to the extent that the diversity crusade plays a role in that failure, there is cause for concern—and a purpose for this book.

# ONE

# Overview

The coloring of the news is one of those stories that have been happening more or less invisibly for some years. By December 1992, it was not only in the cultural air, but very much on the table at the joint Diversity Summit Meeting of the American Society of Newspaper Editors and the Newspaper Association of America. This get-together had the unmistakable air of a tent revival, full of grim jeremiads, stern calls for repentance and holy roller zeal. Diversity had been fast becoming one of the most contentious issues in American society and in American journalism, responsible for polarizing, if not balkanizing, more than one newsroom around the country. Yet only one side of the issue was present in this crowd. Speaker after speaker got up to declaim in favor of diversity and to warn of editorial sin and financial doom if this cause was not embraced.

The Newspaper Association of America is a publishers' organization, concerned with advertising, circulation, and other business-related issues. The American Society of Newspaper Editors has a different brief, concerning itself with the broad issues of news coverage and the news-gathering process—with journalism proper. The nature of their relationship is often likened to that between Church and State; when the two sides are in agreement, it is often a cause for anxiety, at least among the journalists who are always fretting about the perception that they are sacrificing editorial integrity for the sake of ad sales or circulation figures. But on that day in December, the two sides were definitely on the same page and no one was worried about a loss of objectivity.

From one corner came a declaration that diversity was crucial if the news industry was to realize its mission of "service to democracy." From the other corner, a promise "not to stop until we have met our goal of an industry that reflects the diversity of our society." Most of the big-shots in that room hadn't gotten their hands inky in years. But if they had tried to distill the essence of the meeting, their headline might be: "Diversity: Makes Good Editorial Sense; Makes Good Business Sense Too."

Sitting on a bench in the back of the hotel ballroom where guests of the conference were allowed to observe proceedings, I wondered whether I had fallen into some kind of parallel universe where reality was turned inside out. Journalism, as I had known it, was distinguished by its gratuitous cynicism, brash iconoclasm and ready impertinence. As *Washington Post* columnist Richard Cohen has said, practicing it well requires a "religious belief in absolutely nothing, a conviction that nothing can be taken on faith." But in this room at least, the normal rules of engagement seemed to have been turned on their head, and all the gospel hours of "testifying" that I was hearing produced a sense of cognitive dissonance.

On another level, though, the zealotry was entirely understandable. In the preceding few years, the cause of diversity had become a crusade across the length and breadth of the American media, and would be a defining and dominating force in journalism in the decade to come. Almost every day after that 1992 meeting, one could hear echoes from it in newspaper stories and nightly network broadcasts. Diversity was the new religion, and anybody who wanted to be anybody in the news industry had to rally behind it.

At news organizations both large and small, print and broadcast, managers were rushing to change "the way we view each other and the way we view the news," in the words of Arthur Sulzberger Jr., publisher of the *New York Times*. They were embracing an array of measures designed to increase minority representation both on their news staffs and on their news pages. In a profession historically wary of championing social causes, diversity had become *the* social cause, a path to salvation that would both improve the quality of American journalism and make it more attractive to an increasingly diverse set of readers.

To increase the racial and ethnic diversity of their staffs, almost every major news organization has mounted a "pluralism plan" with aggressive hiring and promotion goals, and created a special "diversity steering committee" to oversee it—the "Diversity or Die" committee, as Sulzberger jokingly called his organization's task force in his Diversity Summit speech. In some places, such as the *New York Times*, the *Los Angeles Times*, and the *Philadelphia Inquirer*, top editors have openly admitted to relying on quotas, favoring less qualified minority candidates in filling positions, and violating hiring freezes when minority journalists have been in short supply. Nearly all major news organizations have created special internship and training programs for nonwhites. At the *New York Times,* three out of four James R. Reston Reporting Fellows, participants in a prestigious internship program for college students, were minorities in 2001. At the eleven newspapers owned by the Tribune Company—parent of such publications as the *Baltimore Sun, Newsday* and the *Los Angeles Times*—there is a special two-year internship program devoted exclusively to nonwhites, with no corresponding company-wide training program for nonminorities.

News organizations have also shown support for a variety of special fellowship programs for "multicultural management" which have been instituted to help nonwhite journalists increase managerial skills so they are more desirable candidates for promotions. To further the goal of putting minorities in decision-making positions, newsroom managers have also developed special mentoring programs, and have tried to boost the visibility and status of talented minority journalists by sending them off to prestigious mid-career enrichment programs like Harvard's Nieman Foundation Fellowship.

At an increasing number of news organizations, the pay and promotion opportunities of senior editors is linked to the number of minority journalists they hire, retain and promote. At the Time-Warner magazines, for example, new editor in chief Norman Pearlstine has decreed that 10 percent of the bonuses managing editors can receive should be linked to how successful they are "at hiring and promoting minorities." Those editors who can show measurable gains make more money. Those who don't will find their salaries and career prospects diminished. And even where pay has not been pegged to recruitment, there have been deliberate efforts to insulate nonwhites from the layoffs and force reductions that have been common in the news business over the last several years.

Some of the larger news organizations have created positions for special diversity development editors, or, as at the news networks, positions with titles like "Senior Vice-President, Diversity." Often their sole task is to prospect for desirable minority candidates, but at some news organizations they sit in on daily news meetings and contribute to coverage decisions. These development editors are a fixture at minority job fairs, where first-time minority job seekers, as well as seasoned pros, find a reception many of their nonminority peers often envy. Recruiting of first-time job seekers and poaching of those who already have positions elsewhere also take place at the national conventions of the various minority journalists' associations, such as the National Association of Black Journalists, the National Association of Hispanic

Journalists, the National Lesbian and Gay Journalists Association, and the Asian American Journalists Association. These conventions often pursue a political as much as a professional agenda. But the conflicts of interest don't seem to faze senior managers, who attend faithfully, underwrite special projects, throw lavish parties, and release minority staff from daily duties so they can attend.

To increase the amount and the sensitivity of the coverage given to minority issues, many news organizations have created special beats and columns reserved for blacks, Latinos, Asians, gays, and self-identified feminists; these special vehicles are used to articulate what the news industry refers to as "separate and distinct minority points of view." The broadcasting industry has made analogous moves, triggering heated competition for the right "faces of color" to anchor the news or cover certain beats. Some news organizations have launched special syndicated features, making the work of prominent minority writers available to smaller papers without the resources to recruit their own.

Most of the major newspapers have an in-house "ombudsman," and often as not, especially at the larger urban papers, those promoted into these positions have been minorities. Other news organizations have developed ethnically and racially sensitive "style guides" which advise writers and editors of the proper terms to be used in writing about various racial and ethnic groups or addressing certain ethnically or racially charged issues. In 1999, for instance, the style manual used at the *New York Times* counseled that reporters and editors avoid using "voodoo" as a term of disparagement, since "voodoo is a religion with many followers" who might get upset by hints that it might involve "irrational beliefs."

Still other newspapers have pursued sensitivity through revised photo policies, taking pains to avoid using images that show minorities in unnecessarily negative or stereotypical ways. At some places, special minority review committees vet certain news pieces before publication or broadcast and strategize with editors on how best to cover a particular minority community. In 1992, for instance, the *San Jose Mercury News*, which had been chided for the lack of ethnic faces in its news pages, established what it called a "change pod" made up of five reporters and an editor who would focus on the influx of Latino and Asian immigrants transforming Silicon Valley. "It was an explicit recognition by the paper that it hadn't gotten the job done," the team director declared.

In some news organizations, managers have issued what are called "mainstreaming guidelines" to ensure that stories reflect proper ethnic and racial balance in sources cited. To assist in such mainstreaming efforts, newsroom managers have devised a variety of tools, from color-coded charts hanging on a newsroom wall to special computer programs that track the number of times a minority source database has been consulted by a particular reporter over a set length of time. Such measurements are often incorporated into a reporter's or editor's employee evaluation. Another way news organizations have sought to enforce sensitivity is through the "content audit," in which standardized techniques are used to measure how minority groups are portrayed in pictures and in print, highlighting areas for improvement.

And like the rest of corporate America, newspapers and broadcasters have relied heavily on special "diversity management" seminars. In these sessions, special "diversity consultants" encourage employees to air their complaints about ethnic, racial and gender dynamics within the newsroom, in an attempt to get colleagues to realize how ingrained cultural assumptions of the "dominant" (i.e., white male) culture have hurt both the feelings and the career prospects of nonwhite employees. Top editors have gone away on two- or three-day diversity retreats where they engage in elaborate role-playing games, complete with props and costumes. In preparation for these retreats, managers have been asked to consult specially prepared reading lists said to represent the "authentic voices" of the nonwhite communities into which they want to gain insight.

Encouraging and expanding all of the diversity initiatives by individual news organizations have been the complementary efforts of various professional organizations and foundations. The American Society of Newspaper Editors, for example, has created a position for a special diversity director. In April 2000, the Freedom Forum, underwritten by the Gannett Corporation, announced a program that places more than a hundred minority journalists in special intern programs around the country. The Freedom Forum also established another program that pays for a minority journalism training program at Vanderbilt University. In 1995, the Ford Foundation put money behind the issue of news media diversity, hiring a special program officer to manage grants to various minority journalist organizations. In the year 2000, Ford gave $400,000 to the National Association of Hispanic Journalists and an equal amount to the National Association of Black Journalists.

Some of these steps taken on behalf of diversity are worthy and long overdue. Historically, given the poor record of the press in covering marginalized communities, American journalism really might have an obligation "to compensate for its historical mistreatment of people who are not white, male, or heterosexual," as one journalism professor put it in a letter to the editor of the *Columbia Journalism Review.*

Measured in April 2000, the proportion of minority journalists in newsrooms was 11.6 percent, well below the goal of roughly 25 percent which the American Society of Newspaper Editors promised it would reach by the year 2000—a figure that would have required the industry to make one out of every two hires a minority. This shortfall has been the source of considerable grumbling, with many minority journalists charging the industry with retreating from its stated commitment. But while minority representation in journalism lags behind that of some professions, including psychology, architecture and economics, it is higher than in medicine, law and academia. In many news markets the percentage of minority journalists employed exceeds their proportion of the available labor pool.

Such gains have meant that many talented minority journalists who may have been passed over in a less enlightened era have been given a chance, and have acquitted themselves impressively. The number of nonwhites who have won Pulitzer Prizes (for excellence in print) and Peabody Awards (for broadcasting) is substantial. And whereas the topmost rungs of journalism were completely white a short time ago, journalists of color now occupy them in greater numbers, or are poised just below in key positions as foreign correspondents and city editors, awaiting the day when they will take over the reins. As I write in mid-2001, minorities occupy the position of managing editor or assistant managing editor at some of the biggest and most prominent daily newspapers in the country, including the *New York Times*, the *Los Angeles Times*, the *Washington Post* and the *Boston Globe.*

With more minorities and a greater regard for what are considered "distinct minority perspectives," the press is certainly no longer an all-white bastion focused on all-white precincts of power, where slights and offensive stereotypes go unnoticed and unchallenged. News organizations now use a wider radar screen to monitor their communities, and the expanded reportorial range has encouraged, at many points, gritty, incisive stories that may not have been produced before, or produced as readily. As a result, the realities of minority life that were once excluded from mainstream view are more accessible.

Having greater racial and ethnic breadth on staff also pays dividends in moral authority, as minority reporters often enjoy a license to weigh in on touchy issues that white journalists are reluctant to approach. At the *Washington Post*, for instance, it was a black reporter,

Vanessa Williams, who was able to explain that D.C. mayor Marion Barry's support for the death penalty did not represent pandering to white voters, as many whites in the newsroom assumed, but was a reflection of the black community's growing endorsement of capital punishment.

Yet improved access and greater breadth often come at considerable costs, as the push for diversity has also fed a climate of racial grievance and accusation, undermining newsroom morale and collegiality.

White journalists blame the obsession with diversity for encouraging racial favoritism and double standards, and for crimping their career prospects so that higher-ups can collect fatter bonuses for minority hiring and advancement. In a 1996 study, 40 percent of whites thought lower standards for promotion were applied to blacks. They also frequently complain that race, ethnicity and gender play an unfair role in assignment policies; that managers indulge behavior from minority colleagues (including racist behavior) for which they themselves would be fired or demoted; and that diversity management seminars often amount to little more than Maoist-style self-criticism sessions that create the very racial and ethnic divisiveness they are supposed to help overcome.

Meanwhile, blacks complain about glass ceilings, about lip service from white managers more interested in appearances than real diversity, and about being pigeonholed in Black or Brown beats and being restricted to weekend duty, known at ABC News as the "Third World Ghetto." Minority reporters and editors also complain about their lack of decision-making powers, and express resentment over the feeling that many are there simply to educate whites in what is and is not racially or ethnically offensive.

Sitting front and center at the 1992 Summit meeting, *New York Times* publisher Arthur Sulzberger Jr. put it well when he described a breakdown of communications on his multiracial diversity management committee that had its members "at each other's throats." The "cultural change" involved in diversity, he said, had proved to be "hard, brutal stuff." Sulzberger could have been previewing the complaints of the entire industry which followed his lead in the years to come, embracing diversity without really debating it much, and thus finding itself in a quagmire of diversity-related troubles.

• At the *Miami Herald*, for instance, diversity seems to have been a major reason why a paper once considered one of the country's premier training grounds for national journalists has become, according to *Time* magazine, "a shell of its former self."

Taking over the paper in 1989, publisher David Lawrence committed the *Herald* to an aggressive multicultural vision that would help Miami show the rest of the increasingly diverse United States of America "how you work it out." Under Lawrence the paper hired dozens of Latino reporters, introduced sensitivity training in the newsroom, and created special Latino sections and editions. In a city with a rapidly expanding potential Latino readership, these steps made good journalistic and business sense, Lawrence believed. But some saw problems in the offing. "Will the *Herald* pander to readers to avoid making them mad?" the *New York Times'* Celia Dugger asked. "Will the paper stay away from tough critical reporting because it makes some readers uncomfortable?"

At the time, Lawrence said the answer to these questions was no. But in the following years, many at the paper said otherwise, particularly when it came to the city's ethnically assertive and politically influential Cuban community. According to some, instead of providing the city with honest, fearless coverage of the news, the paper pulled its punches, shying away from rigorous, searching pieces that might call into question the assumptions of Cuban Miami and the actions of its political elite. As one veteran reporter told the *New Republic,* "We quit doing tough stories." The paper was particularly wary of questioning the separatist mind-set of the Cuban community, for whom assimilation "was not on the agenda," as one Miami journalist explained.

One of the most vivid illustrations of the *Herald*'s ethnic pandering was its coverage of the Elián González affair in 1999 and 2000. According to an analysis made by the *New Republic,* the paper demonstrated a pattern of foot-dragging in reporting news developments that supported the return of the seven-year-old Cuban boy to his natural father, allowing itself to be scooped several times by out-of-town competitors. The *New Republic* account also described intense ethnic fractiousness at the paper. Cuban journalists and newsroom staff fell prey to ethnic partisanship that diluted the newsroom's professional detachment on the story, the *New Republic* said. The prickly chauvinism of this newsroom clique also became a headwind for the paper's best and most aggressive reporters, whose commendable efforts were met with charges of anti-Cuban bias.

Columnist Liz Balmaseda caused an uproar when she was photographed outside the house of the González family in a prayer circle. Balmaseda complained to both the paper's editor and the publisher about what she considered the *Herald*'s unsympathetic coverage of the Elián affair; her complaints eventually led to a special meeting between the publisher and the paper's Cuban-American reporters.

Eventually, the atmosphere in the whole newsroom became so strained that unprecedented departmental meetings were held to instruct journalists to refrain from humor that could be deemed insensitive. Tensions were particularly sharp the day federal agents raided the González family home to take the boy into custody. "I'm sure that you are all enjoying what took place in Little Havana and that you will have lots of fun celebrating this move," one young Cuban reporter wrote to his Anglo colleagues on the paper's internal newsroom bulletin board.

• At Gannett Corporation's *USA Today,* a longstanding policy required that editors regularly run photos of minorities above the front-page fold. This, said minority journalists who worked there, let the paper give a sense of the world that moved beyond the "traditional white power structure." But in 1993 Gannett took its picture policy one step further. Members of *USA Today*'s diversity committee now began to comb through every article appearing in the paper on a daily basis, examining the ethnicity of those who were quoted in each story—a process known as "mainstreaming" that seeks to make the pool of experts and authorities that the paper relies on mirror "the face of the country." Reporters didn't have quotas per se for sources, but percentages were worked up and written into evaluations. Assisting this process was a computer database that not only coded sources by race and gender but also gave management a record of how many times individual reporters have logged on to the database. (A related development at Gannett was its "All American Contest," a program covering its ninety-plus other newspapers, tying bonuses, promotions and compensation packages of senior editorial managers to their efforts to increase newsroom diversity and enhance sensitivity to minorities.) In 1997, succumbing to pressure from critics both inside and outside its newsroom, *USA Today* scaled back its mainstreaming policy; although the company still kept numerical tabs, it no longer made these numerical scores part of journalists' individual evaluations.

• At the *Los Angeles Times,* the nation's second-largest metropolitan daily, serving the most diverse (and fragmented) city in the country, a buyout plan was offered in 1992 in an effort to trim newsroom editorial staff. Management was shocked when nearly 10 percent of the newsroom staff took the buyout, four times the number expected. Many were senior editors and reporters in the prime of their careers, including several award-wining journalists. According to sources, the exodus was a reflection of plummeting morale. In the aftermath of the 1992 Los Angeles riots—or "rebellion," as the *Times'* many black staff members called it—management exacerbated racial strains by aggressive affirmative action efforts, including a hiring freeze for white males.

Typical of the steps that poisoned the air at the *Los Angeles Times* were the 1993 "Guidelines for Racial and Ethnic Identification," an amendment to the paper's official style guide that many took to be a parody of a politically correct speech code. Reflecting the heavy hand of powerful minority factions at the paper who were inflamed over what they said was "insensitive" coverage of the riots, the guidelines proscribe such "insensitive" or "offensive" terms as *deaf, Hispanic, alien, Dutch treat, illegitimate, grandmotherly, crazy, lame, middle-aged, tribal, WASP,* and *bi* (for bisexual). The guidelines also counsel writers and editors to avoid characterizing immigration in terms that are negative, as in "tidal wave of immigrants," and they explain that since there is no such thing as a mother who does not work, there cannot be "unemployed mothers."

• Diversity-related controversy erupted again in the *Los Angeles Times* newsroom when new publisher Mark Willes, who took over the job in 1997 in the face of a five-year decline in circulation, proposed the creation of a new section aimed at Latino readers. Claiming such a move was condescending, 108 reporters and editors signed a protest letter denouncing the idea. But within a few months there was more turmoil. In May 1998, Willes told the *Wall Street Journal* he wanted to make the *Times* more appealing to women and minorities by producing stories that were "more emotional, more personal, and less analytic." He also announced a plan to set specific numerical goals for increasing the number of women and minorities quoted in stories and used as sources, and to pay editors partly according to how their reporters met those targets. Citing an internal survey that showed that white males are 80 percent of the paper's subjects, Willes said, "People want to feel like the paper is theirs. They can't do that if the paper is a fundamentally white male newspaper."

Reporters and editors reacted negatively to what many saw as little less than "a quota plan for sources." Some cracked jokes at Willes' expense, and wondered aloud whether there would be goals for each minority group or just minorities in general, and whether they were supposed to guess a source's ethnicity or race in an interview or ask directly. Others confronted Willes at a newsroom staff meeting, saying his assumption that blacks and Hispanics would be more interested in an article in which blacks and Hispanics were quoted was "patronizing and insulting." Calling the plan a "manipulative, market-driven sales approach," assistant Metro editor Bob Baker told the *Washington Post*, "We spend our whole lives denying we write stories a certain way to sell papers and now we're being asked to play that card to appeal to people's most superficial qualities, their race or gender."

Still more controversy arrived in September of the same year when the paper announced the formation of a "Latino Team," comprised of eleven members including reporters from business, sports, and the general news departments. The team would meet daily and plan coverage of Latino issues throughout the paper. According to associate editor Frank del Olmo, the paper's highest-ranking Latino, the idea is "to try to get us far ahead of the curve on Latino stories." But those familiar with the *Los Angeles Times'* hypersensitivity toward Latino issues wondered whether the creation of the team might make it even harder to discuss the hard realities of immigration, bilingualism, assimilation, and other stories that the paper has long been accused of glossing over, spreading an even thicker layer of ethnic protectiveness over contentious subjects at the heart of California's dramatic demographic transformation.

• At the *New York Times*, publisher Arthur Sulzberger Jr., galvanized by the 1992 Diversity Summit Meeting, has repeatedly stressed that diversity is "the single most important issue" facing his paper. According to Sulzberger, "We can no longer offer our readers a predominantly white, straight male vision of events and say that we, as journalists, are doing our job." He has also said that "you can't merely bring in Hispanics or African Americans or Asian Americans and hold them to a standard that says 'Fine, you're in, now behave like a white male.' "

Though bettering the paper's coverage in some ways, Sulzberger's efforts have also produced sharp dissension within the ranks, triggering accusations of both double standards and lingering racial prejudice.

In 1991, editor in chief Max Frankel launched what he called his "own little quota plan," under which he would quicken the pace of minority recruitment by hiring one nonwhite for every white hired. (Under pressure he later backed away from the idea.) Frankel also came under pressure when he admitted at a forum at the Columbia Graduate

School of Journalism that because of political considerations he would hesitate to fire a black female reporter if she was "less good"; minority staffers at the *New York Times* said that Frankel was being patronizing and that his admission threw their competence into doubt.

More diversity-related controversy at the *Times* involved a lawsuit filed in 1996 by former culture editor Angela Dodson. According to Dodson, senior editors gave her the editorial position but did not share real decision-making power with her because she was a black woman with family responsibilities. According to Dodson, the paper's much-vaunted commitment to diversity was hollow on the uppermost levels. What made Dodson's lawsuit even more embarrassing for the *Times* was that Dodson named diversity czarina Carolyn Lee, the paper's assistant managing editor, as one of her primary tormentors, along with the current editor in chief, Joseph Lelyveld, who has made diversity one of his top newsroom priorities.

• Another high-profile embarrassment surrounded the dismissal of *Boston Globe* Metro columnist Patricia Smith. In 1994 Smith became the paper's first black female columnist, winning a nomination for a Pulitzer Prize in 1998 and a writing award from the American Society of Newspaper Editors the same year. After subjecting her work to the periodic checking that all columnists face, *Globe* editors confronted Smith in June 1998 with charges that she had fabricated quotations and made up fictitious people in at least four recent columns. Moving swiftly, the paper's top editors asked for her resignation, which she submitted the same day.

Former colleagues at the *Chicago Sun Times* said this was not the first evidence of Smith making things up, and cited a 1986 incident when she worked there. At the time, the *Sun Times* ran a correction, but Smith was not dismissed. Many in the newsroom felt that her editors had invested so much in her success—and the affirmative action plan she represented—that they accepted an alibi from her that they would not have accepted from a white staffer in the same position.

In the wake of Smith's resignation from the *Globe*, the paper combed through several years' worth of her past columns and found that the pattern of fabrication stretched back to 1996, involving at least fifty-two additional columns. But the real bombshell news involved editor in chief Matt Storin's confession that three years earlier he had significant indications that Smith had been engaging in fabrication, but had not taken disciplinary action because he did not want to be regarded as singling out a black woman.

For many at the *Globe*, the incident focused longstanding, unspoken concerns about diversity. In a blistering attack on the *Globe*'s racial anxieties, Smith's fellow Metro columnist Eileen McNamara denounced Smith and her "enablers," saying that Smith's rise had "everything to do with race." According to McNamara, "An honorable commitment to open these pages to people long unrepresented led to a less than honorable trade-off. Patricia Smith's images were so mesmerizing, her rage so galvanizing that we chose not to see the deceit at their core. It was the worst sort of racism that kept us from confronting the fraud we long suspected…. A white institution is paying now, just as much as a black columnist." Replying, Smith said her colleague's attitude clearly showed that she was considered "the nigger who came to dinner and just wouldn't leave."

• Patricia Smith was barely out the door when the *Boston Globe* became engulfed in another racial controversy involving another of its star Metro columnists, Mike Barnicle. A white, twenty-five-year veteran of the paper with a loyal following among Boston's white working class, Barnicle was accused of stealing material from a book by comedian George Carlin. Nervous about being charged with a racial double standard in the wake of the Smith case, *Globe* editor Matt Storin asked for Barnicle's resignation. But Barnicle's allies in the national media, including NBC's Tim Russert and CNN's Larry King, successfully lobbied on his behalf. To throw Barnicle overboard for such a relatively minor infraction, these defenders argued, would be sacrificing him to an irrationally rigid sense of journalistic justice. Storin backed down, giving Barnicle a two-month suspension instead.

The backpedaling set off a fury in the newsroom. Many editors and reporters at the *Globe* long suspected that Barnicle had fabricated material for some of his stories, though they had no evidence of it. Many newsroom colleagues also felt that Barnicle was a relic of an earlier time, and that the politically conservative white working-class community he was said to represent was on the wrong side of history— and of Boston's surging nonwhite demographics.

Fifty angry staff members, most of them minorities, signed a petition protesting the decision to retain Barnicle. According to one Hispanic reporter, keeping him was a sign that the *Globe* was "a racist institution." Weighing in from his perch at the *New York Times*, which owns the *Globe*, editorial page editor Howell Raines said the bottom line of the Barnicle episode was that "a white guy with the right connections got pardoned for offenses that would have taken down a minority or female journalist."

Barnicle did resign after he was unable to counter charges that he had fabricated a story in 1995—but not before the *Globe,* and its commitment to diversity, showed embarrassing signs of strain. "It's been a terrible time," managing editor Ben Bradlee Jr. told a national media reporter, just after Storin chewed out his city editor for requesting yet another meeting with minority staffers. "It just can't get any worse."

• Diversity has been a source of bitter racial tension at the *Washington Post* too. According to a controversial exposé in the *New Republic* in late 1995, hiring and promotion have caused rancor and contention among the staff. While whites charge that the paper's diversity effort has compelled it routinely to hire minorities whose credentials and competence have been less than standard, blacks claim that they are held to *higher* standards and constantly labor under a racial stigma. The problem of lowered standards for minorities was confirmed in an internal memo that the paper's development editor wrote to her superior, in which she complained that the paper would fall short of its minority hiring goals unless it became more "flexible and creative" in the way it measured whether minority candidates were "ready" for the job.

• At the *Wall Street Journal* in 1994, minority journalists who took offense at a piece by a *Journal* opinion editor circulated a petition demanding that the editor be chastised. The disputed piece had been written freelance by Amity Shlaes for the *Spectator,* a British political magazine, and discussed the racial implications of the high rate of criminality in the black community, a subject that the American press widely regards as taboo. The petition called on editorial management to bar Shlaes from using her institutional affiliation in any subsequent freelance efforts, a demand that management rejected. Nevertheless, the petition made its point. "The circulation of newsroom petitions against journalists who transgress certain ill-defined PC boundaries (generally on race and gender issues) has become an ever more common feature of American newsrooms," wrote media critic Scott McConnell, noting similar efforts at other news organizations. "It is in its way a quite effective way to chill free expression—more so than a formal speech code—and few writers are likely to feel comfortable expressing unpopular ideas after being targeted."

• Newsroom harmony at the *Philadelphia Inquirer* was damaged by a 1996 incident involving a female staffer scrolling through the computer files of Art Carey, a Style section humor columnist, for signs of alleged "insensitivity to women." An old-guard journalist, Carey had previously poked fun at a local feminist icon, and had made a few risqué references to her that some considered demeaning. Defending her own action, the reporter said, "We have rules at this paper about sexism and racism. You simply cannot say demeaning things about minority groups in this paper."

• There's diversity-related trouble even at the entry levels of journalism. Following suggestions from the American Society of Newspaper Editors (ASNE) to boost the number of minority reporters and editors through internship programs, many news organizations have restructured their internships so that only nonwhites may apply. One of them is the *Boston Globe,* which has used the program in conjunction with other diversity efforts to achieve a 17 percent minority representation in the newsroom, well above the industry average. Another is the *New York Times,* which has been known to interview prospective interns at graduate journalism schools on a "minorities only" basis, prompting complaints from excluded whites.

In 1996 the *Globe* became the focus of a racial discrimination complaint filed with the Equal Employment Opportunity Commission (EEOC) after a twenty-three-year-old University of Kansas senior, David Wilson, was told by a *Globe* staffer that he could not even submit an application to the paper's internship program because he was white. Wilson, who had been an intern at the *Kansas City Star,* filed a complaint with the EEOC, saying, "It was kind of a slap in the face to say 'We're not even going to look at you.'"

Finding in Wilson's favor, the EEOC determined that the internship was indeed open only to nonwhites and that Wilson had a basis for a suit. At that point the *Globe* announced it was changing the internship program to include all applicants regardless of race. "We are no longer calling it a minority internship program although we certainly encourage minorities to apply," the paper's spokesman said.

• Even those organizations where the diversity agenda is unquestioned have seen acrimony and accusations arising from it. For most of 1998, the various professional organizations representing journalists of color in the pro-diversity "UNITY" coalition were wracked by dissension. At issue was whether they should cancel their planned UNITY '99 convention in Seattle scheduled for July 1999. Members of the National Association of Black Journalists said they should move the convention out of the state of Washington in protest of the state's Initiative 200, a measure to ban race preferences that would appear on the ballot (and ultimately pass) in November. But other minority organizations were not so inclined, being worried that such a protest might harm the perception of professional impartiality. The quarrel grew so heated that at one point the Unity leadership actually called in a professional diversity trainer to clarify the cultural differences among them. "We couldn't get past one group feeling that their concerns were more important than another group's," said the president of the National Association of Hispanic Journalists.

During the late 1980s I spent a number of years reporting and writing about South Asia, one of the world's most ethnically riven places. I had no ideological predispositions in the matter of ethnic issues or identity politics when I began working there. After a few years as a frontline witness to the tragedy of ethnic violence, however, I left with the understanding that identity politics could be extraordinarily divisive, capable of polarizing a country's political affairs, undermining its economic productivity, weakening its educational institutions, and straining the bonds that hold people together as one nation. The experience also taught me that journalists can play a role in either accelerating the process of ethnic fragmentation or containing it, depending on how committed they are to resisting identity politics and to eschewing the politicization of information.

Given what my South Asian experience revealed to me, it was unsettling to watch the mounting potential for cultural and political fragmentation here in the United States early in the 1990s. Rapidly changing demographics fed by increasingly nonwhite, Third World immigration were combining with a liberal cult of race, ethnicity and gender to mount a broad attack on the sense of a common American identity and the ideal of race-neutrality in public life.

While Americans once automatically saw themselves as a nation of individuals relating to one another through a common culture forged in "the melting pot," the new multicultural vision demanded that America be viewed as a "nation of nations"—a mosaic composed of separate ethnic, racial and gender blocs, each with its own cultural reference points, and each to be judged with respect to the rest of society by its own distinct values and standards. This was a vision that celebrated differences over consensus, and spurned what historian Arthur Schlesinger, in *The Disuniting of America,* referred to as a "transformative identity" based on "the historic promise of America: assimilation and integration." The multicultural vision also supported ethnic, racial and gender grievances against the oppression borne of "white male hegemony," and demanded compensatory preferences to help the aggrieved groups overcome their injury.

This shift from melting pot to mosaic represented a profound change in the ground rules of society, with far-flung implications for the shape of politics and civic culture. In effect it represented a vast national experiment, calling all the old givens into question. Whereas we used to emphasize the melding of individuals into an American whole and tried as much as possible to shun race and ethnicity as factors in the conduct of public life, now we were stressing group identity as a legitimate consideration in making laws and shaping social policy. Whereas colorblindness was once regarded as an uncontested article of liberal faith and the key to the liberal ideal of equality, it was now being disparaged as a defense of the "unleveled playing field." Liberals were once the champions of racial transcendence; now they were fast becoming the biggest exponents of racial determinism—the belief that race, ethnicity, gender and sexual orientation matter above all else.

As antithetical to the core values of traditional liberalism as the new identity politics was, it also defied the sustaining journalistic ethos that traditional liberalism had shaped. For this reason, the press might have been expected to scrutinize closely the premises and assumptions of identity politics, to challenge its attendant cant, and to point out its undesirable consequences where appropriate. Instead, much of mainstream journalism was giving it a pass or, even worse, becoming a vehicle for it.

Rather than pay attention to ground realities, and the prickly and difficult problems associated with changing demographic and social facts, journalism seemed to have become detached, and trapped in airy abstraction. Tough questions that should have been asked about developments such as bilingual education, immigration policy, gay rights, and racial preferences were not surfacing. Pieties crying out for intellectual puncturing—*Diversity is strength! Demography is destiny! Treating people equally means treating them differently!*—were allowed to march forward unexamined. Stories that might have explored the downside of diversity, its wobbly, unexamined assumptions, or its internal contradictions were either ignored or reported with euphemism and embarrassment, as through a fog of avoidance. Unpalatable facts got an airbrushing, while critical voices remained unsought or unacknowledged. Instead of questioning whether multiculturalism was something we really wanted, and letting the American public decide, the press treated it as an immutable *fait accompli,* ignoring competing perspectives and contradictory information that might have cast another light on the concept. The sins of omission were as bad as those of commission, and brought to mind Orwell's famous observation that propaganda is as much a matter of what is left out, as of what is actually said.

On immigration, for example, journalists have tended to embrace a highly romantic, sentimental and historically distorted script which assumes immigration to be an unqualified blessing and minimizes its costs. As the urban historian Peter Salins puts it, the core questions associated with immigration are: "What are we going to become? Who are we? How do the newcomers fit in—and how do the natives handle it?" But it's clear that if the press asks itself these questions at all, it does so in only the most superficial fashion, gliding over realities that might otherwise curb its enthusiasm.

This is so even when evidence of the downside is obvious, as it was in 1992 in New York's Washington Heights, when the justified use of deadly force on the part of a white undercover patrolman was labeled police racism by the *New York Times* and the three-day riot by illegal immigrant Dominican drug dealers was portrayed as justified community outrage. The media script also tends to work hard at filtering out uncomfortable realities that might legitimize calls for tighter controls on newcomers, such as alien criminality, high rates of dependency on social services, the adverse impact that high rates of immigration have had on wages, and the quality of life in areas where newcomers have concentrated. When these realities become unavoidable, as when authorities discovered illegal Thai immigrants living in slavelike conditions in a fortified California sweatshop in 1996, and when illegal aliens tried to blow up the World Trade Center in 1993, journalists will pounce, as they might on any sensational story. But if they explore the conditions that allowed such things to happen, it is almost always after the fact, and after the authorities have taken the lead.

Calls for regulating immigration through enhanced border control and limits on the number of immigrants who might become dependent on the state are in keeping with the legacy of Progressive reforms from the turn of the century, which have historically proved to be key factors in staving off nativist restriction. But contemporary journalists, seeing nativism in almost anything that challenges the doctrine of open borders, have generally scoffed at these old policies. The press has heaped unbridled scorn on reform measures such as the 1996 Immigration Reform Act and the 1994 California Proposition 187, dismissed

as "racist" even in the face of sizable nonwhite support. It has also consistently—and glibly—proclaimed the futility of border enforcement
in a way that makes immigration appear to be an unrestrainable force of
nature.

The subject of cultural difference—another facet of immigration—
also produces journalistic avoidance, or tepid cultural relativism.
Ignoring the precedent set by journalists at the turn of the century who
confronted problems associated with unassimilated newcomers as a
way of making a case for reforms designed to help absorb them into
the mainstream, the press today either turns a blind eye to these problems, or throws its influence behind policies that work against the
process of acculturation and transformation. As the *New York Times* put
it in a long 1998 series on the new "transnational" Third World immigrants, assimilation to an American norm has become, in the eyes of
many, "a dated, even racist concept."

The antagonism to assimilation runs across a variety of fronts,
but is starkest in the coverage of bilingual education and efforts to
reform it. "Reporters just can't see this issue beyond their own ideological bent," said Alice Callahan, a left-wing Episcopal priest who
works with Latino sweatshop workers in Los Angeles, most of whom
supported Proposition 227, a measure against bilingual education, in
1998. "I have been surprised how unwilling they are to entertain a view
of this issue different from their own preconceived view no matter what
the facts are."

Like the anti-assimilationist bias in the coverage of immigration,
the diversity script on race downplays the value and accomplishments
of integration, affirming a subtly separatist sense of black cultural identity in a way that rebukes the race-neutral ideals that guided journalism
in the civil rights period. As a result, news organizations have shown a
decided lack of rigor in reporting on such touchy issues as black cultural separatism. The same cultural relativism—with its implicit double
standards—seems to lie behind the reluctance of many news organizations to explore the more troubling realities of the black underclass:
illegitimacy, welfare dependency, crime, drugs and other manifestations
of antisocial behavior, pathology and dysfunction. Rather than concede there are major problems in black America in order to muster
public support for solutions, the orthodoxy encourages a skittish fear of
feeding pernicious stereotypes.

Reporters who do violate politically correct racial pieties to take
on completely legitimate journalistic subjects often find themselves
charged with racism, or with racial treason, depending on their color. Of

this hypersensitivity, one former *Washington Post* editor said, "The *Post* sees this as enlightenment, but it is really another form of racism because it is based on condescension and fear."

The script on race also tends to mute the reporting on unflattering incidents of black racism and black anti-Semitism as in the case of the *New York Times'* coverage of the anti-Semitic violence in Brooklyn's Crown Heights in 1991, and its coverage of a massacre in a Harlem department store in 1995. When an embarrassing state report came out two years after the Crown Heights riots, the *Times* was forced to run a front-page mea culpa admitting to "blindspots" that made its original reporting "so deficient as to be misleading."

Meanwhile, the press is fixated on the idea of rampant and irredeemable institutional white racism, particularly in the criminal justice system, where white police racism is assumed and facts to the contrary take a back seat. At times this willingness to see racism everywhere has led the press to rush off and cry wolf without grounds, to play into the hands of racial arsonists with agendas, and to deny the reality of racial progress in order to perpetuate a corrosive theology of racial grievance and justify the continuation of racial preferences. Although the facts behind the 1996 wave of arson attacks on black churches in the South were complicated, for instance, news organizations were quick to declare that Mississippi was burning once again. When contradictory facts emerged in isolated corrective reporting, newspapers, television and newsmagazines did not give them appropriate space or attention, leaving behind the impression that we still had not progressed much from the racism of 1963.

The same went for the alarmist reporting in the wake of the Amadou Diallo shooting in New York in 1999, when the *New York Times* tried to paint a picture of minority citizens being just as threatened by racist police as by the criminals the police were trying to neuter. Although the available facts suggested that the police were more restrained than in recent memory, the *Times* painted a picture of white police out of control, much to the detriment of racial harmony and effective police protection of the very minority citizens on whose behalf the *Times* was crusading.

With respect to gay and feminist issues, diversity's enhanced sensitivity has purged news coverage of many of the pernicious stereotypes that governed reporting and commentary in the past. But it has also given the coverage a decidedly partisan edge. Whether the issue be the integration of gays and women into the military, AIDS, abortion, gay marriage or gay adoption, the press has tended to side with gay and feminist interest groups, trimming its news-gathering zeal to filter out realities that might undercut the cause.

The script on gays and feminists also tends to depict any objections to their causes—however well grounded in constitutional, moral or institutional traditions—as outright bigotry, worthy of cartoonish portrayal. Those journalists who voice conservative perspectives—or defend those who do—know they can expect blowback, as much from gay activists in the community as from those within news organizations themselves. After writing a column criticizing gay activists at Harvard in 1997, for instance, conservative *Boston Globe* columnist Jeff Jacoby was attacked by gay newsroom colleagues—including two of his copy editors—as well as the paper's ombudsman, who called Jacoby's work "offensive" and "homophobic." Describing the "chilling effect" such internal criticism has, Jacoby said: "A lot of gay activists think that any point of view different from theirs is not only wrong, but so illegitimate and beneath contempt that it doesn't even deserve to be considered. I know up front that if I want to write about this topic, I have to be prepared to run a gauntlet and to jump a lot of hurdles—not among the readers who I think mostly agree with me, but right here in the newsroom."

In terms of bias, though, no subject bears the mark of the new diversity orthodoxy more than the emotionally divisive issue of affirmative action and the politics of racial preference. For years, most of the national press treated affirmative action with little journalistic rigor and scant regard for contradictory facts. No matter how weighty (or grim) the evidence, as in the case of Dr. Patrick Chavis, most of the journalistic establishment has not been above performing a little cosmetic surgery of its own in order to preserve the correct image.

In recent years there has been more readiness to examine the operational details of preference programs, mainly because of newsworthy efforts on the state and national level to roll back such programs. But the press continues to demonstrate its ideological attachment to affirmative action in the energy it spends discrediting efforts to eliminate preferences, such as California's Proposition 209 in 1996 and Washington State's Initiative 200 in 1998. "There was a reflex in the coverage that started with the assumption that people in [the pro-209 movement] had bad motivations, racial motivations," observed Ronald Brownstein of the *Los Angeles Times.* The ideological slant comes through as well in the hysterical, exaggerated way the short-term consequences of these rollback efforts get reported, as in the much-hyped 1997 "Resegregation of Higher Education" story. Contrary to what so many journalists predicted, steps to end racial preferences in university admissions did not result in "lily-white" campuses. In fact, Asian students, not whites, gained in percentage representation, and those minorities who were displaced from the elite schools actually ended up in places more appropriate to their academic qualifications, where they would graduate at higher rates than before. And by mid-2000, the percentage of minority students throughout the University of California system, the focus of most of the "resegregation of higher education" coverage, was up overall.

To be sure, I am painting with a somewhat broad brush here, and have chosen to concentrate my analysis on the reporting and editorials of major national newspapers like the *Washington Post* and the *New York Times*, and to a lesser degree on the major broadcast news outlets. This is because the coverage problems I have spotlighted are often most glaring here and because these organizations have disproportionate influence as self-conscious enforcers of the diversity dogma. Of course, even the worst offenders are not offensive all the time, and their editorial boards are hardly Politburos. Let me also say emphatically that the organizations on which I have chosen to focus are still capable of rising above orthodoxy and producing some inspired and objective reporting. But I think the examples and case studies in this book will show that the overall ideological atmosphere is one-sided, especially when it comes to diversity.


Asked to account for why there has been so much bad reporting about diversity, many of the reporters and editors I approached simply blamed the restrictive conventions of the news-gathering process: daily deadlines, reportorial ranks stretched too thin, the difficulty in finding an acceptable news peg to make a story complex and alive. Yet the reporting and re-reporting I have done have shown me that a new taboo against the skepticism that is supposed to be a journalist's greatest asset has been a more significant factor.

Moreover, efforts to expand newsroom representation by ethnicity, gender and race have not been accompanied by any corresponding effort to expand or enhance intellectual or ideological diversity or an appreciation for it. Diversity, it turns out, is only skin deep. Surveys done over the course of the last two decades consistently show that journalists on the whole are today more liberal than the average citizen, and that the influx of women and minorities has only accentuated that imbalance since these groups are measurably more liberal than others. At some news organizations, especially those most committed to diversity, having liberal values has practically become a condition of employment. People with more traditional or conservative views have a hard time getting through the door, and if they do get through, they are wary of revealing their views.

The problem is not an active liberal conspiracy. Rather, it is one of an invisible liberal consensus, which is either hostile to, or simply unaware of, the other side of things, thereby making the newsroom susceptible to an unconscious but deeply rooted bias. The answer is not affirmative action for conservatives, but rather a recognition that this bias exists and serves as an invisible criterion affecting the hiring process.

Journalism is a profession that prides itself on its maverick outspokenness and its allergic reaction to preconceived notions. Yet in today's media climate, some notions are considered beyond scrutiny—including the merits of the diversity agenda. "I deplore the fact that the issue is so sensitive that reporters don't want to talk by name," one Washington bureau chief told me, hastening to add, "I don't want to contribute to that, but I would rather not be noted by name either." Indeed, in many ways news organizations have become the same kind of dysfunctional cultures as those found on the multicultural university campuses, where transgressions against the dominant line of thought can result in hostility and ostracism.

Another important reason why the diversity agenda has been inimical to sound journalism is the way the search for distinct minority viewpoints and voices has opened the door to ethnic, racial and gender cheerleading. Most minority journalists have no problem upholding the goal of professional detachment and nonpartisanship, but many younger journalists, particularly members of minorities, see objectivity as a reflection of "white" cultural values. This scorn for objectivity has encouraged a form of relativism in which facts lose their currency, and concerns about feeding anti-minority stereotypes, or undermining community self-esteem, triumph over candor and factuality.

While the political preoccupations of Latino, black or gay reporters vary sharply, the sense of advocacy they share is often animated by the same concerns. One of them is a sense of obligation to protect and uplift the group. This can create a conflict of interest between being a good journalist and being "a loyal brother" working to advance "the liberation of an oppressed people," as black columnist Jack White of *Time* magazine described his own dilemma to a group of students at a 1997 Columbia School of Journalism seminar. Minority journalists tend to exert a tremendous amount of peer pressure on each other, chastising those who are seen as airing dirty laundry in public or offering ammunition to the enemy. They are also guilt-baited by black political figures and activists who like to scold them for having become "an elite class" which has forgotten that "we are still in a racist nation," as a Dallas city councilman put it at the 1994 convention of the National Association of Black Journalists.

Inside the newsroom, the activist impulse has sometimes translated into obstructionism by mid-level minority editors who either discourage racially sensitive pieces, or sidetrack, gut or kill them once they are further into the pipeline. Outside the newsroom, that activism has fed the increasing politicization of the various minority journalists' associations. In recent years, all of them have taken explicit stands on political issues, and often sponsor workshops at their annual conventions where activists advise attendees on the best way to spin various political issues back in the newsroom.

The fear of being labeled racist, sexist or homophobic makes many white reporters reluctant to challenge this newsroom advocacy. As a *New York Times* reporter told a writer for *Esquire*, "All someone has to do is make a charge of racism and everyone runs away." And instead of taking hard-line stances against racial and ethnic cheerleading or the prickly hypersensitivity that mistakes rigorous editing for prejudice, many managers respond with solicitude because they don't want open ethnic conflict on their staff or they are worried about jeopardizing their careers. One of my *Los Angeles Times* sources said that "a large responsibility lies with the fifty-year-old, white males who find it easier, as a company, to give in to these groups than to deal with the real problems."

Not to be ignored in assessing the impact of diversity doctrine is the false perception reigning in the profession that this cause is the moral successor to the Civil Rights Movement of the 1960s. Many top editors who cut their teeth as young reporters covering civil rights in the South seem still to be fighting the last war in their effort to reconfigure the newsroom, ignoring today's more complicated ethnic and racial picture.

Among other things, the conflation of civil rights with diversity has extended the shelf life of the outdated paradigm of white oppression and nonwhite victimization, which the media invokes to justify a compensatory system of group preferences. It has also allowed diversity supporters to rationalize and excuse their own excesses and failings. When asked about complaints that the diversity campaign encouraged news organizations to go easy on minority groups, the *New York Time's* Arthur Sulzberger Jr. told *Newsweek's* Ellis Cose, "First you have to get them on the agenda."

Most significantly, though, seeing diversity as the next phase of the Civil Rights Movement has also given the whole media debate about it an overly righteous, moralistic air. This has made it difficult to discuss more subtle issues with the dispassion they require, and has also tended to encourage racial McCarthyism toward critics of the effort by dividing the world between "an enlightened us and unenlightened them," as one *Philadelphia Inquirer* reporter put it. As a result, "the whole debate gets lowered to a grade school level of oversimplification" with little effort expended to see the other side, complained former *Los Angeles Times* reporter Jill Stewart.

Such moral preening makes it hard for supporters to accept criticism too. When their diversity effort was disparaged in the lengthy *New Republic* exposé, *Washington Post* editors went into a frenzy, attacking the integrity of the writer and the racial bona fides of the magazine. *Post* publisher Donald Graham sneeringly offered the *New Republic* his suggestion for a new motto for the magazine: "Looking for a qualified black since 1914." Reacting in similar fashion, editors at the *New York Times* have dismissed criticism of the paper's slanted coverage as "unhealthy and unhelpful," "just pathetic" and ideologically motivated "drivel" tinged with implicit racism.

Supporters of the diversity agenda promised that it would benefit minority groups that have long been marginalized or maligned, and that it would encourage the formulation of policies needed to accommodate the changing demographics of multicultural America. But when you look at the political effects such a journalistic agenda encourages, you can see the law of unintended consequences in full operation.

Are new Americans really helped by journalism that bolsters bilingual education, depriving immigrant children of the ability to speak and read English, in order to maintain traditional identities? And are immigrants, who are disproportionately victimized by alien criminals, really better off when newspapers shy away from hard-hitting reportage about crime out of deference to "community sensitivities"?

There are also many legitimate questions to ask about the impact of journalism that indulges the antisocial behavior of the black underclass as a romantic rejection of "white norms" and holds black leaders to a lower standard than whites. After all, blacks are usually the ones harmed by such antisocial behavior, and by the political corruption of black officials. Is the goal of black inclusion really enhanced by reporting that sees racism everywhere, or does this reporting in fact encourage such an incapacitating sense of victimization and alienation that true inclusion and integration have become impossible?

And what about the thousands of gay men who became infected with the AIDS virus while journalists fretted about feeding pernicious stereotypes of gay promiscuity, failing to report on the dangers of bath houses and sex clubs as aggressively as they should have? *Newsday* columnist Gabriel Rotello told an audience at the 1995 National Lesbian and Gay Journalists Convention: "It has gotten to the point that we [gay men] are the biggest consumers of [these] mistruths and misconceptions about the AIDS epidemic and it is us who are dying."

The diversity crusade has had other unintended consequences too—some affecting the media. Research suggests that besides driving down morale and encouraging attrition, the diversity effort has not become "the cornerstone of growth" its supporters said it would be. Much to the chagrin of news organizations who thought they could leverage diversity to bolster sagging readership and viewership, the new minority readers and viewers never really materialized. In fact, the push for diversity has driven away many white, middle-class readers and viewers who often find the ideologically skewed reporting on diversity sharply at odds with their sense of reality. Many in this alienated white middle class have embraced the alternative news of conservative talk radio—arguably the Frankenstein monster created by the PC press—as well as the upstart Fox News Network, increasingly seen as a breath of candor and balance in comparison with its network rivals.

In the end, though, the press's diversity crusade has performed its greatest disservice to the country's broader civic culture by oversimplifying complicated issues and by undermining the spirit of public cooperation and trust without which no multiethnic and multiracial society can survive. Instead of making public discourse intellectually more sophisticated, the diversity ethos has helped to dumb it down. Instead of nurturing a sense of common citizenship, the emphasis on diversity has celebrated cultural separatism and supported a race-conscious approach to public life. And instead of enhancing public trust—a critical element in the forging of consensus on the thorny social issues we face—the press's diversity effort has manufactured cynicism through reporting and analysis distorted by double standards, intellectual dishonesty and fashionable cant that favors certain groups over others.

The task of building a workable multiethnic and multiracial society is daunting, but by coloring the news, the diversity crusade has made it even more problematical. As one perceptive reporter at the *San Francisco Chronicle* reflected: "The ultimate goal is a society with as much racial and ethnic fairness and harmony as possible, but we can't get there unless we in the press are ready to talk about it in full."

# TWO

# Race Issues

J ust a few weeks before the school year began in 1996, the Washington, D.C., School Board voted to approve a $360,000 proposal to establish an Afrocentric academy for boys. Part of an experiment with charter schools, the Marcus Garvey School, as the academy was named, would offer an alternative course of study infused with Afrocentric themes for some eighty students, most of them boys in grades 4 through 12. It would be run by a self-described "clinician and psycho-education consultant" named Mary Anigbo who until recently had been running a private school along the same lines as the plans for Garvey out of her D.C. home.

The subject of private Afrocentric academies has generated contention all by itself, but the use of tax dollars to underwrite Afrocentric programs within the larger public school system is even more controversial. While supporters say the curricula in these schools will spur an enthusiasm for learning and a sense of self-esteem in black children who have been failed by "Eurocentric" public schools, critics disdain what they say is the movement's crackpot scholarship and deplore the use of public money to subsidize racial separatism.

In Washington, D.C., the subject is especially prickly. The school system was turned upside down in 1993, when it was learned that teachers preparing to launch the city's first Afrocentric education program were trained for the project at an unlicensed and unaccredited university founded by the program's director, whose credentials included a master's degree from the same place. Furthering the scandal was the disclosure that the director and her husband had been paid nearly $250,000 to develop a curriculum guide for the program but had done virtually no work beyond a five-page outline.

Given this backdrop, it would be only natural to assume that the Marcus Garvey proposal would have been subjected to considerable scrutiny by the press, especially given the exceptional racial militancy that drove principal Mary Anigbo's educational philosophy. In her charter application, Anigbo had asserted that many minority children suffer from "Cultural Familial Retardation" and that they have been victimized by the systematic "destruction of black civilization." Anigbo wrote that the Marcus Garvey School would teach standard English as a foreign language (the "native" language being Ebonics), and that the students, mainly boys, would wear military-style fatigues and be disciplined according to principles of a traditional African village, while calling the principal "Mama Anigbo."

Despite these unusual trappings, the proposal received little attention from the public or from school board members. More to the point, the local media said barely a word. The *Washington Post*, which had devoted absolutely no attention to the Marcus Garvey proposal before the actual vote, ran a 560-word item the day after the proposal was approved. Buried in news about the fate of the eight other magnet school applications the school board had considered that night was a half-sentence reference to the Garvey approval, saying the school was "intended to offer a 'culture sensitive' education for African American boys."

Reporter Susan Ferrechio, although she worked for the conservative *Washington Times*, had actually written sympathetically about the Marcus Garvey school when it was still at the proposal stage, filing two positive articles emphasizing Mary Anigbo's desire to "change the moral fiber of the district's youth through a new kind of public education." Planning to write a story that would chronicle the progress and the problems emerging in the first semester of the Garvey experiment, Ferrechio tried to call the school to set up an appointment to interview Anigbo in early December 1996. When she got an "out of service" recording on the phone, she drove over to the school, hoping to meet with the principal in person. Ferrechio entered the building through an unlocked side door at about 3:15 P.M. and, following standard procedure, went to the principal's office and identified herself to the secretary there as a reporter. Told that the principal was down the hall teaching, she waited in the office for about ten minutes, then proceeded down the hall, escorted by a student. On the way she spoke casually to the student about school life, and jotted down the student's name and phone number so she could interview him later.

According to Ferrechio, principal Mary Anigbo flew into a rage upon learning that she had been speaking to students without her consent, and demanded to see the legal pad Ferrechio had used to write down the student's home information. At that point, Ferrechio says, she tried to head for the office door but was stopped by Anigbo, who grabbed for the legal pad. A secretary, a school guard, and seven to eight students joined in, kicking, hitting and pulling at Ferrechio, ripping the pad from her hands and pushing her out the school door, with Anigbo calling her "white bitch" and advising her to get her "white ass out of this school." As Ferrechio left the premises, two boys followed her down the street, threatening her with physical violence as she looked for a phone booth.

The principal would later say it was the white reporter who was to blame. Claiming that Ferrechio stole a notepad off a desktop, Anigbo alleged that she refused to give it back when asked, and then started to punch and grab at Anigbo when she pulled the notepad back. At some point, Anigbo said, Ferrechio threatened them all with a can of mace and a knife before being ushered out the door.

There were conflicting accounts of round two of the contretemps as well, when Ferrechio returned to the school about an hour later, escorted by a photographer, another reporter and two police officers, to get her notepad, which had more than a month's worth of notes and phone numbers on it. According to Ferrechio and the police officers, the group was assaulted by students and staff, who wrenched the photographer's camera away from him and hurled highly charged racial epithets at the black officers, calling them "fake-ass cops" who were "working for the white man." According to Anigbo, it was the police who were to blame for the ensuing altercation, which erupted when she demanded that the photographer stop taking unauthorized photos in a school.

The judge hearing the case when it eventually went to trial in July 1997 convicted Anigbo of assault and theft, charges which could have earned her a year and a half in jail, and did cause the school board eventually to revoke the school's charter.

Besides its obvious racial dimension, the story certainly raised important questions of public accountability. How exactly did someone with Anigbo's temperament and racial attitudes get her hands on nearly $400,000 worth of public money and win charge over the education, welfare and character development of young adults? Such concerns grew when it was learned that Anigbo had been charged ten years earlier with assaulting two women who were trying to serve her a subpoena at her home, slashing one so badly that she required twenty-five stitches.

The police also released information on the background of Calvin Gatlin, the security guard who was involved in the fracas. Gatlin, who was Anigbo's nephew, had a felony record including convictions for armed robbery, car theft and cocaine possession. As recently as a year before he started working at the school, Gatlin had been in serious trouble with the law.

Responding to these concerns, and with one of its reporters as a central character, the *Washington Times* gave prominent play to the Marcus Garvey incident. For several days straight the story ran on the front page, illustrated by exclusive photos the *Times'* photographer had taken when he had returned to the school with the two policemen and Ferrechio. Local television stations gave the incident heavy play too. With Ferrechio very badly bruised, and the police officers and photographer confirming her account of the return trip to the school, it was hard to deny that something terribly wrong had happened.

Yet all through this, the reaction of the *Washington Post,* a virtual synonym for fearless and independent reporting since Watergate days, was oddly hesitant. There was no acknowledgement of how the paper had dropped the ball by not holding the school's mission and leadership up to closer scrutiny. Although an incident like this would certainly have gotten banner coverage had the racial roles been reversed and a black reporter assaulted by a racist white school principal, the *Post* initially played the Garvey story on the inside pages, making very little effort to determine what actually happened, and treating the conflicting accounts of the incident as if they were of equal weight. The paper also made frequent and conspicuous use of the term "alleged"— as in "the alleged assault"—which in context deflated Ferrechio's credibility as a victim and as a reporter. In fact, in the first week after the confrontation at the school, before Anigbo's troubling legal and financial background was disclosed, the *Post* gave prominent space to black political activists like former NAACP president Benjamin Chavis and Nation of Islam activist Malik Shabazz who rallied to her side, blaming the white media and threatening racial violence.

And even when it did begin to report the story more aggressively, the *Post* left unexplored significant gaps and angles that might have given the public a better sense of what had happened and why. As reported in the *Washington Times,* for example, Anigbo was familiar to many on the school board, some of whom may have known about her legal and financial troubles before they gave her nearly $400,000. Yet the *Post* ignored this important background information. And while the paper mentioned that racial politics were a factor in the board's decision to approve the school's charter, it did so only in passing, ignoring the significant story of how racial politics had set the stage for the ensuing trouble.

The most disturbing aspect of the *Post*'s coverage, though, was the response of the paper's prominent black columnists. Colbert King, a member of the editorial board who writes a regular column under his own byline, dismissed the outrage of public officials who had condemned the incident and remained silent on the incendiary remarks of activists who had come to Anigbo's defense.

Yet King's bland dismissal of the Garvey case didn't compare to the rhetoric of another *Post* columnist, Courtland Milloy, who called it "an incident undeserving of its fame." Ignoring the violence against Susan Ferrechio and the questions the case raised about public accountability, Milloy wrote: "The eagerness with which whites have seized on this case is astounding. Their outrage at the perceived slight against a white woman at the hands of a black is matched only by the sheer absence of any concern when whites do worse to blacks.... It's as if whites were engaged in a desperate bid to absolve themselves of racism by going to any length to prove that blacks are racist too." He turned Ferrechio into a symbol of white arrogance, describing her as a white "Missy" tossing her hair into Mary Anigbo's face. Milloy closed his tirade by writing that if in fact Anigbo did tell Ferrechio to get her " 'white ass out of here,' then I think I know how she feels."

Many in the *Post*'s newsroom, angered by the column's crude tone and racist language, thought Milloy had crossed a line. Had a white columnist written anything so racially blunt, these *Post* staffers held, he or she would have been fired, or at least severely chastised. But the *Post*'s editors neither issued an apology nor disciplined Milloy. The only response to the column was a following piece by Geneva Overholser, the paper's ombudsman representing readers' interests, which was a study in racial double standards. Overholser's column noted the furor Milloy's column had triggered, but somehow also managed to hold it up as a valuable contribution to "diversity." Quoting a white reader who was outraged, she took pains to note that black readers were elated at the presence of a black columnist who "can tell folks what they wouldn't otherwise hear."


The media's minority critics and their white liberal sympathizers frequently assert that the press conspires to portray African-Americans in a negative light. This institutional racism, they allege, undermines black America's self-esteem and feeds white America's anti-black attitudes by stoking offensive racial stereotypes such as the scheming welfare mother, the crack whore, and the shiftless young man always in trouble with the law.

Much of this case against the media is made from within. In her much-acclaimed book, *Volunteer Slavery* (1993), former *Washington Post* reporter Jill Nelson maintains that "black folks" exist mostly as "potential, pathological, scatological slices of life waiting to be chewed, digested and excreted into the requisite number of column inches in the paper." Echoing and adding to this charge, former *Newsweek* reporter and current ABC News reporter Farai Chideya denounced the media for peddling "cultural misinformation" about African-Americans. In *Don't Believe the Hype* (1995), Chideya writes that "American journalism is often misleading, myopic, and unreliable when it comes to detailing the lives of African Americans.... In journalism's game of connect the dots, black has come to symbolize crime, reckless childbearing, moral turpitude and pathology." Agreeing with both of these authors in his *Waking from the Dream* (1996), *Los Angeles Times* correspondent Sam Fulwood asserts that "Newspapers tend to tell one side of the truth about the black community and it is usually the negative side."

Yet the *Washington Post*'s coverage of the Marcus Garvey incident, along with scores of other stories similarly miscovered by the *Post* and other news organizations, suggests that the double standard runs much more often in the opposite direction. Rather than hold blacks to higher collective standards, newspaper, magazine and television journalism has set the bar much lower, implicitly endorsing a kind of cultural separatism that minimizes the value—sometimes even the possibility—of common cultural standards for all Americans.

Such an outcome represents a compromise of basic journalistic standards and practices. More importantly, it represents a betrayal of the legacy of the Civil Rights Movement and its core integrationist ethos, which many journalists of that day took considerable risks to advance by their courageous reporting in the face of real danger. Many of those journalists would be happy to see the gains in minority representation that the diversity agenda has produced, but they would probably be disenchanted to see the way that diversity has infected the news reporting process with racial ideology and orthodoxy, and with a nervousness about confronting basic, if uncomfortable, facts.

In today's "city room of many colors," as *Newsweek* calls it, a new mindset reigns in which racial identity and racial nationalism trump yesterday's ideals of civic wholeness. Black cultural deficits are viewed solely as a function of white racism, while "cultural uplift" is rejected as condescending white cultural hegemony. In *Someone Else's House: America's Unfinished Struggle for Integration* (1998), author Tamar Jacoby writes that "Blacks and whites think they are formed by different cultures and they are part of another America." If this is so, diversity journalism bears some of the blame for this melancholy outcome, which could not have been imagined during the halcyon days of the Civil Rights Movement four decades ago.

If reporting on the cultural liabilities of the underclass during the Civil Rights era generally resisted the lure of identity politics, the implicit assumption of much news coverage now is separatist, supporting a reluctance to hold blacks to the same standards as whites.

The general journalistic resistance to the broad subject of problems faced by the black underclass was amply illustrated in the furor over Dinesh D'Souza's controversial book *The End of Racism* in 1995. This was a provocative, sometimes harsh examination of race relations in America, emphasizing what the author calls black "cultural deficits." *Dissent* editor Sean Wilentz wrote in the *New York Review of Books*, "Inquiries into these matters cannot be dismissed as prima facie racist. It would be strange if the experience of slavery and segregation had not left behind some pathologies in black American culture." Nevertheless, mainstream journalists reviled both book and author. Jack White, a black *Time* magazine columnist, said that *The End of Racism* was full of "obscene ideas" and "specious scholarship" and that the book's publication proved that "bigotry sells books."

Exaggerated racial sensitivities have taken their greatest toll on the debate over the staggeringly high black illegitimacy rate. In 1965, when Daniel Patrick Moynihan first tried to draw attention to the problem, the rate was 25 percent. By 1996, it exceeded 75 percent. Recently, a consensus on how to address the problem has begun to emerge, focusing on marriage and recognizing the adverse impact of illegitimacy on society in general and the black community in particular. But at almost every turn in the debate over illegitimacy—including whether or not it is "racist" even to use the term—the press has been reluctant to admit the seriousness of the problem and has disparaged proposals floated to address it, even as the public embraces them.

Trying to delegitimize the entire issue, Rosemary Bray of the *New York Times Magazine* wrote in 1992 that arguments about black illegitimacy were based on "insistent, if sometimes unconscious racism." Bray maintained that "ideologues" have "continued to fashion from whole cloth the spectre of the mythical black welfare mother complete with a prodigious reproductive capacity and a galling laziness accompanied by an uncaring and equally lazy black man in her life who will not work, will not marry her and will not support his family."

Echoing that racial defensiveness was *Newsday*'s Les Payne, who in 1996 wrote a Mother's Day tribute to what he called "the most maligned moms in America." Invoking the shades of past oppression, when slaves were deprived of the legal right to marry and in effect were forced to bear children out of wedlock or not have them at all, Payne saluted "All the young and teen-aged single black parents over all the generations who have so heroically prevented black genocide in this republic."

One of the best-known examples of media hypersensitivity on the issue of black illegitimacy was the 1990 controversy at the *Philadelphia Inquirer* over an editorial suggesting that teenage mothers be given the contraceptive agent Norplant to reduce pregnancies. "All right, the subject makes us uncomfortable too," read the editorial, written by Donald Kimmelman, a former Vista volunteer, and approved by Donald Boldt, the paper's editorial page editor. "But we are made even more uncomfortable by the impoverishment of black America and its effect on the nation's future." Kimmelman said the intent of the editorial was to stimulate debate over an unsettling subject, one that was all too often avoided in the public's larger discourse on race and poverty.

Instead of stirring reasoned debate, however, the editorial triggered widespread anger, especially among the *Inquirer*'s minority staff. Many black reporters and editors read it as meaning that the answer to poverty was to reduce the ranks of black people. The president of the Philadelphia chapter of the National Association of Black Journalists called it a brief for "cultural genocide." Charging that the editorial showed the "white male bias rampant in American society," the *Inquirer*'s minority staff circulated a petition calling for Boldt's ouster and held two protest meetings where they branded both Kimmelman and Boldt racists.

Cobbling together an apology for the editorial, Boldt and Kimmelman granted that their suggestion had been "misguided and wrongheaded" and that the editorial itself had been "fatally flawed not by its ideas but by the way it had put things, especially its conflation of race and contraception." Not long after the apology ran, the editorial page announced that in the future all editorials would have to be approved by the entire thirteen-member editorial board, in effect giving its three minority members veto power over any controversial position. Using the Norplant furor as leverage, minority staff were able to make a power play to bolster the paper's "pluralism plan." A special "minority monitoring committee" was formed to review coverage of all racial issues. Additionally, a freeze was put on the hiring of white men so that more journalists of color and women could be brought aboard—

a plan that editor Maxwell King hailed as the "most aggressive" quota plan in the country.

Later on, Boldt backpedaled in a piece written for the editorial writers' professional journal, *The Masthead*, saying that the apology had entailed "needless groveling." He also bemoaned how political correctness had turned "an important discussion of inner city poverty" into "a separate…largely irrelevant argument about racial sensitivity." Much more significant was the climate of racial intimidation and cynicism that the episode left in its wake, and the way it prompted many on the paper to tiptoe around sensitive subjects for fear of stepping on yet another racial landmine. After the episode Boldt said, "I'm aware how much easier it would be not to take up arms against a sea of troubles. Every pressure on me is pulling me in that direction. No one will punish me if I become bland and boring." More recently, a colleague at his paper admitted that in matters of potential racial controversy, the prevailing rule was: "When in doubt, chicken out."

That is the lesson Sandra Evans, a *Washington Post* reporter, learned after spending several months researching the neglect and abuse of children in suburban Prince Georges County, Maryland. The piece examined the broad subject of dysfunction in the child welfare protection system through the eyes of a white social worker, emphasizing how a huge caseload of teenage mothers was overburdening a system that simply wasn't set up for such numbers.

Such accountability reporting was in the best tradition of progressive muckraking. But when Evans filed her story, her editors spiked it, explaining that it looked like a white social worker was trying to impose her values on a black world. In about as clear a distillation of the new journalistic *Zeitgeist* as one could find, Evans explained (approvingly, according to a *New Republic* account): "The paper's trying very hard to make sure that people see the diversity of the people around us and not judge them by subjective standards. And ultimately if you're white and middle class, you're going to see the world through white middle class eyes."

Even reporters of color have had problems in reporting on underclass issues. Leon Dash of the *Washington Post* wrote an award-winning series in 1995 chronicling three generations of a black family headed by a single mother named Rosa Lee. The series' leading theme was the intractability of underclass crime, poverty, welfare dependency and drug addiction. It was itself a tribute to the spirit of untrammeled inquiry, annoying orthodoxies of both the right and the left through its eye-level view of problems normally discussed in terms too abstract to capture the complicated realities involved.

Dash won the Pulitzer Prize for his effort, yet he became a pariah of sorts among his black colleagues. Complaining loudly that the series fed pernicious racial stereotypes, Dash's newsroom critics demanded that editors let them vent in grievance sessions, during which they accused editors of trying to make the black community look bad. In response, editor Leonard Downie issued a series of memos promising to assign more uplifting "solution" stories. Dash is now teaching journalism at the University of Illinois.

Dash ran afoul of the *Post*'s piety police yet again in late 1998 with another story about unflattering underclass realities that focused on the transformation of a pair of teenage brothers from fairly ordinary children into convicted murderers. The piece's raison d'être was fairly clear. As Dash explained in the prologue, the "juvenilization of violence," including a skyrocketing teenage murder rate, has been horrific, especially in Washington, D.C. The story of the two brothers' transformation, wrote Dash, "illuminates a lost generation and the harsh reality that nearly one-third of black American men in their twenties are in prison, on probation or parole."

Dash was unsparing in his description of the chaos in which the boys were raised. Their father was a drug addict and an alcoholic. After their mother left him, she moved the family around and lived in an open lesbian relationship with another woman. Growing up in the face of precarious family finances and little parental control, the two were easily swept into the violent world created by D.C.'s booming drug trade. Attempting to settle a score with a rival drug dealer who had shot at one of them one day, for instance, the brothers stalked and killed him while they were out doing laundry for their mother in the middle of the night. "Now look at you, you bitch-ass nigger," the shooter yelled as he towered over his victim after putting a bullet through his back. Then he extended the pistol again, pumping ten more shots into the man's body before running back to his brother in their car, laughing as he did.

Dash's chilling story cast a light on the malfunctioning moral compass of children as they developed into stone-cold killers—an important dynamic to understand in any debate about inner-city pathology. Yet he was pilloried once again for the same offenses that irritated the racial censors in the Rosa Lee series. Even such otherwise racially candid national journalists as *Post* columnist William Raspberry were dubious of his efforts. "What was the point and purpose of this reportorial investment? What do we know now that can help us better address the problem?" Raspberry asked skeptically, obviously doubtful of the legitimacy of Dash's endeavor. "What is the payoff—socially, journalistically, ethically—for intruding into the lives not just of teenage felons but also of their families and friends?" (To be fair, Raspberry did let Dash have the last word: "Your questions suggest that I ought to be prescribing instead of describing," he responded. "But that's somebody else's job. I'm a reporter, not a policy wonk.")

An even greater journalistic uproar greeted the publication of photojournalist Eugene Richards' *Cocaine True, Cocaine Blue* in 1994. A study of hard-core dependency in America's inner cities, the book is full of searing images of crack addiction, and the degradation and violence it brings to the lives of those controlled by it. Richards hoped the book would spark a debate about crack addiction and the racial and social injustices he saw behind it. Instead, he found himself accused of "representational racism."

Richards, a thin and stoop-shouldered man, served in his youth as a Vista volunteer editing a community newspaper in the Klan-dominated Mississippi Delta, and then spent more than twenty-five years putting his considerable artistic talents to the service of social activism, earning a reputation as one of America's most accomplished photo-documentarians. Intrigued that even someone with such impeccable liberal credentials could run afoul of the new diversity censorship, I took a ride with Richards one day back to the bleak streets of East New York, one of the three neighborhoods he photographed over the course of four years. He told me about the fate of his project.

*Cocaine True, Cocaine Blue* is a collection of one hundred images gleaned from the four years Richards spent in East New York and Redhook in Brooklyn, and in North Philadelphia—then some of the most drug-plagued places in America. The photographs are accompanied by a text composed of equally gripping journal entries and transcriptions of taped interviews conducted with addicts, their families, and drug dealers. (This is supplemented by material gathered by Edward Barnes, a reporter who had worked on an assignment with Richards for *Life* magazine). Together the words and images evoke a world of violence, misogyny and abjection, its pages rendering perfectly the Dante-esque tableau of wasted, rubble-strewn streets and blighted lives.

A few months before the book came out, seven of its pictures were printed in the December 1993 *New York Times Magazine*, including the close-up cover shot of a deranged-looking woman clasping a syringe in the few front teeth she still had. Although the *Times* editors made a determined effort to show whites, Hispanics and blacks in roughly equal proportion, a storm immediately erupted in the black community, which felt that it was harshly portrayed by this and other photos. The most controversial shows a black woman with a baby strapped to her back, on her knees performing what looks like oral sex on a john in a crack house. On the wall behind them are pictures of Malcolm X and Martin Luther King.

Within a week, a group of prominent black clergymen and politicians signed a letter of protest to the *Times*. Sparing no rhetorical expense, an editorial in the *Amsterdam News*, a paper serving New York's black community, declared the pictures to be "the most demeaning and degrading imagery we have ever seen in a reputable news organ anywhere in the world." A group called the Committee to Eliminate Media Offensive to African People, or CEMOTAP, mounted a demonstration outside the *Times*, and black agitator Al Sharpton, who called Richards a "crack-smoking photographer," threatened a boycott of the paper if *Times* executives did not meet with its members.

According to CEMOTAP spokeswoman Betty Dopson, Richards was "a degenerate, a loser, and a parasite who lives off the misery of unfortunate people, particularly blacks." Dopson also claimed that Richards had staged the image of the woman with the baby and the john in the crack house, and she offered a $1000 reward for anyone with information to prove it.

*New York Times* executives declined to meet with Al Sharpton and CEMOTAP. But the charges did resonate on the pages of the *Times Book Review*, which ran its review of *Cocaine True* on February 5, 1994. Written by *Times* editorial writer Brent Staples, who had declared, in a signed editorial a few months before, that there was no such thing as "political correctness," the review managed to praise Richards's oeuvre and disparage this recent book at the same time.

Drugs were indeed a scourge in the African-American community, Staples admitted. Yet he still wanted to know "why nearly all the people in these photographs are black?" Asserting that "the vast majority of addicts in America are white" and that the white aspect of drug addiction is "consistently invisible in the media," Staples insisted he was not asking for "equal opportunity representation of drug abuse," but he did ask, "Couldn't Mr. Richards have found a setting where most or at least half the drug addicts are white?"

Staples also suggested that Richards had staged the prostitute and john photo. "Fortuitously or by plan," he wrote, "the scene is bracketed by pictures of Malcolm and Martin Luther King on the wall behind them." When I asked Staples if he had any evidence to support this serious charge—alleging a breach of ethics that *New York Times* photo editors I spoke with said would cost a photographer on their staff his or her job—he huffed, "You mean did I do any reporting, go out there and talk to people? No I did not."

Richards says he had initially worried that he might be describing the problem of inner-city crack addiction out of context; but after researching the demographics, he realized he was right. The book's focus is people held by drugs, a disproportionate number of whom happen to be black or Hispanic, he asserted. "The last thing I noticed about the pregnant women smoking crack, the addicts dying after shooting up, the young girls prostituting themselves, the drug boys with the automatic weapons, or the mothers grieving for their dead children was their skin color."

Reflecting on his ordeal as we drove by methadone clinics, open-air drug markets and vast stretches of junkie desolation in East New York that day right in the middle of the flap, Richards described the lessons he had learned. During meetings with CEMOTAP representatives at the International Center for Photography, Richards said he began to wonder whether the status anxieties of some middle-class and professional blacks, including some of the journalists who attacked him, might be discouraging frank discussion of underclass problems.

Perhaps more unsettling is what the experience has taught him about his own profession and the regrettable climate of correctness that seems to permeate it. As we cruised (carefully) out of East New York, junkies skulking on its desolate corners, Richards was anxious about his role and that of the tradition of socially concerned photojournalism he represents. He worried that racially or socially problematic issues "will get buried." Richards lamented,

> There are certain subjects now that you just won't be able to deal with. It means that people will be very reluctant to touch any kind of sensitive racial story. It's all so depressing, how they let these skewering minor issues get in the way of seeing the real problem. An editor may say, "Okay, go out and look at the drug war for us. But stay away from this and this, and make sure you don't focus too much on that and that." It's probably the most terrible form of censorship.

Another problem difficult to address as fully and frankly as needed is that of black crime. Many black journalists claim that the media exaggerates the rate of black criminality in pursuit of what *Philadelphia Inquirer* columnist Acel Moore calls "the demonization of black men." In fact, print and broadcast reporting are often skittish about the subject.

The result is airbrushed reporting that both downplays the scale of black criminality—according to a recent ACLU study, nearly a third of all black men between the ages of 17 and 35 are either in jail, on probation or on parole—and paradoxically, at the same time, paints this development as the result of racism in the larger culture.

Under the reign of diversity, for example, crime coverage has been systematically purged of "inessential racial information." While this is good in cases where race is not important, as when a criminal has already been apprehended, in many other cases such an omission seems irresponsible. In May 1993, for instance, two women were raped, sodomized, beaten, and robbed after being followed into their apartment building in the West Side neighborhood of Chelsea at 2 A.M. According to police, the assailant took the two at knifepoint to the tenth floor stairwell where they were assaulted. The attacker fled the scene and was still at large when the papers ran the story the following day.

Police had given out a description of the suspect, identifying him as a black man between 25 and 30 years old, muscular, and between 5 feet 10 inches and 6 feet tall, wearing a long-sleeved sweatshirt. It was hoped that the information might solicit help from the public, who could call in on a special number. It was also hoped that the information might warn other potential victims to be on guard. The city's other papers ran the racial identifier, but the *New York Times* did not. Purging the suspect's color, all its report said was that he was "muscular." In a similar case in September 1996, with one woman raped and another locked in a closet, the *Times* again failed to disclose the racial identity of a black rape suspect still at large.

Another racial story where important identifying information was withheld, this one from the heartland, involved the March 2000 slaying of Kayla Rolland, a white first-grader, by a six-year-old black classmate in Flint, Michigan. According to eyewitnesses at the scene, the boy had taken a loaded .32-caliber handgun from his uncle's house, brought it to school and shot the girl in front of a large group of other first-graders. The boy then put the gun down and walked away, without showing any emotion in the aftermath.

The case represented a macabre human-interest story, but as details about the killing came to light, it also had various implications for liberal social polices, particularly the failed policies aimed at keeping dysfunctional inner-city families intact. According to social welfare authorities, the boy's father had six children by three different women and was in jail for cocaine possession and burglary. The boy's mother, homeless at the time, had sent him to live with her brother, whose residence was considered an "active drug location" (read: crack house). The boy had been suspended before for stabbing another classmate with a pencil, prompting intervention by social welfare workers, who filed a report declaring that the mother was "involved with drugs."

Such a laundry list of parental dysfunction might have made the accused a prime candidate for removal from parental custody. But the Michigan Family Independence Agency, the office responsible for making such determinations, did not do so.

In addition to reporting on the killing of Kayla Rolland, news organizations might have gone on to explore the implications of the social policies that contributed to the tragedy. But the coverage not only failed to probe deeper into the philosophy of the Michigan Family Independence Agency, it also shrouded the racial identity of the killer, which was important to a full understanding of the case.

In its first report, the *New York Times,* mirroring the racial discomfort of most of the national media, failed even to mention that the boy who killed Kayla Rolland was black. And instead of raising questions about the failure of the child welfare system that had led to the boy's access to guns in his uncle's crack house, the *Times* established the official liberal media "storyline" on the case by spotlighting President Clinton's reaction: the case showed the necessity for gun control legislation, especially handgun locks. "Why could the child fire the gun? If we have the technology today to put in them child safety locks, why don't we do it?" Clinton said.

A *Times* report the next day did include facts about the family dynamic that gave rise to the tragedy, but its recitation was incomplete, leaving out some aspects of the boy's background having to do with his race, which still went unmentioned. Instead there was a generalized pathos, captured by the front-page headline: "A Life of Guns, Drugs, and Now, Killing, All at Age 6." Only days later did the national press finally release the fact that the boy was black, leaving the serious moral problems in the inner city that create such tragedies as the unseen iceberg below this tip.


If sins of omission plague contemporary journalism's appreciation for the realities of black crime, so do sins of commission, in the form of significant solicitude toward certain criminal figures who are idealized as "outlaws" bedeviling a racially oppressive white society.

This syndrome has been especially apparent in mainstream reporting on the world of rap music. An example is a 1996 *New York*

*Times Magazine* profile of "The Godfather of Rap," record executive Suge Knight, written by Lynn Hirshberg. Then the head of the immensely profitable Death Row Records, Knight was—until his arrest and incarceration—a larger-than-life character, cut from gangster cloth of old. Besides having a reputation for violence himself, he ran a stable of recording artists up to their eyeballs in trouble with the law: Snoop Doggy Dogg, who went to trial on accessory charges to murder in Los Angeles; Tupac Shakur, who did prison time for raping a fan in a hotel room and was finally killed in a shootout; and Dr. Dre, who served five months in a work-release program for violating parole on an earlier assault charge.

The piece was carefully written, noting Knight's proclivities for violence and the allegations of extortion and intimidation associated with his style of doing business. But Hirshberg romanticized Knight, striking a fawning tone that let him off the hook in a way that she probably never would have done were her subject a white entrepreneur inhabiting such a nether world. She quotes without particular censure his repulsive misogyny: "A dog is better than a woman. They are always happy to see you…. If you don't call them they don't care. They don't say, 'Where have you been?' " Knight's thinking was clearly juvenilely antisocial, as he crowed about loving to ride in a bouncing low-rider simply because it is illegal. He was also unapologetic about his use of violence, explaining that "You have to realize one thing: results."

Hirshberg saw Knight and his world as a phenomenon unto itself, apart from conventional standards: "They move at their own time, they do things their own way. Suge and his boys are grand. Men without women, they believe the masculine code defines everything." When Knight was finally sent to prison after violating his probation by participating in a beating—a beating that led to the eventual retaliatory killing of Tupac Shakur—the *Times* buried the news inside the paper, also neglecting to mention Knight's groveling before the judge and his promises (unpersuasive, as it turned out) never again to produce another rap song "with the word nigger in it."

Radical chic was also evident in the *Washington Post*'s celebratory coverage of black cop-killer Terrence Johnson when he was finally paroled after seventeen years in prison in February 1995. Arrested as a fifteen-year-old on charges of robbing a coin-operated laundry of $29.75, Johnson was put into a detention cell, where he grabbed a policeman's gun and shot two cops to death. Johnson said he was acting in self-defense and that he had killed the officers to protect himself from racist brutality.

The Terrence Johnson case became a local cause célèbre, and the racial divisions it exposed have been likened to the O. J. Simpson case. To whites, Johnson was a stone-cold cop killer, a demented teenage outlaw; to blacks, he was a martyr to a racist criminal justice system that had long abused black men. Originally charged with two counts of first-degree murder, he was convicted by the jury of one count of manslaughter and found not guilty by reason of insanity in the other. At his sentencing, where Johnson received the maximum of twenty-five years to life, blacks shouted for his freedom, and whites—particularly white cops and family members of his victims—for a lifetime of incarceration. A *Post* reporter would later write, as if the issue were filled with great moral complexity, that Johnson was "damned by some, deified by others and neither side saw much gray." Over the years, Johnson's supporters in the black activist community used their influence to get his petitions for parole a considerable amount of publicity. Although the efforts were denied four times running, they ultimately bore fruit when he finally won his release.

Having given Johnson's appeals generally sympathetic coverage, the *Post* greeted the news with a long celebratory profile by Jon Jeter. It portrayed Johnson as a disciplined and focused man ready to resume life, a man who had "managed redemption for a murderous act long ago." In breathy tones, the article explained that Johnson had completed a college degree while behind bars and was planning on going to law school. While it acknowledged the resentment of the slain police officers' families over Johnson's parole, it did not quote them.

This changed man was not entirely transformed, however. After he lost his law school scholarship, he grew financially desperate. In late February 1997, accompanied by one of his brothers, Terrence Johnson tried to rob a suburban Maryland bank, only to put a bullet in his own head when the robbery was foiled and he found himself surrounded by police.

Yet the cause of Terrence Johnson survived his own death, becoming a vehicle for pummeling the white system for robbing black men of spirit. Writing in her weekly column in the *Post*, Dorothy Gilliam spoke of Johnson sympathetically, adding, "There are still hundreds of thousands of young black men in prisons to be saved." Writing in the Outlook section, reporter Patrice Gaines blamed the system's callousness, claiming that the truth was, "Terrence Johnson died before he lifted that gun to his head. While no one was looking, his spirit slipped away." Only the more sober, and candid, William Raspberry saw a different picture: "Black people always seemed to see something special in

Terrence Johnson. He was always a good-looking kid, well-spoken, and well-possessed. He seemed to be headed somewhere.... Even now, many of us will find it hard to confront the possibility that maybe he was just a good-looking smooth talking thug all the while."

The tendentious kind of reporting that is done in the shadow of race could also be seen in an April 2000 *New York Times* report on drug crackdowns in minority neighborhoods, headlined "Anti-Drug Tactics Exact a Price on a Neighborhood, Many Say." Written by Metro reporter David Barstow, it was published in the aftermath of the killing of Patrick Dorismond, a black man shot by police in an undercover drug operation gone awry. This case had raised questions about the aggressive police tactics supported by Mayor Rudolph Giuliani and the racial profiling that allegedly followed.

The police insisted that profiling was not an issue and that Operation Condor, the aggressive anti-crime campaign that had done much to clean up marginal areas blighted by drugs, simply went into neighborhoods where crime statistics said it was needed. Trying to refute this claim, reporter Barstow traveled out to Brooklyn along a tattered, crime-ridden strip called Rugby Road. There he tried to examine the impact that Operation Condor was having on the mostly black and Latino residents. "The major sentiment," he wrote, was of a "police precinct that mindlessly imposes the mores of Maybury on what is a classic rough and tumble Brooklyn neighborhood—working class, Democratic, ethnically dazzling, full of swaggering striving characters who are not greatly shocked by a little vice."

Equating efforts to halt narcotics activity with "mindlessly imposing the mores of Maybury" was bad enough, but even more ridiculous was the way Barstow signed off his report. " 'I'm going to Connecticut,' huffed one resident—a resident who had been arrested in one carefully orchestrated sting operation for dealing 12 bags of heroin from his apartment building. 'I don't want my kids raised in this chaos.' "

Minority critics both inside and outside of the media charge that the press subjects black leaders to a higher level of scrutiny as part of a "plan" to deprive the black community of effective leaders who can challenge white supremacy. Yet there is substantial evidence that the contrary is true. In fact, concerns about appearing overly harsh on black political figures have led news organizations to pull punches in a way clearly suggesting double standards.

Nowhere is racial solicitude starker than in the *Washington Post*'s long dance around the personal misconduct and political malfeasance of Marion Barry, the city's first black mayor. As Tom Sherwood and Harry Jaffe noted in the book *Dream City*, Barry's drug and alcohol habits became clear to most political observers shortly after he first took office when he was seen doing cocaine in public and consorting with a number of women at a strip club. Yet the *Post* continued to support him, and repeated their original endorsement twice more when he ran for re-election. In his third mayoral election bid in 1986, the endorsement specifically cited Barry's efforts to fight drugs, even though the city's political circles were churning with talk of unreported instances of the mayor's own drug abuse.

This period was also marked by softball coverage of other troubling aspects of Barry's mayoralty, particularly its corruption and ineptitude. According to reporters and editors in the *Post* newsroom at the time, writers trying to pursue stories about malfeasance, cronyism, or egregious instances of patronage in city agencies met with consistent frustration. Although Milton Coleman, the paper's city editor at the time, had shown considerable journalistic courage in reporting Jesse Jackson's "Hymietown" remark in 1984, he was less bold when it came to taking on Barry and other black political figures in his own back yard. At one point, Coleman was spiking stories so routinely that the Metro staff he supervised rose up in revolt, leading to a highly charged confrontation in the newsroom, but very little toughening of the coverage itself. As a result, the public was left in the dark about the city's increasingly dysfunctional schools, police force, public housing, and child welfare services, to name but a few of the city services and agencies that declined on Barry's watch.

The *Post*'s reluctance to confront Barry head on was a function of white guilt, racial idealism and condescension. Embodying the white establishment, *Post* editors apparently felt that any criticism of Barry in its pages would be taken as a challenge to the "home rule" which had taken the largely black district decades of agitation to win. According to Juan Williams, then a *Post* correspondent who had written for the editorial page, the paper had a view that "black politics were in their infancy and it would be unfair to hold them to the same standard."

Not to be underestimated, too, was the solidarity of some of the paper's black editors and reporters. In many parts of black D.C., where hostility to the *Post* is reflexive, these black staff members were generally seen as "Toms" doing the master's bidding. According to reporters at the paper, Barry was skillful at roiling these troubled writers. "Did your white editor tell you to ask that question?" he might respond if a black reporter pressed him too hard at a news conference. Indeed, Barry seemed to enjoy getting in the face of the *Post*'s most senior people as well. Asked point blank over lunch one day by *Post* editor Ben Bradlee Jr. whether he was using drugs, the sweating and stammering mayor said he wasn't, and that his slurred words resulted from a speech impediment.

Increasingly concerned about the perception that it was covering for the mayor, the *Post* finally took off the kid gloves in 1990, reporting that the D.C. police had cancelled a drug raid on a hotel when it was learned that Barry was in the room they planned to hit. This story did not get the prominent play it might have, but subsequently the paper started to devote much more attention and resources to the Barry story. It even assigned a reporter, Lee Hochstadter, to tail the mayor on a vacation trip to the Caribbean where he was staying with an associate suspected of procuring both drugs and women for him. When Barry returned to Washington, the paper shadowed his movements and staked out his house.

For many white reporters at the *Post*, Barry's eventual arrest was a vindication, lifting a sizable cloud that had hovered over the paper for not coming down hard on him sooner. But many black reporters continued to feel anger over the perception that there had been a setup in order to bring a powerful black man down. Many minority journalists at the *Post* were also alienated by the "white self-satisfied contentment" brought out by the arrest, as former *Post* writer Jill Nelson recalled in her memoir, *Volunteer Slavery*. In the months following Barry's arrest and leading up to his trial, Nelson wrote, many of her white colleagues had 'indicted, tried and convicted him. No punishment was good enough, even lynching."

After limited editorial calls for Barry's resignation, the *Post*'s coverage began to turn again in his favor. The paper bought into the Barry camp's themes of redemption and rehabilitation, and gave lots of space to conspiracy theories alleging that the mayor was being persecuted by the white power structure in the District in order to discredit black self-rule. The *Post*'s coverage of the conspiracy story was credulous, filled with unfiltered quotations and unsubstantiated allegations by blacks that Barry's case was one where "race played a central role." A story headlined "Backlash over Barry Case: Many Blacks Are Wrestling with Ambivalence" featured black voices who claimed that Barry was being singled out because he represented a threat to white business interests and because his administration empowered blacks. According to Jill Nelson, whose byline appeared on this piece, the Barry case was a "de facto conspiracy on the part of the US Attorney, the *Washington Post*, and sundry others to *get* Marion Barry." Furnishing crack and putting him together with one of his old lovers, "the US government—and not only in this instance—is just as bad."

Despite her clear preconceptions about Marion Barry, Nelson accepted an assignment to the team of reporters who would write about his trial, and later admitted to playing the role of "sullen disgruntled Mau-Mau" in meetings where coverage was discussed and planned. After testimony by several women who said Barry had raped them, Nelson convinced the editors to use the word "coerce" instead of "rape." "No use of the 'R' word," she would later crow. "Now that's spin control!" When Barry was found not guilty on all but the most insignificant count, Nelson was relieved. Calling the joy at the verdict "a black thing" that whites wouldn't understand, she wrote that the victory celebration she attended that evening was "about the vindication of a reality as perceived by many blacks."

Faced with the prospect of Barry's return to the mayor's office in 1994, the *Post* editorialized against him. But it was still possible to discern reluctance to report fully and frankly on the Barry comeback. According to some at the paper, reliable tips on voter payoffs and fraud were not pursued with vigor, and the fact that Barry was surrounding himself with many of the same cronies who had gone to jail during his earlier administrations was ignored. Again the *Post* ceded Barry the opportunity to define the story line of his re-election bid as one of redemption—a man's triumph over his own inner demons—and the racism of the system.

The re-election coverage was also marked by a decided effort to minimize the racial polarization in the voting, which couldn't have been starker. While blacks voted overwhelmingly for Barry, whites gave him only 10 percent of their votes. Yet in analyzing the vote, the *Post* chose to ignore the larger black-white polarity and to highlight instead the electoral patterns within the black community. Thus the headline of the lead article announcing the challenger's victory: "Barry Win Transcends City's Barriers: His Supporters Came from Many Classes, Sections of the City."

In the wake of Barry's re-election, news of congressional moves to strip him of essential mayoral powers, along with a decision to remove authority from such symbolic government agencies such as the board of education, were reported in a straightforward manner. But their larger significance—i.e., the failure of the poisoned politics of racial demagoguery that were practiced so long and so destructively by Barry—was not addressed. And moves to stabilize the District by stripping local authorities of much of their power—moves that were long overdue and represented the city's only hope of salvation—were the target of sniping. According to *Post* columnist Dorothy Gilliam, the takeover represented a white "war against the city" of Washington—a "coup" that had overthrown democracy itself. In May of 1997 she wrote: "With Congress as the city's revitalized overseer, the District has gone from being the nation's last colony to its last plantation."

With the city in shambles and the mayoralty stripped of most of its power, Barry decided not to run for office again. The *Washington Post's* editorial page called this "a much welcomed decision" that was "certainly best for the nation's capital." Given the decade's worth of misreporting and underreporting, the editorial was at best justice delayed. Yet in some quarters, the Barry cult lived on. "Sure at times he plumbed the depths of racial politics," wrote reporter Kevin Merida. But in quoting Barry admirers extensively, Merida also drew a picture of the disgraced mayor as a role model for young blacks, a symbol of black self-government, and a man who would "turn out to be a historic figure."

Coverage of black political figures also tends to wink at the politics of excommunication practiced by black intellectuals and political activists on those who dare to dissent from liberal racial orthodoxy. The rhetorical abuse heaped on those who do speak out is often ugly, and would certainly be deemed impermissible if it came from whites. Yet political reporters and commentators often either ignore it or echo it, with black journalists functioning as hit men against those painted as "traitors to the race."

There was no critical coverage to speak of on the vicious attacks on former Connecticut Republican congressman Gary Franks by his colleague William Clay, a Democrat from Missouri, both of whom are black. Perhaps this was because the press was predisposed to be suspicious of Franks as an "anomaly" given his long record of voting against measures sponsored by the Congressional Black Caucus, his support of Clarence Thomas's Supreme Court nomination, and his votes for welfare reform and against race-conscious redistricting.

In issuing a bizarre, ten-page press release to celebrate Franks' loss of his congressional seat in 1996, Clay broke all bounds of civil discourse in his charge that Franks promoted "a foot-shuffling, head-scratching Amos and Andy brand of Uncle Tom-ism" and that he "gleefully assists in suicidal conduct to destroy his own race." According to Clay, black conservatives like Franks were "Negro wanderers," driven to "maim and kill other blacks for the gratification and entertainment of ultraconservative white racists."

Clay's broadside was about as ugly as it gets in American politics, and spoke volumes about the lack of tolerance for dissenting positions in the black political world. Editorial writers who routinely denounce right-wing hatemongers and bemoan the loss of civility in public discourse should have denounced Clay too. But aside from a *Wall Street Journal* editorial decrying this "stunning propensity for cruelty" and insistence on ideological conformity, no major paper took Clay to task. And except for a small item in the *Washington Post* that poked fun at Franks even while recording Clay's derisive comments, no other news organization of national stature paid much attention at all.

Solicitude toward unbecoming behavior on the part of black political figures appeared again in the wincing attention paid to Jesse Jackson when it was revealed in January 2001 that he had fathered a child out of wedlock with a colleague in his Rainbow Coalition organization. The *National Enquirer,* which broke the story, reported that Jackson, who has been considered the moral center of the black political establishment and was a spiritual advisor to President Clinton during his adultery crisis, was making child support payments of $3000 a month to his former mistress. Quickly trying to get ahead of the story, Jackson immediately confessed, declaring, "This is no time for evasions, denials or alibis."

In reporting Jackson's admissions, however, the *New York Times* buried its story on page twenty-one, a position much less prominent than what a conservative political activist of equal stature to Jackson would earn if he or she had produced an illegitimate child and was supporting it with a nonprofit corporation's funds. And even though the story got more visible play from other news organizations, few looked at the moral implications of Jackson's behavior—certainly fair game considering that he had tried to claim the role of America's "moral conscience." Instead, most "insider" journalists followed a story line about the political skullduggery that may have been behind the *Enquirer's* disclosure. Some of them charged that Republican political operatives may have played some part in bringing the scandal to light so as to discredit Jackson on the eve of the inauguration of President George W. Bush, at which Jackson was expected to be a leader in street protests. Thus the reverend got a free ride and was able to return to the limelight a few days after promising to closet himself with his conscience for several months.

Meanwhile, the press has become more insistent in denying that any black racism toward whites exists. In case after case, black-on-white attacks are treated as nonevents, while the reaction is fierce when the opposite occurs. According to the standard media script in which whites are oppressors and blacks are victims, the latter can't be racists because, being a minority, they lack the economic and political power to institutionalize or systematize their anti-white animosity. In support of this politically correct cliché, former *New York Times* columnist Anna Quindlen wrote, "Hatred by the powerful, the majority, has a different weight and very often different effects than hatred by the powerless, the minority. Being called a honky is not in the same league as being called a nigger."

Yet just because slavery and segregation have left a harsh legacy doesn't mean that journalists should give short shrift to the problem of black racial animosity, which through the 1990s grew deeper and more widespread and found powerful institutional expression in the form of militant organizations such as the Nation of Islam. Like the white racism of old, black racism makes a shared civic culture impossible. As Harvard law professor Randall Kennedy, himself black, wrote in a May 1997 *Atlantic Monthly* cover story, history has taught that the oppressed will oppress whomever they can once the opportunity presents itself. "Because this is so," Kennedy maintains, "it is not premature to worry about the possibility that blacks or other historically subordinated groups will abuse power to the detriment of others."

One especially piquant example of journalistic indulgence toward anti-white racism among blacks was a 1998 *New York Times* essay by reporter Lena Williams, headlined "It's the Little Things." Williams' piece, which eventually grew into a book with the same title, ostensibly examined the "looks, stares, offhand remarks and other facts of everyday life" that blacks find offensive and irritating about whites' behavior toward them. But it was really an apology for anti-white anger, framing uncivil and racist actions by blacks as a variety of historical reparation. In Williams' eyes, a black man violently pushing his way through a crowd of whites was not simply loutish, he was "a brother fed up with eating crow, as in Jim." Everything was excusable because of past racism.

A string of black-on-white assaults in the Washington, D.C., subway system in early 1994 elicited similar rationalizations. These attacks were clearly racially inspired. In one incident, a white woman was harassed by a group of black teenagers who cried out, "Let's kill all the white people!" In another, a woman was threatened with rape. Yet the

*Post,* in an obvious bid to minimize the criminal nature of the misconduct, reduced the trouble to a "clash of two cultures" in which the perceptions and racial stereotypes of the older white passengers were assigned equal weight to the misconduct of the teenagers, which was explained away as youthful rowdiness.

Refusal to acknowledge the reality of anti-white racism is particularly evident in coverage of black-on-white crime. According to some surveys, in the 1990s blacks were at least three times more likely to commit hate crimes against whites than the other way around. Yet in case after case, media coverage either refuses to acknowledge the racial subtext of such crimes, or fails to subject them to the same scrutiny used when the racial roles are reversed. This is so even in cases where the racial motivation is clear-cut, as in a 1994 case when a gang of black teenage muggers confessed to police that it had intentionally limited its violent attacks in a Brooklyn housing project to elderly whites. Police reports had one culprit admitting, "We made an agreement not to rob black women. We would only take white women. It was a pact we all made. Only white people." Yet such details did not find their way into the stories run by the *New York Times.* The same omission occurred in coverage of other instances of black-on-white attacks, even when the assailants were heard calling their victims "white bitch," "white ho" (whore) and "white KKK bitch," as they were in an April 1997 attack on a white matron by a gang of New York City high school girls on a bus.

The pattern was apparent once again in the spring of 1997 when three white teenagers, a girl and two boys, from the rural Michigan town of Highland hopped off a freight train they were riding and were then attacked by a gang of up to a dozen black youths in a hard-bitten area of Flint, Michigan. The gang raped the girl and shot one of the boys to death. Coverage of the crime left it unclear whether race was a factor in the attack, but it is almost certain that if the attackers had been white and the victims black, race would have been explored in earnest and there would have been more coverage than a small, one-day story.

By now there is enough of a backlog in cases where acknowledged black racism was involved to make a prima facie case against contemporary journalism. In the boycott of a Korean-owned produce store in Brooklyn in early 1990, for instance, black protesters called Korean owners "yellow monkeys," and organizers with troublesome racial track records urged neighborhood residents to avoid shopping with "people who do not look like us." For more than three months, the boycott got little attention from the city's major news organizations.

Charging a double standard, the *New York Post*'s Eric Breindel asked, "If this was a long-term boycott of a *black*-owned store by a band of Ku Klux Klanners, it would have long ago been a national story. Why should the rules change when the victims are Korean?"

The double standard was even more dramatic in the *New York Times'* misleading coverage of anti-Semitic riots in Crown Heights, Brooklyn, in the summer of 1991. Sparked by a tragic accident in which a seven-year-old black boy named Gavin Cato was killed after a car driven by an Orthodox Jew named Josef Lifsh swerved out of control trying to make a red light, the rioting extended over four nights in late August. Reacting to rumors that the Jewish ambulance corps that arrived at the accident scene had ignored the boy to take care of the driver, blacks in the neighborhood went rampaging through the streets, jeering at Lifsh and shouting "Jews! Jews! Jews!" before turning their anger on police. That night Yankel Rosenbaum, a Hasidic scholar from Australia, was returning to the neighborhood on the subway when he was confronted by a gang of up to twenty black youths shouting, "Get the Jew!" He was beaten, kicked and stabbed, and he later died at a Brooklyn hospital. Meanwhile the rioting continued, as blacks threw bricks and bottles and burned police cars. The disorder was not quelled until the fourth night, when Mayor David Dinkins, himself the target of rocks and bottles, finally ordered the police to crack down. By the end of the rioting, scores had been hospitalized and the working-class neighborhood, where blacks and Hasidic Jews had always managed a gingerly coexistence, lay fractured in mutual recrimination and suspicion.

The *Times* noted that the vast majority of people arrested during the riot were black. It also relayed a vivid report of a mob of black youths chanting "Heil Hitler!" in front of the headquarters of the Lubavitchers, one of New York's most prominent Hasidic groups. Yet almost every other aspect of the story was mishandled or skewed, in a way that seemed to excuse or minimize the racist actions of the black community and the militant leaders who incited it. In the days following the accident, for example, the *Times'* news analysis searched for "context" as a way of blaming societal racism and excusing black mobs for their misdeeds. Such reporting was clearly consistent with the "justifiable rage" theory of civic unrest in America that legitimated explosions of unrest in aggrieved minority communities. A *Times* news analysis was headlined "For Young Blacks, Alienation and a Growing Despair Turn into Rage." Anna Quindlen, then a columnist at the *Times*, visited a grim housing project in Crown Heights and asked, "What must you feel if your whole life is a slur, if you read the handwriting on the wall of your existence and the graffiti seem to say: 'Who cares.' "

By putting the events "in context," journalists could see the violence as a "culture clash" between two groups equally at fault. A *Times* headline, for example, declared, "The Bitterness Flows in Two Directions." The story explained that "the Hasidim are often the focus of anger because of the widespread belief that they receive special treatment from the police and other city institutions and get help that blacks sorely needed in a time of dwindling resources." But was this "widespread belief" founded on facts? The *Times* didn't ask and didn't tell. By contrast, *New York Newsday* went the extra step and mounted an extensive investigation into those charges, reporting that little evidence existed to support the accusations.

At Gavin Cato's funeral, banners commemorating the accident victim shared space with others bearing messages such as "Hitler did not do the job," while street agitator Al Sharpton caricatured Jews as "diamond dealers." While the *Times* reported the "diamond dealers" slur, it ignored Sharpton's other incendiary remarks at the funeral, where he compared Gavin Cato to slain civil rights leaders and drew parallels between Hasidim and supporters of apartheid. The *Times* also gave easy treatment to another black clergyman, Rev. Herbert Daughtry, who accused Hasidic Jews of abusing their power and likened them to the Ku Klux Klan. (It was not until fourteen months after Yankel Rosenbaum's murder—when Lemerick Nelson, the sole suspect prosecuted for that killing, was acquitted—that the *Times* got around to expressing "shame and alarm over anti-Semitic violence that recalled the pogroms of czarist Russia and Eastern Europe.")

While the violence of the Los Angeles riots in May 1992 surpassed the Crown Heights violence that preceded it, the coverage followed a similar pattern. This problem afflicted almost all the news organizations involved, but it was most acute at the *Los Angeles Times*. Notwithstanding the Pulitzer Prize it won for its riot coverage in 1992, the paper's reporting and commentary seemed to pass through an ideological filter in a way that raised serious reservations about the accuracy, balance, and ultimate honesty of its content.

More than half of those arrested in the disturbances were black; the bulk of the rest were Latino, many of them illegal aliens with little stake in the riot's larger racial dynamic. Yet to the *Los Angeles Times*, the riot was one in which all of the city's various ethnic and racial groups participated equally. A front-page piece reported that those arrested for arson "ranged from career criminals to a USC professor's son," and an op-ed piece by Jesse Jackson in the riot's first days spoke of "a terrible rainbow of protest."

The *Times* followed the same script as nearly all major media in portraying the violence as the product of a long history of oppression, and thus an expression of "justifiable rage." The Rodney King acquittal was merely the spark. A front-page story asserted that "most middle class blacks understand why [the riot] happened. It was inevitable, driven by an anguish that transcends class lines among blacks—an anguish so deep it cried out for something extraordinary to be done in response." Upbraiding local broadcasters for calling rioters "thugs and hooligans," *Los Angeles Times Magazine* writer Itabari Njeri criticized the "reluctance to view those nights of rage as a revolt, not a 'riot' "—placing the word *riot* in quotations marks everywhere it was used in the piece. Given no "socially sanctioned place to express their despair over the injustice of the system, they [young black men] release their distress where they can."

The *Los Angeles Times* lacked candor in discussing another crucial dimension of the riot: black anti-Korean racism. According to Njeri, answering the question of whether black attacks on Asians constituted racism depended on how racism was defined. She then repeated the shibboleth that racism was strictly a matter of "racial prejudice plus power," something blacks supposedly didn't have. Making the issue of black accountability even fuzzier, Njeri said that the violent acts were an expression of "internalized oppression."

The *Times'* reporting ignored the media's role in fanning the riot, especially the leading role played by the *Times* itself in stoking public indignation over the Rodney King verdict. All too ready to damn the jury, the *Times* exaggerated the fact that the jurors came from all-white Simi Valley, and that many of them had police and military in their families. The *Times* also ignored the factors that influenced the jury in its decision to acquit. (Instead of mentioning the high-speed chase and King's irrational responses when he was finally apprehended, the *Times* simply kept referring to him as a "black motorist.")

In the national coverage of the riot, it was hard to surpass the tendentiousness of ABC's *Nightline*. Offering a platform to members of the very gangs that were later held responsible for starting the riot and for attacking white trucker Reginald Denny in an assault famously captured by an Los Angeles news station's sky-camera, *Nightline's* Ted Koppel turned himself into a near-parody of racial chic. He told the two gang members he had invited onto the show that he was impressed by what they had to say and by the eloquence with which they said it—but failed to mention that both "Monster" and "Bone" had served hard time, the latter for murder.

Koppel's lack of critical focus was most marked, and most objectionable, when it came to the targeting of Koreans, who, though representing a fraction of the city's retail establishments, suffered more than half of the arson attacks and looting. According to "Bone," it was no big deal to burn down liquor stores since there were too many "owned by Koreans" in the black community to begin with. The Koreans "send their kids to college with our money," he insisted, adding with a chuckle that to burn down their stores was simply a matter of "renovating our neighborhood."

Koppel also did not probe the reaction of certain black public figures when he questioned them, too, about the anti-Korean attacks. According to John Mack, another guest on the same *Nightline* segments where the gang members appeared, the situation wouldn't improve until Korean merchants "stop blowing black customers away"—a reference to the shooting of black teenager Latasha Harkins by a Korean grocer some months before, an incident that the local media reported with incendiary irresponsibility. Yet in the battles between Korean storekeepers and black "customers" in the months before the riot, thirteen Koreans had died and only one black—a salient statistic that Koppel failed to note as a correction to Mack's propaganda.

Another illustration of mainstream journalism turning a blind eye to black racism is the coverage by New York papers of the December 1995 arson slayings at a Jewish-owned clothing store in Harlem. The attack on Freddy's Fashion Mart on 125th Street was the culmination of a long and bitter protest mounted by several dozen black militants angry that a well-known record store next door would be losing its lease to allow Freddy's to expand. The decision not to renew the lease was the landlord's, a Harlem church called the United House of Prayer for All People. Still, picketers aimed their venom at the storeowner, an orthodox Jew named Fred Harari, and called on Harlem residents to join them in boycotting Freddy's. Although the protest had significantly curtailed business, picketers were feeling considerable frustration because it had not yet driven Harari to close up shop. According to various accounts, some of the picketers were talking of taking more drastic action.

On Friday, December 8 one of the protestors, a fifty-one-year-old black man named Roland Smith, barged into the store, set the place on fire, and started shooting store employees. "It's on now!" Smith screamed. By the time the smoke had cleared, seven people working at the store were dead, along with Smith, who had taken his own life.

Evidence suggested that the incident had a strong racial component. The protesters had called a security guard there a "cracker lover,"
had shouted "Don't buy from crackers" to passersby, and had made
threats to come back to Freddy's "with 20 niggers to put the Jew in a
casket." Eyewitness accounts of survivors also said that Roland Smith
had spared a black girl in the store and called one employee a "damn
Jew" before shooting him. Yet in the first days of coverage, the *New
York Times* ignored these reports and said it was wrong to reduce the
incident to "a simple morality tale reeking of prejudice." The attack was
"the work of a madman, not a flashpoint in the complex relationship
between black and Jew, black and white," according to *Times* reporter
Carey Goldberg.

The *New York Times'* reporting on Roland Smith was telling. An
ardent black nationalist, Smith had refused the military draft in the
1960s, telling the judge that as a black man he was a "subject," not a
citizen of the United States. Long on the fringes of the black militant
community, Smith had served prison time in the early 1990s for strug-
gling with a police officer in Florida and making threats to kill him,
before moving to New York and becoming a street vendor, while agi-
tating against city efforts to remove unlicensed vendors. "Everything to
him was a conspiracy against black people," a fellow vendor told the
*Times*. "It was always, 'Cracker this and cracker that.' "

But instead of interpreting this record as evidence of unhealthy
racial preoccupation, the *Times* depicted Smith as a man of "principle,"
explaining that he lived "an ardent credo" of black "self-sufficiency"
and "resistance," and that his actions inside Freddy's were not criminal per se, but a strange act of suicide in protest against the
"institutional force" of white racism.

Racial avoidance also seemed to be behind the *Times'* soft-focus
profile on the protest's leader, a well-known figure in black activist circles named Morris Powell. According to a column by the *Daily News's*
Mike McAlary that was sourced by senior police commanders, Powell
had a long record of racial extortion and violence, and a history of organizing "protests" against Korean merchants, who were made to pay
sizable sums so that the protesters would go away. According to police,
Powell had been arrested in 1984 after breaking the skull of a Korean
woman who had touched a picket sign during one particularly bitter
demonstration. Powell, said one senior law enforcement official, was a
"social arsonist" who "ignites the racial inferno and then cashes in on
the madness."

Yet to the *New York Times*, Powell was "an elder statesman" among
the city's street vendors, who offered colleagues advice on "how to

avoid skirmishes with police." He spoke "softly," the *Times* reported, "in measured tones." And while the *Times* did report that Powell had made an appearance at a rally in Brooklyn where he laced his comments "with racially offensive rhetoric," it neglected to note that Powell too had called Fred Harari "a cracker"; that he had set up a protest at another white-owned business the day after the Freddy's tragedy; that in memorializing Roland Smith he had called him a victim of a "white setup" and asserted that accusations of black racism were unfounded because "not one white person died."

On the day of the fire, the *Daily News* reported that protesters had been overheard singing "Freddy's dead" in a kind of gloating triumph. The next day, the *News* reported that the protesters had taken up position at Bargain World, another Jewish-owned business they were battling with, chanting, "Don't buy from the cracker, he ain't like you." Later in the week, at a rally at Brooklyn's Slave Theatre—a temple of black militancy overseen by the Reverend Al Sharpton—several speakers praised Roland Smith as "a hero and a martyr," and Morris Powell drew applause when he said "cracker" storeowners were "stealing our dollars." There was also cheering when Betty Dopson, the chairwoman of the Committee to Eliminate Media Offensive to African People, insisted that the Harlem incident "was caused by the Jew, not the brother who had the psychic breakdown." Yet these incidents either were ignored altogether by the *New York Times* or made their way into the paper slowly several days after they had been reported elsewhere.

In fact, when the *Times* did try to assign responsibility for the incident, it did so in a way that sounded like blaming the victim. In a profile of Fred Harari, reporter Matthew Purdy noted his "unvarnished" and "blunt" demeanor and the "insular world" in Brooklyn where the Orthodox Harari lived at far remove from the Harlem neighborhood where he made his living. Purdy descended even further into stereotypes when he wrote that protesters saw the situation as "an effort by a greedy Jewish businessman to evict a black-owned record store." The profile also neglected to say that it was not Harari who had refused to renew the popular record store's lease, but the United House of Prayer for All People—the black church across the street.

The *New York Times'* most egregiously misreported racial angle, however, was the toothless and partisan coverage of the role played by Al Sharpton. Although he had a long record as a racial firebrand and political scoundrel, the *Times* treated Sharpton's 1993 Senate bid favorably, retouching certain unattractive aspects of his past to burnish his image as an up-and-coming black statesman. A Sunday *New York Times*

*Magazine* profile of Sharpton, headlined "The Reformation of a Street Preacher," noted his past as "an irresponsible, inflammatory, race-baiting agitator hungry for publicity," although it failed to mention his more incendiary deeds and utterances during the Crown Heights riot of 1991, as well as provocative actions at other equally tense moments in New York's recent racial history. According to the *Times Magazine*, Sharpton was now "softer, more focused, more intellectually polished."

Sharpton had been an early supporter of the Freddy's Fashion Mart protest and had allowed his name to be used on a flier calling for a boycott that circulated in Harlem. He had also made a personal appearance at the picket line in front of the store, where he was captured on store security cameras denouncing "white interlopers" and urging protesters to defend "this brother"—the record store owner— by boycotting Freddy's. Sharpton had made other statements about Freddy's too. On radio broadcasts he said the closing of the record store was part of a strategy to eliminate "our people" from doing business and that would be "a sin and a shame and a disgrace" if it happened without a "major reaction and major protest from us." In the *Amsterdam News,* the most prominent news organ in New York's black community, Sharpton was quoted as saying, "We intend to run the company out of here."

While the *Daily News* and the *Post* reported Sharpton's more racially inflammatory statements, they did not make their way into the *Times,* or did so in a manner that minimized their significance. Typical of the *Times'* supportive coverage was the Sharpton profile by reporter Charisse Jones that ran a little more than a week into the episode. Appearing in the Metro section under the headline "Sharpton Buoyant in a Storm," the profile characterized Sharpton as playing the role of "consoler, conciliator and political jouster," and ignored the damning evidence that had been building up around him for weeks, Jones' piece did not mention his "white interloper" comment, and allowed him once again, despite documented statements to the contrary, to insist he was unaware of some of the anti-white and anti-Semitic comments that protesters had made. The piece also let Sharpton characterize himself as a victim in the whole affair. "In my life I've had to walk alone sometimes," Sharpton told Jones. "I've been lied on, I've been talked about, mistreated, stabbed and indicted. But through it all I've learned to trust in Jesus. I've learned to trust in God. It's only a test."

Another recent illustration of the media's tendency to sidestep uncomfortable realities of black racism involved the case of Ronald Taylor, a thirty-nine-year-old black Pennsylvania man who killed three people and wounded two others, all white, in March 2000. According to authorities, Taylor had grown enraged when managers at his Wilks-burg, Pennsylvania, housing project sent white maintenance workers to fix something in his apartment. He shot the two maintenance workers, killing one. Then he set his apartment on fire and walked to a Burger King a mile away, where he shot another white person before going across the street and shooting three others at a MacDonald's. After that, Taylor stormed a building used as a senior citizen and children's day care center, taking hostages before finally surrendering.

It would not have taken much digging to find a racist antipathy to whites in the background of Taylor's rampage. According to the Associated Press, which quoted the surviving maintenance worker, Taylor had shouted, "You're all white trash racist pigs. You're dead." Other published reports the day after the shootings had him barging into the home of a friend, saying, "I'm not gonna kill any black people. I'm gonna kill all white people." Witnesses cited in these reports also had Taylor reassuring a black hostage he took in the senior citizens' center. "Not you, sister," he allegedly said to one fearful black woman when he threatened to shoot others there. But in the *New York Times* account, which ran on the inside pages, these remarks went unreported. Taylor's possible racism was alluded to only in a reference to the local mayor's statement that the matter was "being investigated."

After finding racist and anti-Semitic literature in his home, the FBI finally labeled Taylor's actions a hate crime, which forced the media to report it as such. To some, the lag was odd. As a writer for the webzine salon.com put it: "What took so long? Why did the media, which normally promote not only the idea of hate crimes but of hate crime legislation, have to wait for the FBI to make this designation?"

When five black teenagers robbed and murdered a restaurant deliveryman in Queens, New York, in August 2000, the coverage provided yet another example of the aversion to reporting the racism behind some black crime. The five youth—all from reasonably solid, middle-class homes—had phoned in a $60 takeout order to a Chinese restaurant near JFK Airport, luring the deliveryman, who was also the restaurant's owner, to a secluded, vacant house. There, the boys covered the man with a sheet and wrestled him to the ground, choking him. While the man was on the ground, one of the boys bludgeoned his head with a brick, killing him. The group then fled to one of the attacker's houses, where they ate the food the man had been trying to deliver. When caught a few days later, all the boys confessed to some level of involvement, leaving a city once again stunned by what seemed to be a case of inexplicable violence involving what were not known as "troubled teens."

The anti-Asian bigotry present in some predominantly black urban neighborhoods was completely ignored in the *New York Times* reporting of the case, which was surprisingly minimal anyway, given the heinousness of the crime. Instead, the *Times* chose to focus on the reactions of the attackers' parents, presenting them in a victimized light. "And so now between waves of tears and anger and disbelief . . . five stunned families find themselves confronting a nightmarish tangle of questions." As for focusing on the real victims, the wife and family of the murdered deliveryman, the *Times* waited six months, until February 2001, to get around to it, and then framed the story as if the City of New York, by failing to provide the woman with the social services she needed to stay afloat, were the bad guy.

If journalists have had difficulty acknowledging cases of individual black racism, they've had an even harder time with its institutional embodiments. The press came down firmly on Louis Farrakhan and his Nation of Islam when it emerged into the national spotlight in 1984 during Jesse Jackson's first run for president (and Farrakhan called Judaism a "gutter religion"). But with the increasing power of the diversity ethos, there has been considerable reluctance to criticize Farrakhan since then. In the years leading up to the Million Man March on Washington, D.C., in late 1995, with his stature in the black community rising, news organizations became much more timid in their coverage, apologizing or ignoring the anti-white racism that is at the core of both the man and the movement.

In March 1994, a three-part *New York Times* series attempted to explore the "real" Farrakhan. All three segments were assigned to black reporters. The series touched upon some of the less appealing aspects of Farrakhan and his movement, but in the main it defended the Muslim leader by making him seem less extreme than evidence suggested he was.

The *Times'* Chicago bureau chief, Don Terry, set the apologetic tone in the first installment. Thirty-second sound bites, he wrote, have turned Farrakhan "into a one-dimensional character: the black twin of David Duke." Lost in the outcry over his public remarks about Judaism is "how politically and socially conservative Mr. Farrakhan actually is," Terry contended. "The problem of racial nationalism is a real problem," said a hate crime "expert" Terry quoted. "But Minister Farrakhan is a minor player. There are much bigger white players who don't get the same level of criticism and that's unfair."

More airbrushing came in part two of the series, by reporter Steven Holmes, which examined problems with the controversial security guard business maintained by the Nation of Islam (and funded in part with tax dollars), but failed to mention a long list of extensive allegations made against Farrakhan's other business enterprises. In an apparent attempt to restore a sense of balance, the *Times* series closed with a harder-edged piece by reporter Michel Marriott, filled with criticism of Farrakhan from leading black intellectuals like Ellis Cose and Albert Murray. Farrakhan's separatism and hate-charged hostility, said Murray, were nothing but "a bunch of ignorance." The piece also included opinions of leading black political figures like New York congressman Major Owens, who likened Farrakhan to Hitler and said many of his followers were "looking for someone to hate." Yet Marriott still managed not to cross the party line and expose the appetite for demagoguery in the black community that makes Farrakhan acceptable. In his story line, Farrakhan may be an extremist, but it is white racism that drives blacks to the extremes he represents.

In some news reporting and analyses of the Million Man March itself, there were signs that reporters, particularly younger African-American reporters, had embraced much of the militant black nationalism that Farrakhan stood for. According to Nathan McCall, a reporter on leave from the *Washington Post* who published an essay in the paper's Outlook section even as he was negotiating to ghostwrite Farrakhan's autobiography, complaints about Farrakhan from whites were "a smokescreen to conceal their blanket contempt for any black man who attempts to lift us up." A *New York Times* analysis by Don Terry closed with a certifying statement by a Howard University political scientist, Ron Waters, who downplayed the significance of Farrakhan and insisted that the march "belongs to the people and they have taken it over."

The reporting of the march was often marked by a triumphalist tone. The *New York Times* ran a front-page feature piece about a busload of black men on their way to the march from Atlanta. Running under the headline "A Bus to the Black March: 31 Men, Hope and History," Michel Marriott's piece said that the twelve-hour journey "was less to a place than an appointment with black hope, history and renewal"—an "appointment with destiny," as one fellow traveler put it, that answered "our ancestors' call." Practically every gesture, expression and observation was felt to have a special significance, Marriott wrote breathlessly. "At times even the bus itself seemed to carry a symbolic meaning," he maintained, the reverse image of the "slave ships of old."

Equally swept up, the *Washington Post* carried a front-page article saying that the rally "created the sheltering atmosphere of a family reunion" and that participants "were washed in a warm sense of brotherhood." Another story, purporting to analyze the "meaning" of the event, was even more gushing, describing a scene "overcome . . . with the sights, sounds and spirit of a community renewing itself in a day-long myth-shattering celebration of smiling faces, slapping hands, upbeat voices, hugs and goodwill." Calling it "liberating and inspiring—an awakening," *Post* columnist Dorothy Gilliam said the event was "a day to remember, a special success."

Farrakhan's two-and-half-hour speech was filled with calls for self-reliance and personal accountability, as well as race-baiting and weird theorizing. The *New York Times* acknowledged the Farrakhan speech's dependence on "conspiracy theory and numerology" on the front page. The *Washington Post,* however, buried its analysis of the speech in its Style section, and treated it as it might a humorist's routine. A similar kind of avoidance could be discerned in the coverage given the speech by the television networks, which were careful to filter out the loopier references to Afrocentric numerology as well as Farrakhan's boast that God had chosen him to lead the march.

The most selective coverage came from the *Los Angeles Times.* Giving not even a passing nod to the self-aggrandizing and less-than-pacific remarks that had filled Farrakhan's oration, reporters Sam Fulwood and Marc Lacey called his speech "a searing demand for self discipline," and wrote: "Instead of the fiery speeches that are his trademark, he [Farrakhan] struck a conciliatory tone by paying tribute to all other religions."

Over the course of the next year, the solicitude toward Farrakhan and his movement continued. A number of profiles of Farrakhan, all with a revisionist cast that very deliberately skirted or minimized such issues as the Nation of Islam's bizarre, racist mythology involving mad scientists from thousands of years ago. In particular, there was a three-part series on National Public Radio advancing the notion that Farrakhan was a misunderstood figure and that his anti-Semitism was exaggerated. While violin music played in the background, the clip closed with Farrakhan declaring, "Music expands my breast to include the beauty of human beings—all human beings."

Less than six months after the Million Man March, however, early in 1996, the effort to establish Farrakhan's mainstream legitimacy ran into a serious roadblock when he went on his "World Friendship Tour" to a string of African and Middle Eastern countries hostile to the United States, such as Libya, Iraq, Iran, Sudan and Nigeria. During these visits, Farrakhan made speeches denouncing America. At one point in Iraq, he compared the impact of United Nations sanctions on the regime of Saddam Hussein to the Holocaust. In Libya he was offered $1 billion from dictator Muammar al-Khadafy, who said it would help Farrakhan establish an army of black men in America ready to fight the white racist power structure.

Some news organizations like ABC News and the *Washington Post* were quick to report the story, but others that had invested heavily in the newfound political legitimacy of Farrakhan were clearly hesitant. For more than a week after the story first broke the second week in February, there was not a single mention of the controversy occasioned by the trip in the *New York Times*, even though it had a correspondent in Sudan about the same time Farrakhan visited there.

Returning to the United States, Farrakhan was quick to lash back at his critics. In a speech carried on C-Span during Savior's Day ceremonies in Chicago, Farrakhan denounced his attackers, particularly Congressman Peter King, for demanding hearings, mistakenly charging that King, in fact a Catholic, was a Jew. "The Jews put the Romans on Jesus," Farrakhan insisted. "And the Zionists are stimulating and pulling the strings in Washington.... I have warned you that Allah will punish you. You are wicked deceivers of the American people. You have sucked their blood. You are not real Jews.... You are the synagogue of Satan. And you have wrapped your tentacles around the U.S. Government. And you are deceiving and sending this nation to hell." Farrakhan's tirade was neither reported in the *Times'* news columns nor denounced on its editorial page. Nor did the fallout from the speech seem to affect the overall standing Farrakhan had won in the journalistic community. Members of the National Association of Black Journalists gave Farrakhan a standing ovation when he addressed their 1996 national convention.

This skewed coverage of large national issues involving race is perhaps not so surprising considering the indifference that has greeted racial problems occurring within the American newsroom itself. Public expressions of racial animosity made by certain black reporters toward white colleagues are typically met with avoidance and denial. In *Volunteer Slavery*, her memoir of her years with the *Washington Post*, Jill Nelson causally refers to "ignorant whites." *Los Angeles Times* reporter

Sam Fulwood III, in his memoir *Waking from the Dream*, describes how an apparently well-meaning and insightful story suggestion from a friendly white colleague made him want to "grab her by the throat and shake her like a rag doll." Fulwood also confessed that when a white editor rewrote the top of the story that grew out of the aforementioned suggestion—the story was to focus on the political appeal of Colin Powell in the black community—he wanted "to rip his lungs out."

Anti-white feelings form a dominant theme in *Makes Me Wanna Holler*, Nathan McCall's account of his transformation from a convicted felon to a reporter at the *Washington Post*. In the book he brags that as a young man, he discovered that "fucking up white boys made us feel real good inside," and that even as a successful professional, "sometimes I wanna do that now…take one of those white boys where I work and bang his head against a wall or stomp him in the ground until all the stress leaves my body." According to McCall, "Nothing I know, not even Olympic sex, relieves tension as completely as when we used to fuck up white boys."

It would be hard to imagine such racist sentiments coming from white reporters; indeed, anyone who was fool enough to utter them publicly would also have to know they would probably kill a career. Yet these black journalists have been celebrated and their anti-white racism heralded as an "honest" reaction to a racist newsroom culture. Appearing on the *Today Show* during the publicity tour for *Makes Me Wanna Holler*, McCall was lobbed this fraternal softball by NBC's Bryant Gumbel: "Its been written that being black in America is like being a witness at your own lynching. Why didn't your experience make you more resentful than you are today?"

If the press pushes evidence of black racism into the periphery of its vision, it has no trouble staring down the racism of whites. Despite the progress that American society has made, the press still clings to a view of race relations in which racism is seen as a force deeply imbedded in the psyche of white America and in a broad spectrum of America's institutions, from the criminal courts to corporate boardrooms, army barracks to mortgage banks.

Contrary to the view that prevailed during the Civil Rights era, when America was seen as flawed but perfectible, the press now sees racism as perdurable and even growing worse. Of course, from time to time there are exceptions, such as the impressive fifteen-part, six-week-long series that the *New York Times* published in 2000 called "How Race

Is Lived in America," which managed to catch many of the subtleties and the sense of historical progress often lacking in most of the paper's daily coverage. But the overall picture that the average news consumer in America gets is a bleak one. Insisting on the inherent victimhood of people of color, news reporting tends to exaggerate the problem of race. The press would have us believe that racism lurks everywhere, ready to violate nonwhites at any opportunity, and to erode the tenuous progress that has been made over the last fifty years.

The journalistic establishment never tires of celebrating the Civil Rights Movement itself, yet its own reporting would make it seem as if the struggle's gains have been minimal. For Pulitzer Prize winner (and former *Washington Post* ombudsman) E. R. Shipp, for example, the thirty-year anniversary of the 1964 Civil Rights Act and 1965 Voting Rights Act brought only disillusionment. " 'Free at last. Free at last,' we cheered back then," she wrote. "Never guessing that nearly 30 years later many of us—those who seem to have made it and the many more who clearly haven't—would still be singing the Billy Taylor song: 'I wish I knew how it would feel to be free.' "

For the *New York Times,* the thirtieth anniversary of the Civil Rights March in Selma, Alabama, in 1965 was an occasion for the headline "In Selma, Everything and Nothing Has Changed." Whether the *Times* was ready to acknowledge real change was questionable, though. According to Gay Talese, who was sent back to Selma to reflect on his experience there as a young reporter, the *Times* had a photograph of an interracial couple being married at Selma City Hall. But the picture—a white bride and a black groom who was an aide to a mayor who had once been part of the bigoted ruling elite—did not run for reasons, Talese suspected, that involved more than managing editor Gerald Boyd's insistence that images like that had little news value. Rather, the image of racial amity was problematic to the story line.

Even the FBI's 1997 decision to reopen the infamous and still unsolved 1963 Birmingham church bombing investigation became an occasion to reassert black victimization. Closing his account of the announcement to look once again into the thirty-year-old case, *Times* reporter Rick Bragg allowed one black Baptist minister to complain that "black life is still not considered as valuable in this country."

The one institution that has been attacked more than any other in discussions of race is the criminal justice system. The activist party line that the justice system is institutionally biased is one that journalists have become much more ready to echo, whether the facts are there to back it up or not.

Consider the notion that the war on drugs is basically a war on blacks and that the penal system represents "concentration camps" for black males, as *Washington Post* columnist Courtland Milloy has written. A March 1996 report in the *Washington Post,* for example, said that African Americans in California were sentenced under the "Three Strikes" law at a rate thirteen times higher than whites, and that 83 percent of those sent to prison under the law were there for nonviolent offenses, primarily involving drugs. "If you were writing a law to target blacks one could scarcely have done it more effectively than three strikes," the *Post* reporter quoted one activist. Left unsaid, however, was that most of those imprisoned for drug crimes under the three strikes law have long criminal records involving a variety of other crimes, some violent, and that the last drug offense is merely the final act in a destructive criminal career. Also not noted was the fact that those in prison for drug crimes are usually there for trafficking offenses, not mere possession, which makes the idea of racial victimization a little harder to sustain.

An ideological commitment to seeing the criminal justice system as institutionally racist is also evident in the resistance of the press to research contradicting that presumption. In early October, 1996, for example, the Center for Equal Opportunity, a conservative research organization, issued a report disputing the widespread claim made by liberal activists that whites are more likely to be acquitted of serious crimes than blacks. Analyzing Department of Justice data, the study concluded that, in fact, conviction rates for blacks were actually lower than for whites in 12 of the 14 most serious felony categories including robbery, rape, and assault.

Coming on the eve of the O. J. Simpson verdict's one-year anniversary, when questions about the system's basic racial fairness would be raised once again, the report was timely and provocative. Despite the center's aggressive efforts to publicize the report, however, journalists ignored it. Instead, their Simpson coverage centered on a spate of stories affirming the notion of systemic racism. The *Washington Post,* for example, discussed the racial implications of mandatory sentencing guidelines, reporting that black defendants received slightly longer sentences than whites. And a few months later, the *Los Angeles Times* explored the issue of racial disparity in homicide investigations, asserting that the system appeared "to devalue the lives of low income people and minorities."

Media insistence on the inherent racism of the justice system is starkest and most sustained in relation to cases of alleged police brutality. One such case occurred in January 1994, when the son of one of New York's most prominent Muslim clerics, seventeen-year-old Shu'aib

Abdul Latif, was shot by police in a dimly lit basement of a Brooklyn apartment house. According to police, officers responding to a gun call had chased Abdul Latif into the basement, where he scuffled with them and made a grab for one of their guns. But according to the boy's family, as well as alleged eyewitnesses, Abdul Latif was shot in cold blood with his hands raised over his head as he tried to surrender.

The officer who shot Latif was black, as was the officer who was accidentally wounded in the course of the struggle. So was the inspector assigned to investigate the shooting. Yet the black community insisted Abdul Latif's death was yet another instance of police racism.

While the city's other papers were careful to describe the incident's ambiguity, the *New York Times* painted the boy as a martyr and gave unwarranted space to unsubstantiated charges by the boy's family that officers involved in the shooting were racist and that a cover-up was under way.

A week after the January 4 shooting, for example, the *New York Post* reported that the youth had been arrested as a minor on charges of selling crack the year before and that his friends said they suspected the boy had become involved in drugs again. *New York Newsday* ran with this information too, adding that police maintained they had found twenty-four vials of crack and $83 in cash on the floor of the basement where he had been killed. Yet on the same day, the *New York Times* ran a profile of the boy under the headline "Slain Youth Is Called Nonviolent." According to reporter Felicia Lee, Abdul Latif was the "painfully shy" son of a cleric who dreamed of being a carpenter as he worked in the family business, studied for the GED and "tried to negotiate the gritty streets of East New York as a practicing Muslim." While the family members Lee interviewed did admit he had dropped out of school and had one minor scuffle with the law, for turnstile jumping, they said he was a young man who shunned drugs and violence. The boy's uncle—incidentally a news clerk at the *Times* named Ismail Abdul Karim, who had tutored the boy four times a week when he was not working in his father's food distribution business—insisted, "This boy ran away from violence at all costs. He was not one to mix it up." And although it had no direct evidence to substantiate the charge, the article also gave considerable space to family members who accused the police of racist misconduct. "A lot of the police are not as professional as they ought to be," the boy's father, the Imam, insisted to Lee. "Many of them are racist, fearful of young black men and Hispanic men, and when they see one they think right away they have a gun."

This article proved embarrassing to the *Times*. The paper backtracked the next day, publishing what was in essence a retraction.

According to *Times* reporter David Firestone, "A picture began to emerge yesterday of the teenager's involvement in the drug-soaked world of the neighborhood where he was killed." Relying on information from law enforcement sources, Firestone explained that Latif had been convicted in March 1993 on charges of carrying twenty-two vials of crack, a class B felony, and had been sentenced to five years of probation. Quoting four teenage friends of Latif who lived in the building where he was shot, Firestone said that Latif was not a drug dealer or user but "worked as a courier for a local drug dealer, holding drugs for the dealer in exchange for cash."

Still another case illustrative of the knee-jerk readiness to see racism in law enforcement and the administration of criminal justice involved what soon became a celebrated traffic incident on an upstate stretch of the Florida turnpike in April 1997. After abruptly cutting off another driver without having used his turn signal, black Miami police major Aaron Campbell was pulled over in his Ford Explorer at about 7:30 P.M. by Corporal Richard Mankewich of the Orange County Sheriff's Department. Campbell claimed that Mankewich had stopped him for no good reason, and quickly grew truculent. After a struggle he was eventually charged with battery against a police officer and resisting arrest.

According to a videotape from a camera mounted on the patrol car, Campbell handed over his license, but almost immediately accused Mankewich of "fucking with people from Dade County." Although identifying himself as a police officer, Campbell refused to show Mankewich his police identification card when asked. After a certain amount of back and forth, Campbell, who was armed and admitted so to Mankewich when asked, called the corporal a "fucking liar" and then grabbed his license back, referring to Mankewich as "bitch" and "boy" and declaring that he would take no ticket from him.

Told by Mankewich that he would either have to hand back his license or go to jail, Campbell refused and demanded to see a supervisor. He also refused to keep his hands away from the waistband pouch that carried his weapon, balking at Mankewich's orders to keep his hands on top of his head and, after that, to get down on the ground. Warned that he would be hit with pepper spray if he continued to ignore the corporal's commands, Campbell then ran away from Mankewich and a second deputy who had responded to Mankewich's radio call for assistance. He was chased about a quarter-mile before surrendering, and then was cuffed and taken in to be booked. (At a trial in 1998, Campbell was convicted of resisting arrest.)

With the facts of the case unequivocally documented on videotape, it was hard to argue that Campbell had been a victim of anti-black police racism. Yet *Nightline*'s Michele McQueen tried to make Campbell out to be the one who was wronged. Echoing charges from black officers in Miami who were nowhere near the scene that Campbell had been pulled over on the basis of racial profiling, McQueen also allowed Campbell's supporters to claim that Corporal Mankewich had purposefully tried to provoke him by being rude. Invoking the history of bad encounters between police officers and black males along "a dark road at night," McQueen herself sought to excuse Campbell's behavior: "Was it possible that Major Campbell was frightened too?" Closing the show, host Ted Koppel cited Campbell's rank and the expectation of respect that went along with it, and said that it was "not hard to understand why Major Campbell felt that a senior white police officer might have been treated differently." Not addressed was the fact that Campbell had refused to show his police ID, which meant that in fact he had never established his rank to begin with, and that this might have made the patrol officer reluctant to accord him the respect Campbell assumed he should have.

But at least *Nightline* got the facts of the case correct in its report, unlike the *Washington Post*'s Michael Fletcher, whose piece tried to make the arrest of Aaron Campbell look like the Return of Rodney King.

According to Fletcher, after he read a short dispatch about the Campbell case that ran on the AP wire on May 22, he and his editor decided that the story would make a good piece for the *Post*'s national news section. To their minds the story was part of a larger pattern of racism operating within the ranks of police officers. As Fletcher later wrote in his piece, the incident was "the latest in a series of violent confrontations between white police officers and black officers who were off-duty or working in plainclothes."

Making no mention of the fact that Campbell had refused orders to keep his hands away from his weapon pouch or that he had called Corporal Mankewich a "bitch" and "boy," Fletcher, a black reporter often assigned to stories involving racism and civil rights, gave an abbreviated version of the standoff that made it seem explicable only in terms of racial animus on the part of the police. Then he described the officers as having jumped Campbell from behind, spraying him with pepper gas after he had "tried to walk away." It was as if the incident had taken place in a parallel universe.

Media obsession with racist police brutality hit frenzy level in response to the February 1999 shooting of Amadou Diallo by four white officers in the Bronx. Diallo was a twenty-two-year-old West African immigrant street peddler living in the Soundview section of the Bronx, who recently had lied to immigration officials about his status, claiming to be a torture victim from Mauritania instead of the well-off son of a middle-class Guinean. Just after midnight he was approached by four officers in the NYPD's elite, but controversial "Street Crime" unit. Though its aggressive "stop and frisk" tactics had been credited with leading to a dramatic reduction in the amount of gun-related street crime, the unit also stood accused of harassing minorities while pursuing this goal.

The police officers that night were patrolling the area in response to a rash of shootings and to the activities of an armed serial rapist who might have been responsible for up to fifty-one sexual assaults, ten in Soundview alone. While cruising in an unmarked car, the officers saw Diallo pacing back and forth and peering suspiciously into the windows in front of his dimly lit apartment building doorway. They stopped the car, identified themselves as police officers and demanded that Diallo stop. Instead, he continued into the vestibule of the building and tried to go inside.

The officers ordered Diallo to come out and put his hands where they could see them, but Diallo pulled out something that one of the officers thought was a gun. "Gun!" one officer yelled, and the rest fired forty-one shots, nineteen of which struck Diallo, killing him. It was only after the ten-second incident was over that they realized that what Diallo had in his hands was a wallet, which he apparently had taken out of his pants pocket to show the officers as identification.

With so many shots fired in such a seemingly senseless killing, Diallo's death raised immediate suspicions that the police had overreacted and that race had played a role. Had Diallo been white, the charge went, the officers might not have been so reflexively fearful or assumed his actions had criminal intent. But unmentioned in the inflammatory reporting of the incident were mitigating facts that could have explained, if not justified, the shooting.

As James Fyfe, a former New York police officer and criminologist at Temple University, wrote in the *Wall Street Journal*, the killing could have been seen as an honest mistake made by four men with limited information in the course of a dangerous action. It was more akin to malpractice than murder, wrote Fyfe, who often appears as an expert witness *against* the police in brutality cases but appeared for the defense in this one. It was also noteworthy, Fyfe observed, that the shooting was perpetrated in a completely unintentional manner, unlike other recent high-profile cases of police brutality, such as the upsetting sodomy that had been perpetrated on Haitian immigrant Abner Louima in Brooklyn in 1998.

Yet from the moment the Diallo case was first reported, the *New York Times* presented it as a classic instance of racist police misconduct that exposed the dark underbelly of the Giuliani administration's bid to clean up New York City. The Diallo case, insisted the *Times* in both its editorials and its feature articles, was typical of an abusive police culture, exemplifying the kind of treatment that minority residents had come to expect in a city that was "taking on the sinister colorations of a police state."

One of the ways that the paper advanced this image was by the sheer amount of space it devoted to the case. In the first two months after the shooting, the *Times* ran an average of 3.5 stories per day on it, many of them beginning on page one and then jumping inside, where they were decked with multiple sidebars. The saturation coverage climaxed on March 26, when news was announced that Bronx district attorney Robert Johnson—who had publicly stated he saw no difference between what the policemen did and "any other individuals who roll up beside a building and open fire"—filed second-degree murder charges. On that day, the paper went with nine Diallo stories, putting the case on par with wars or major international disasters.

The fact that the officers were to be tried for murder, and not a lesser charge that reflected a lesser degree of intent, was fine with the *Times*. Columnist Bob Herbert wrote, "Black New Yorkers are in a fury over the cold-blooded killing of Mr. Diallo. His death is seen by most blacks as simply the latest tragic manifestation of the ruthless and humiliating treatment of ethnic minorities that is part of the daily routine of so many cops in this city." Yes, it is true, Herbert continued, that crime has dropped and that most cops are solid citizens. "But it is also true that there is a frightening number of violent, racist, sadistic and in some cases homicidal police officers who spend much of their time terrorizing people. And that behavior is widely seen by black New Yorkers as being tolerated, if not condoned, by Mayor Giuliani."

If Herbert and the editors at the *Times* had looked carefully at police department statistics, however, they would have discovered that the Diallo shooting was hardly typical at all of Rudy Giuliani's New York. In fact, it was an aberration. The eleven police shootings in 1999 represented the lowest number of civilian deaths in the city in twenty-five years, and showed a police department much more careful with the use of lethal force than during the administration of David Dinkins, the city's first black mayor. Shootings per officer had dropped 67 percent between 1993, the last year of the Dinkins administration, and 1998, the year Amadou Diallo was shot. In 1993, the police made 266,313 arrests and killed 23 people; in 1998 they arrested 403,659, killing only 19. Even as the department grew by 36 percent, the absolute number of police killings and the rate of fatalities per officer fell. In addition to showing that the NYPD was more cautious than at any other recent time, the data also showed it less likely to inflict harm than almost any other similarly sized urban police force. In 1999, the NYPD had 0.48 fatal shootings per 1000 cops, while the predominantly black cops in Washington had 3.12.

Another way the *New York Times* underscored what it cast as racist brutality was by the erroneous picture it presented of minority antipathy toward the police, creating a perception that nonwhite residents felt under siege and that, as an early April editorial put it, they had "exchanged the fear of crime for a fear of the police." A late March report, running under the front-page headline "In Two Minority Neighborhoods, Residents See a Pattern of Hostile Street Searches," typified the tone of the reporting. "The treatment down here is crazy," one neighborhood resident was quoted as saying. "Stop and frisk, harassment. The average person down here has no faith in police officers." Said Shawna Hamilton, a thirty-four-year-old woman who said she had been taken to the police station five or six times in the last five years though not arrested, "Everyone out here is Amadou Diallo. It's just waiting to happen. Who will it be? When will it happen?"

The *Times* was particularly intent on proving the alienation and fear of the West African immigrant community that Diallo belonged to. In an early February report headlined "In a Quest for Peace and Opportunity West Africans Find Anger," reporter Amy Waldman quoted one immigrant as saying, "It makes you wonder whether leaving your troubled home was a mistake. America was supposed to be a safe haven, but if you get shot by the police, where else can you turn to." A week later the same theme was sounded in a second piece headlined "Killing Heightens the Unease Felt by Africans in New York." In this report, another immigrant declared, "We are afraid. We are afraid. I want to go back before someone kills me."

Such reporting led the officers' attorneys to petition for a change in venue where a fair trial might be more likely. In granting the motion and moving the trial to Albany, the judge assigned to consider the motion clearly had the *New York Times* in mind when he bemoaned the "pubic clamor" that news coverage of the incident had generated. In response, the *Times* editorial page lashed out, criticizing the judge for failing to mention "the large amount of balanced press coverage about the defendants."

The public rebuke that the venue change represented seemed to introduce a more sober and at points sympathetic tone to the coverage as the trial approached in the spring of 2000. Emphasizing the officers' point of view that had eluded it the year before, the *Times* seemed intent on corrective reporting, with pieces headlined "For Officers in Diallo Case a Year of Scorn and Isolation" and "Defense Wants Diallo Jurors to See through Officers' Eyes." Yet during the trial itself there were continued broadsides against the police, epitomized by the snide tone of a report examining what the paper said was the "blue wall of solidarity" among officers testifying at the trial, which, the piece insinuated, amounted to nothing less than lying on the witness stand.

The charge of second-degree murder was one that many thought excessive and hard to prove, carrying as it does the prosecutorial obligation to show some degree of intent on the part of the accused. And in fact, the prosecutors did have difficulty, especially in the face of the obvious remorse the officers, one of whom broke down in tears. As predicted, the officers were acquitted.

The verdict triggered a torrent of bitterness at the *New York Times*. The thousands of protesters who took to the streets after the verdict "were understandably outraged that an innocent man had been shot down in his own doorway," the *Times* editorial read, and the verdict demonstrated why "many New Yorkers, especially in minority communities, think the police are a threat to their lives and safety." Bob Herbert's strident commentary at the front end of the Diallo affair lost none of its scalding—and erroneous—edge at the end of it. "The hope here is that the cops who killed Amadou Diallo for the crime of breathing while black will turn in their badges and their blue uniforms and move on. Whatever they do, the problems that they have come to epitomize will remain—the humiliation and brutalization of thousands of innocent New Yorkers, most of them black and brown, by police officers who are arrogant, tyrannical, poorly trained, often frightened, and not infrequently, racist."

Of course, if the malefactors are nonwhite police officers, it's a different story. One clear example of this double standard on police brutality involved a December 1997 case in Brooklyn, when a group of seven off-duty black narcotics officers assaulted a thirty-year-old recreation specialist named Reginald Bannerman. The officers had been socializing loudly in a Crown Heights bar when Bannerman—also a patron, and also black—asked them to quiet down. Taking exception to Bannerman's complaint, the men beat and stomped him outside the bar, firing their guns fourteen times over his head to scare him as they did so. Later that night, a disoriented Bannerman was hit by a subway train. His death was ruled a suicide.

The trial of the officers involved took place at the same time as the trial of the white officers accused of beating and sodomizing Abner Louima. Yet the Bannerman case earned very little attention from the *New York Times,* which did not even indicate the race of the cops in question. To some, this calculated indifference to the racial identity of the attackers seemed odd. "Can anyone imagine [racial agitators] being silent if the only thing different about the Crown Heights incident were that the seven cops involved were white rather than black," asked an editorial by the rival *New York Post.*

In some cases, the press's eagerness to confirm institutional racism in American life extends to information of extremely dubious provenance. In August 1995, a business story that ran on the Reuters news agency wire played on page one of *USA Today* under the headline "Groups Say Crime Reports Affect Hiring." The article maintained that the overrepresentation of young black men in local television crime stories was contributing significantly to the problem of inner-city unemployment. Citing such authorities as the Chicago Urban League, the Reuters/*USA Today* report said that crime reports and the images of depravity and violence on local television discouraged employers from hiring blacks.

Lacking the kind of statistical or quantitative base that might have been expected to support such a conclusion, the story nevertheless generated a significant amount of "bounce." Radio and television talk shows seized upon it for a news peg on which to hang, once again, the demon of racism. Having recently published a piece on the subject of diversity and the *New York Times* in the *Columbia Journalism Review,* I was invited onto a cable news TV talk show, *Talk Back America,* and asked to discuss the report with several other guests.

Linking inner-city unemployment to negative TV imagery seemed dubious to me. Of course, the racism of employers *could* be a factor, and sensationalistic crime coverage *might* be feeding that. But poor education, criminal records, drug abuse, absenteeism and unfamiliarity with appropriate workplace attitudes seemed more likely causes for the problem of joblessness among black youths. On the show I cited the work of liberal black sociologist William Julius Wilson, whose masterful book on underclass dysfunction, *When Work Disappears*, points out that urban employers consider young black males "to be uneducated, unstable, uncooperative, and dishonest," and have sound reasons for that view.

The real problem with the Reuters/*USA Today* piece, however, was not its sociological simple-mindedness, but the way it transformed the mere intuition of a link between media images and black unemployment into a solid social-scientific fact. According to James Lewis, the research director of the Chicago Urban League who was cited as a primary source, that linkage "wasn't based on anything but my imagination," and there was no quantitative analysis that he knew of to back up the connection.

Lewis, whom I had interviewed by phone before going on *Talk Back America,* told me that Sherwood Ross, the Reuters stringer who wrote the initial piece, had contacted him while doing research for a larger story he said he was preparing on the reasons why businesses don't locate in inner-city areas. Ross, said Lewis, asked him if he thought it was *possible* that images of black men on the crime reports on local television news could be playing a role, and Lewis replied that he thought it was indeed possible. Lewis told me that he had meant nothing conclusive by that remark; "It was sort of a derived kind of thing, kind of something I had an intuition about."

The *USA Today* story was a one-day phenomenon with relatively little national impact. Other stories of American racism based on similarly sketchy evidence or outright fraud have become part of the popular consciousness, resistant to corrective efforts, which are usually rendered too late and too little.

This has been the case in a number of high-profile, so-called "bias crime" stories. One such case, from the summer of 1996, involved allegations that racist U.S. Army Special Forces troops at Fort Bragg, North Carolina, had painted swastikas on the doors of black soldiers training there. The story went national almost immediately, grabbing newspaper headlines and network leads. It also made a significant splash politically. Citing it in his acceptance speech at the Democratic National Convention in late July, President Clinton said, "We still have too many Americans who give in to their fears of those who are different from them." While cool on its surface, the subtext of the president's comment was clear: America is such a hotbed of racism that even elite Army units like the Special Forces are not immune.

Two months later, army investigators identified a black soldier as the culprit and initiated procedures to discharge him. But unlike the flood of stories that were triggered by the first reports of the swastikas, neither the networks nor the major national press gave any significant attention to this development. The *New York Times* noted blithely that even if the bogus charge had set everyone on edge, at least it had provided an opportunity for the races to reach out to each other. Said one black preacher quoted by the *Times*, "Out of all that adversity, some good things have come."

Another media-abetted hoax involved the annual gathering of local and federal law enforcement officers in Tennessee called the Good Ole Boys Roundup, where egregious racial misconduct was alleged to have occurred. According to reports that began to circulate in 1995 about a past gathering in 1994, the Roundup was a "racist event" filled with obscene jokes about blacks and crude racial stunts such as a banner emblazoned with letters reading "Nigger Checkpoint." It was also reported that black law enforcement agents who had tried to attend the gathering were given a hostile reception and ordered to leave by the event's organizers.

The number of federal agents said to have attended the event was miniscule—between 120 and 200 in all over the course of ten years' time. At no point did anyone bring forward evidence that these agents had actively participated in the racially offensive conduct. Yet the reports were taken as signs of vast and deep systemic racism in federal law enforcement, particularly the Bureau of Alcohol, Tobacco and Firearms. Responding to pressure from the Congressional Black Caucus and civil rights organizations, the Senate Judiciary Committee held hearings on the subject. The Justice Department launched an internal review during which over fifty thousand federal law enforcement agents were interrogated about their possible participation in the event and any other racist activities they may have joined in or were aware of. (This was a review that civil libertarians, rarely on the side of federal law enforcement, denounced as an abridgement of constitutional rights and an effort to get agents to "name names.") Once again, President Clinton spoke to the nation about the evils of racism, citing the Good Ole Boys Roundup in his "mend it, don't end it" affirmative action speech that June.

Yet even as this witch hunt was going on, it was becoming clear that there was little fact behind the story. In late August, the *New York Times* admitted that much of the information pertaining to the gathering had been taken from a doctored video and were bogus. Also deflating the presumption of racism was the revelation that the leader of the 1994 gathering had in fact told those who complained about the presence of black FBI agents to get lost themselves. Soon, other news organizations were reporting that much of the information they had been supplied about the 1994 event came from National Rifle Association activists out to throw mud on federal law enforcement agencies that they felt were persecuting gun rights advocates. The hoax unraveled further when it was reported that the person who had given the evidence of racist misconduct to the NRA was a white-power activist who had himself been prevented from distributing racist literature at the previous year's Roundup.

These corrective reports, however, came out episodically and had nowhere near the force of the original stories. In the public mind, and in particular the black mind, the Good Ole Boys Roundup and the federal agents mentioned in connection with it remained tarred. (During the investigation into the wave of black church burnings in 1996, for instance, black leaders expressing suspicion about ATF investigators cited the Roundup and the fallout from it as confirmation of their charges of racism.)

The coverage of alleged racist misconduct by high-ranking executives at the Texaco Oil Company in late 1996 also reveals journalists' will to believe the worst about white racism. The Texaco controversy got its start on November 4, 1996, when the *New York Times* published a front-page report claiming that top executives of the company had been caught on secretly recorded tapes making racist comments about minority employees. Based on transcripts of the tapes that were leaked to him by the plaintiff's lawyers, reporter Kurt Eichenwald's story said that senior Texaco executives had referred to black employees as "niggers" and "black jelly beans" and had made disparaging remarks about Hannukah and Kwanzaa. The tapes, Eichenwald suggested, provided an "unfiltered glimpse into one company's senior levels where important decisions—including promotion policies for minority employees—are made."

Described by Wade Henderson of the NAACP as the "functional equivalent of the Rodney King video," the Texaco tapes generated instant national headlines and were seen as yet another sign that racism was still a major force in America—this time in corporate boardrooms. According to the *Washington Post*'s editorial page, the incident showed that "bias in corporate America was alive and well." Bob Herbert of the *New York Times* asserted that "the only thing unusual about the Texaco story was that it was reported." Jack White of *Time* magazine said the Texaco story provided a "rare and revealing glimpse of the bigotry and hypocrisy that still festers at the apex of the corporate world despite three decades of affirmative action."

Much of the news reporting centered on the disparity between Texaco's stated goals of equal opportunity and the realities of its minority hiring and promotion policies. In a detailed racial and ethnic breakout, the *New York Times* reported that "African Americans make up some 12% of the U.S. population, but of the 873 executives at Texaco who make more than $106,000 annually, only six—.07% —are blacks." Such disparity, according to *Times* reporter Kurt Eichenwald, defined a company "that says all the right things but has done too little to insure they have any meaning."

But the evidence used to support the impression of rampant corporate racism in the Texaco story did not stand up to rigorous scrutiny. After listening to a digital enhancement of the original tape, an independent auditor brought into the case at Texaco's request declared that the transcript filed with the court—the same transcript that had served as the basis for the original story—was erroneous. The executive who was accused of using the word "nigger" had in fact been referring to "St. Nicholas," and the term "black jelly bean" was actually an expression used in a company-sponsored diversity management training program.

Although Texaco had brought in the auditor, his reputation was such that his findings and the technical evidence upon which they rested were accepted as accurate by most observers. A week after it had run its original story, the *Times*, tail between its legs, ran a piece on the front page in exactly the same spot as its original scoop, reporting that the racial epithets said to be on the tape were in fact never uttered.

This news, however, did not have the bombshell impact one might have thought it would. Although it placed the story on the front page, the *Times* ran it only in some editions, and the editorial page, which had led the charge against Texaco, gave the correction no notice at all. While incorporating the new, contradictory information, moreover, the *Times* nevertheless still clung to its original interpretation, giving prominent play to civil rights leaders who said that with or without the racial epithets, "the incident is still a damning indictment of Texaco."

News that the tape recording did not really contain what the transcript leaked to the *Times* (and entered into the court record) said it did raised serious suspicion that the plaintiffs in the case may have perpetrated a fraud on the *Times* and on the court. But aside from a *USA Today* story, which quoted *Times* business editor John Geddes defending his coverage by saying that if the *Times* got suckered "so did the court," no one pursued that story. The *Wall Street Journal*'s Holman Jenkins was the only major journalist to report that this wasn't the first time the plaintiff's attorney was caught attempting such a thing. According to

Jenkins, attorney Mike Hausfield had employed a bogus transcript in an earlier case but was caught by the defendant's lawyer before succeeding. Months later Jenkins raised the issue again, demolishing claims made in the meantime that the plaintiff's attorneys had subjected the infamous audiotape to another outside auditor, who allegedly had confirmed that the N-word could in fact be heard. As Jenkins wrote, "It is hard to escape the impression that [these lawyers] did not give a damn what the tape really said."

The Texaco story also raised questions about the relative ease with which the civil rights establishment, capitalizing on a story that proved false in many substantive respects, could intimidate corporate America. Under threat of a national boycott, a $3 slip in share price and calls for a Department of Justice investigation, Texaco suspended two of the executives involved and cancelled retirement benefits for two others without even giving them a hearing. Later, even after the correction was announced and Texaco wasn't in nearly as bad a public relations position, the company nevertheless agreed to a $176-million-dollar settlement of the discrimination suit. It also agreed to one of the most far-reaching plans to foster diversity in hiring and business practices ever consented to by a major American corporation. Some saw the plan as little more than a racial shakedown, and for Texaco, a way to ransom back its public image. Yet with few exceptions the plan was extolled throughout the journalistic establishment. According to the *New York Times*, the settlement would make Texaco "a leader in the struggle for equal opportunity."

*Washington Post* columnist Richard Cohen wrote that the handling of the case clearly underscored a climate of "racial McCarthyism" gripping the nation. "The accusation of racism, unproved though it might be," wrote Cohen, "has become the functional equivalent of what communism used to be." Cohen's was a lonely voice, however. While those ready to read larger lessons into the Texaco racism case were legion when news of the tapes first broke, few were ready to acknowledge what the wider implications were after the hoax was revealed.

In the ranks of press-abetted racial "cry wolf" stories, the black church arson story of 1996 stands in a class by itself. With images of flames licking from steepled wooden churches into dark night skies as anguished congregants stood by helplessly, it was perhaps inevitable that these fires would be seen as a flashback to the 1960s, when Mississippi was indeed burning. As Michael Kelly wrote in the *New Yorker*, the civil rights paradigm is perhaps the strongest in contemporary American journalism. Yet when less ideologically inclined reporters, like Kelly himself, began to unearth hard facts and real evidence, the church arson story stood for something other than racism: exaggeration and dangerous credulity.

Stories about a "wave" of arson attacks against black churches throughout the South began in February 1996 with the *USA Today* headline "Arson at Black Churches Echoes Bigotry of the Past." According to the paper, "an epidemic of church burning" with "scenes reminiscent of the 1960s civil rights struggles" was raging through the South.

The story took on real momentum, though, when the Center for Democratic Renewal (CDR), a left-leaning activist organization formerly known as the National Anti-Klan Network, issued a report on the subject a month later. Claiming to see a surge in arson attacks on black houses of worship—106 since the beginning of 1995—the CDR said that thirty-three of the cases remained unsolved, while twenty-four suspects, all of them white, had been arrested. "Today, our records show that white males between the ages of fifteen and forty-five are virtually destroying many historically black and interracial family founded churches throughout the region," said the CDR report. "A lot like the turbulent 1960s, those who terrorize today are night riders. In most documented cases, white men travel in groups of three to five and do the bulk of their damage under the cover of darkness, during early morning hours—most often between two and six o'clock." In some cases, the CDR added, the acts appeared to have been carried out as part of initiation rites of new recruits into such white supremacist organizations such as the Ku Klux Klan and the Aryan Brotherhood.

The CDR report's sensationalistic tone, with such inflammatory terms as "night riders," limited the coverage it received. Yet the CDR was effective in setting the terms upon which the story was reported: Black churches were being burned down throughout the South at an alarming rate, and white racism—organized white racism, no less—was responsible.

The church arson story spread steadily, unexamined, throughout the media, cementing the idea that history was repeating itself. "A century ago it was lynchings that erupted in a wave of terror against African Americans," the *Chicago Tribune* warned. "Today, an epidemic of criminal and cowardly arson has left at least…churches in ruin."

These claims were repeated in ritualized news analyses, where prominent civil rights leaders and African-American political figures became a veritable echo chamber for the idea of an organized racist assault operating throughout America under cover of darkness. Failing to point out that a significant number of fires had *not* been attributed to racial hatred, a May 21 *New York Times* report quoted Jesse Jackson saying the fires were part of a "cultural conspiracy" against blacks and "reflected the heightened racial tensions in the south that have been exacerbated by the assault on affirmative action and the populist oratory of Republican politicians like Pat Buchanan."

Columnists, particularly black columnists, were the most strident. In mid-March, Barbara Reynolds of *USA Today* said the fires were "an attempt to murder the spirit of black America." Around the same time, Jack White, writing in *Time*, assailed "the coded phrases" of Republican leaders for "encouraging the arsonists" and "playing with fire." White insisted, "there is already enough evidence to indict the cynical conservatives who build their careers George Wallace–style on a foundation of race baiting." Echoing these ideas, *New York Times* columnist Bob Herbert wrote, "The fuel for these fires can be traced to a carefully crafted environment of bigotry and hatred that was developed over the last quarter century." And *Washington Post* columnist Dorothy Gilliam claimed that society was "giving these arsonists permission to commit these horrible crimes."

Reacting to this so-called wave of racist violence and consequent floods of media outrage, the Congressional Black Caucus scheduled hearings on the Hill. The assistant attorney general for civil rights, Deval Patrick, was careful not to affirm charges that the attacks represented a conspiracy of white supremacist groups, but did characterize them as "domestic terrorism."

The story broke wide open at the end of the first week in June, when President Clinton devoted his weekly radio address to the subject. Citing memories of church burnings in Arkansas when he was a boy—memories that journalists who bothered to check the historical record disputed because no churches were burned in Arkansas during those years—Clinton said that "racial hostility is the driving force behind a number of these incidents."

Clinton's remarks, coupled with a second report from the Center for Democratic Renewal, detonated a media explosion. For more than two weeks, the burning of black churches was front-page news around the country, leading the networks' nightly newscasts, dominating editorial page commentary and grabbing the covers of all the major newsmagazines. According to journalist Michael Fumento, who ran a database search for a *Wall Street Journal* article on the subject, more than 2200 stories were done on the arsons in the immediate aftermath of Clinton's radio remarks.

Laced through much of the commentary that accompanied news

accounts were insinuations that the media had been too slow in getting on the story. Writing in the *New York Times,* columnist A. M. Rosenthal said the slowness of the media response was not only "disgraceful, it is disgusting." Rosenthal declared that if white churches were burning "we know what would happen and what would not." Yet even as the frenzy was building, stories questioning the factual data began to emerge, calling into question both the reality of the "epidemic" and its alleged "racist" basis.

The first effort at clarification was by John Lang of the Scripps Howard News Service, who examined federal records and found that roughly the same number of white and black churches were being burned. Lang also noted that many of the fires were in wood frame buildings, which were particularly susceptible to fire, and that many cases of church burning turned out to be the work of psychologically disturbed people committing copycat crimes.

The most significant corrective came, ironically, from *USA Today,* which had probably done more to advance the original "epidemic of racial terror" story line than any other single news organization. In a three-part series that reflected two months' worth of investigation of state and federal records, *USA Today* declared that:

1) There had in fact been no increase in the number of black churches being burned.

2) Black churches and white churches were being burned at similar rates.

3) The rate of church burnings over the last fifteen years had actually been going down.

The paper said racism had been a factor in some of the cases, but not in most. It also noted that in one-third of the arsons, the suspects arrested were actually black. Dismissing the allegation that the fires represented a conspiracy, *USA Today* said the phenomenon had been going on haphazardly for decades and was recently mistaken for something coordinated.

On July 4, Associated Press reporter Fred Bayles, after examining state arson records in the South, said essentially the same thing, reporting that since 1995 the number of black and white churches burned was roughly equal (73 and 75). Although in 12 to 18 of the black church burnings there was evidence that racism had been involved, in another 12 cases the racial issue had not yet been resolved.

A few days later, on the *Wall Street Journal*'s editorial feature page, Michael Fumento declared the story "a myth, probably a deliberate hoax" perpetrated by the Center for Democratic Renewal. Calling the epidemic "all smoke and mirrors," Fumento said there was no compelling evidence of any increase in black church burnings. There was, however, evidence that "activist groups have taken the media and the nation on a wild ride." Fumento charged that the CDR had regularly ignored fires set by blacks and wrongly labeled others as arson. He also said the CDR had neglected to acknowledge that a higher percentage of black churches than white ones were in economically depressed areas, where arson generally occurs at a much higher rate.

The crowning blow, however, came in that week's *New Yorker*, when Michael Kelly, using the *USA Today* series as a base, revealed the truth behind what Deval Patrick had labeled "an epidemic of terror." Citing a case which President Clinton had said was an illustration of "the fires of hatred sweeping the land," Kelly reported that at the time Clinton had cited it, investigators had not yet determined whether it was racially motivated. Since then, they had concluded it wasn't, and had accused an emotionally disturbed thirteen-year-old girl of the crime. This case, Kelly pointed out, "bore no comparison to the systematic efforts of white supremacists during the civil rights years to halt the advance of equal rights for black Americans by bombing and burning dozens of southern black churches." In fact, racism was strongly indicated in fewer than half of the black church fires investigated to date. In most, the fires were set by criminals, vandals or mentally unbalanced firebugs, with a few set by volunteer firemen trying to whip up some business.

In a media world less inclined to see racist motivation, the "fires of hatred" story line, which had been followed up and shown to be erroneous, would have given way to aggressive—and proportionate—efforts to correct public misperceptions and find out how the story had gotten started in the first place. But while the corrective pieces by Kelly, Fumento and others did put a brake on the story's momentum, there were few sizable efforts to correct the overall thrust of the previous reporting or to stage a much-needed journalistic autopsy. And when new information came in that reversed what had previously been said at the story's frenzied peak, the way it was handled proved the old truism that the charge is always on page one and the retraction on page thirty-four.

The June 10 broadcast of ABC's *World News Tonight*, for example, led with a report of two church fires in Texas and an unidentified black minister claiming it was "a matter of pervasive racism." But a few weeks later, when ABC reported that an eighteen-year-old black man had been indicted for both fires, the story was buried deep in that evening's lineup.

In fact, some news organizations ignored the new developments and continued to play the story as before. Scripps Howard, the AP and *USA Today* had already run their reports by the time the *Washington Post* ran Melissa Faye Green's July 1 Outlook essay on the fire at Georgia's Pine Lake Baptist Church. Yet Green was still allowed to write that this particular fire—which actually involved an outbuilding and not the church itself, and was later found to be the work of two disgruntled black contractors—was part of "an effort to turn back the clock to Jim Crow time." Despite mounting evidence to the contrary, the *Washington Post* also ran Dorothy Gilliam's column on July 6 examining "the social and political climate" that "helped create an environment that gives rise to the burning of black churches," and calling this climate "political tinder" for the fires.

Facts didn't stand in the way of the story line in the reporting on President Clinton's address to the NAACP in July, either. During that speech, Clinton had mentioned the burnings in the context of ethnic violence in Rwanda, Bosnia and Northern Ireland, reflecting a view very much at odds with the emerging data. Yet the news accounts of the speech neglected to mention the new information that would have highlighted the president's error.

At some points the reluctance to engage the facts gave rise to serious reportorial disconnects. Fox Butterfield's July 21 *New York Times* piece noted that investigators examining the sixty-seven fires at black churches since 1995 had found "no evidence of a single pattern, much less a conspiracy." Nevertheless, Butterfield still insisted the fires spoke of "racial divisions out of the old south" and supplemented his own analysis with the unchecked rhetoric of civil rights leaders who were still claiming linkage to the hostile racial climate set by Republican attacks on welfare and black crime.

Activists like the CDR and political figures like Assistant Attorney General Deval Patrick had not only cried wolf on this story, they had done so in the most cynical way, tarnishing the legacy of the Civil Rights Movement in the process. But apart from conservative papers like the *Wall Street Journal*, no major news organization condemned them. In fact, Deval Patrick was applauded at the 1996 convention of the National Association of Black Journalists when he said, "Black churches are on fire just like 30 years ago."

Journalists also failed to examine their own role in the fabulated story, or the way an outdated paradigm of white oppression and black victimization may have misled them. In fact, not only was there no institutional self-criticism, there was actually self-congratulation. Even as the real story of the fires was emerging to discredit the original reporting, a panel on the church arsons at the same NABJ convention that cheered Deval Patrick also praised several black journalists for their "initiative and perseverance in bringing the racial aspects of the church burnings to the fore."

A year later, in June 1997, the president's National Church Arson Task Force released a report that completely refuted the notion of a nation-wide conspiracy of hate groups riding in the night. The task force reported that most of the arsons were perpetrated by individuals acting alone, and that one out of every three suspects arrested was black—a rate nearly twice the percentage of blacks in the general population. The report also debunked accusations that the federal government was dragging its feet in trying to get to the bottom of the arson wave. In fact, while authorities investigating arson generally apprehend a culprit only 16 percent of the time, they had made arrests in 35 percent of these cases—more than double the usual rate. The report was also significant in pointing out that many more white churches than black ones were hit in the period between January 1995 and May 1997, contrary to the impression conveyed by the previous year's reporting.

This confirmation that there was no national racist conspiracy got prominent play in some newspapers, including the *Washington Post*, which ran it on the front page. It also got substantial attention on the networks, which either led their broadcasts with it or placed it high in the story lineup. But some of the news organizations that had played up the original story most dramatically virtually ignored this development altogether. Having led the pack during the previous year, the *New York Times* now buried a small AP story on page twenty, under the completely misleading headline "Panel Says Churches Are Still Targets."

# THREE

# Gay and Feminist Issues

I n the middle of the second Clinton administration, spring 1998, the
president was trying once again to make good on his promise of
allowing gay men and women to serve openly in the nation's military services. The "Don't Ask, Don't Tell" policy that the military
accepted as a compromise in 1993 was not working, gay activists and
the administration insisted. Not only were more service people being
discharged under the new policy than the old one, but the armed forces
were losing valuable and expensively trained personnel who found
the military closet still too confining and fearsome and were leaving in
droves for the civilian sector.

On Sunday, June 28, the *New York Times Magazine* published a
cover story about an anonymous gay United States Marine Corps
officer who, the article posited, stood as an emblem of the agonies suffered by closeted gays in the military. The article was headlined
"Uniforms in the Closet," with a subhead that read, "Don't ask, don't
tell has created a world of fear and deceit, alienating 'R' [the anonymous officer] and his friends from their fellow servicemen." The article
was written by regular contributor Jennifer Egan, who spent much
effort depicting the Marine as a straight arrow whom the service would
sorely miss when he left, as he planned to do soon. (In fact he sought
and received an honorable discharge later that year.)

"R" was "fiercely loyal" to the Corps, Egan wrote, "a Marine first
and gay second." The article quoted him as saying, "I know very little
about gay culture," and remarking that he found its hedonism "weary-
ing and empty." He and his friends, the author wrote, "monitor
themselves obsessively" so that nobody could possibly find out they are
gay. "Clinton thought he was doing us this big favor," "R" told Egan,
"and all he was doing was building a brick wall around the closet."

Yet according to a subsequent report in the *Advocate*, a national
gay publication, the *Times Magazine* portrait was naive and the rigor of

its fact checkers left much to be desired. The *Advocate* reported that this supposed straight arrow, allergic to the radical gay lifestyle, was actually Rich Merritt, a captain who had appeared in several gay pornographic movies. According to the *Advocate*'s editor, the story came to light after a reader of the *Times Magazine* story who recognized Merritt from several films contacted the publication.

In response, the *New York Times* ran a follow-up clarification—buried on page twenty-two. Still, editors of the magazine were unapologetic. Although he said "of course" he would have liked to have known about Merritt's involvement with pornography, *Times Magazine* editor Adam Moss declared that this revelation didn't "alter the story's truths."

About a year earlier, in the spring of 1997, the big military story of the day was the impending court-martial of twenty-six-year-old Air Force Lt. Kelly Flinn, the first woman to fly a B-52 bomber. According to feminist groups demanding more aggressive gender integration in the military, Kelly Flinn was a victim of the military's sexist double standard, an impression bolstered by the press, which has taken an even more committed position on the military's sins against woman than on its sins against gays.

A unique and demanding culture whose rules are often at odds with civilian norms, the military has good reason to maintain prohibitions against sex within the ranks and between servicepeople and the civilian spouses of colleagues. Flinn's affair with the civilian husband of an enlisted airwoman showed why. The affair was the focus of much speculation and gossip on Flinn's small, isolated North Dakota air base, as well as a very real threat to good order and discipline, since it appeared to many enlisted people on the base that Flinn had flaunted her rank to grab the enlistee's man.

But Flinn had done other, more serious things to earn the court-martial as well. Having refused several direct orders to cease all contact with the airwoman's spouse, she was charged with insubordination and with lying under oath to the investigators who had first asked her about the relationship. She had also violated the rules against what the military calls "fraternization" between those of different ranks, in a prior affair with an enlisted man. In fact, the Air Force considered these other charges so serious that it had actually decided to drop the adultery charge altogether. Yet to most of the reporters covering the story, few of whom had any military experience, the Flinn case was about adultery and little else.

An April 1997 report by *60 Minutes* was typical. Brought to the

TV newsmagazine by a freelance producer who had a personal relationship with the Flinn family, the report failed to note the fraternization, lying and insubordination charges against Flinn, and failed also to explain the military's reasons for barring the kind of sexual relationship Flinn was charged with having had. To *60 Minutes*, the Flinn case was about the "biblical sin of adultery," a barbaric anachronism in a military culture that had it in for women, particularly strong and symbolic women like Kelly Flinn.

The facts of the Flinn case eventually caught up with the slanted reporting of *60 Minutes* and the other news organizations that took their cues from it. But not before Flinn became a feminist cause célèbre, and the impression of a sexist double standard became cemented in the public mind. Even as Flinn accepted a general discharge and shrank into obscurity, reporters, many of them women, continued to insist on her victimhood and to rail against the institutional misogyny that had shot one of their idols out of the air.

Expanding the newsroom's representation of gays and women and allowing them to write from their unique perspectives is supposed to make the media more sensitive to its history of homophobia and sexism, and better able to grapple with the challenge of redefining traditional sex and gender roles and the social issues such redefinitions will produce. But rather than offer the information to help society assign the proper place to gay and feminist perspectives in public policy, the press has tried to prescribe answers to a number of issues: AIDS, abortion, gays and women in the military, gay marriage, gay adoption. Although there are many journalists able to articulate and defend gay and feminist positions on these concerns, few in today's newsrooms are as willing or able to identify with the cultures and value systems of more traditional institutions such as the military or the church. This narrows the scope of debates that ought to be informed by many different perspectives.

That failing underscore the limits and contradictions of the diversity crusade. Advocates of "inclusion" put a premium on getting inside the value structures of "marginalized" and "historically oppressed" minority cultures, but show considerably less interest in fairly portraying the internal realities of cultures shaped by traditional or conservative values. A press that had a regard for real diversity would, for instance, have been able to characterize the complexity of the clash between the civilian world and the military in its reporting on the Kelly Flinn affair and on the question of lifting the ban on openly gay servicepeople. It would have been able to see that most of those with reservations about changing the sexual status quo are more than simple-minded bigots, and that their concerns represent something more profound and more legitimate than unthinking resistance to change. In the eyes of today's diversity journalism, though, what is valid, right and worthy of tolerance is what matches its own values and political predispositions. Those whose values differ are suspect, and subject to ridicule.

In his book *Straight News: Gays, Lesbians and the News Media*, former CNN reporter Edward Alwood accurately describes the open contempt with which most of the mainstream press once regarded homosexuality. *Time* magazine, in the 1960's, called a same-sex orientation "a pathetic little second-rate substitute for reality, a pitiable flight from life" deserving "no encouragement, no glamorization, no rationalization, no fake status as minority martyrdom, no sophistry about simple differences in taste and above all no pretense that it is anything but a pernicious sickness." *Straight News* also quoted CBS News's Mike Wallace as once saying that the average homosexual was "promiscuous" and "not interested in or capable of a lasting relationship like that of heterosexual marriage."

Indeed, even well into the sexual revolution in the Sixties and early Seventies, gays remained the target of newsroom barbs. Reporting on the famous Stonewall Uprising of 1969, the *New York Daily News* ran the headline "Homo Nest Raided: Queen Bees Are Stinging Mad." As late as 1974, the *Los Angeles Times* referred to gay men on its front page as "fags." Gay reporters and editors also faced homophobia in the newsroom too. Explaining to the *Washington Post* what it was like to come out in the early 1980s at the *New York Times,* reporter Jeffrey Schmaltz spoke movingly of being banished from the Metro desk to the suburbs.

Against this ugly backdrop, the steps taken by the press to enhance the visibility of the gay community and report the subject of homosexuality with more sensitivity are indeed welcome. And the commitment to increasing the visibility of gay reporters and editors in the newsroom has certainly not been a hollow one, especially at the larger daily papers such as the *New York Times*, where three of the paper's top political reporters, an advertising columnist, theatre critic, film critic, architecture critic and classical music critic are all openly gay, along with the page-one picture editor and the top editor of its Sunday magazine. But the notion that the presence of more openly gay reporters in the newsroom has translated into both more and better coverage of gay issues is, I think, without foundation.

The increased presence of gays and lesbians in the newsroom, combined with increased sensitivity to their causes, has intensified the attention given to incidents where gays have been victims of homophobia. Witness the wall-to-wall coverage generated by the murder of Matthew Shepard, the young Wyoming man who was lured from a Laramie bar by two thugs in the fall of 1998, beaten unconscious and left to die, tied to a fence post in sub-freezing temperatures. The implicit assumption of the coverage was that Shepard had fallen victim to the often invisible but always sinister homophobia embedded deeply in American society, a pathology that could be cured only by hate-crimes legislation. On the eve of the killers' trial, Frank Rich wrote in the *New York Times:* "What remains as certain now as on October 22, the day Matthew Shepard died, is that this murder happened against the backdrop of a campaign in which the far right, abetted by political leaders like Trent Lott, was demonizing gay people as sick and sinful."

Given the avalanche of press it received, there are probably grounds to wonder whether the Shepard case might have been over-covered, although the gruesomeness of the murder and the hate that drove it certainly raised it to the level of an important national story. But when homosexuals are the perpetrators of violence instead of the victims, the sense of moral urgency seems to vanish. This is particularly true when the violence touches on the explosive issue of gay pedophilia. A case in point is the 1999 murder of a thirteen-year-old Arkansas boy named Jesse Dirkhising and the 2001 trial of the two gay neighbors who killed him.

According to prosecutors at the trial, the two men had become friendly with the boy and his mother, their next-door neighbors, and one day invited Jesse over to their house. During the afternoon, they drugged Jesse, tied him to a bed, shoved his underwear into his mouth to gag him, and added duct tape to ensure his silence. As one man stood watching in a doorway and masturbated, the other raped the boy for hours using a variety of foreign objects, including food. The two men then left the boy in such a position on the bed that he slowly suffocated to death.

A Nexis search revealed that in the first month after the Shepard murder, the media did 3007 stories about the killing. And when the case finally went to trial in the fall of 1999, it was all over the broadcast news, received front-page coverage in all major newspapers, and was featured on the cover of *Time* magazine. (In all, the *New York Times* ran 195 stories about the case.)

In the month after the Dirkhising murder, however, Nexis recorded only 46 stories. The *New York Times,* the *Los Angeles Times,*

CNN, ABC, CBS and NBC ignored the story altogether and continued to do so through the March 2001 trial of one of the murderers, which resulted in a conviction. (The other assailant later pled guilty.) The *Washington Post* ran but one tiny AP item about the case, along with an unusual ombudsman's defensive explanation of the paper's decision not to cover the case.

According to some network news officials, the Dirkhising story just didn't fit into their tight, twenty-two-minute broadcast format. Others, like ABC spokesman Todd Polkes, considered it "a local crime story that does not raise the kind of issues that would warrant our coverage." This seemed to be the position taken by most print news decision makers too. A *Washington Post* news editor argued that the paper covers only crimes that are local, that inflame local opinion, or that have national policy implications. The Shepard story was news in a way the Dirkhising story wasn't because it "prompted debate on hate crimes and the degree to which there is still intolerance of gay people in this country. It was much more than a murder story for us." When I asked the *New York Times* national news editor why the paper had not covered the story from Arkansas, I received no response.

No one admitted the obvious: that the Dirkhising story was too hot to handle because it raised the explosive issue of gay pedophilia and because it threatened the sanctity of the gays-as-victims script which had attained the status of holy writ in the media. Writing in the *New Republic*, gay journalist Andrew Sullivan had some insight into why there was such disparity between the Shepard case and that of Jesse Dirkhising, and why the press found the latter so difficult to handle. The answer was politics, Sullivan wrote:

> The Shepard case was hyped for political reasons: to build support for inclusion of homosexuals in a federal hate-crimes law. The Dirkhising case was ignored for political reasons: squeamishness about reporting a story that could feed anti-gay prejudice, and the lack of any pending interest-group legislation to hang a story on.... Some deaths—if they affect a politically protected class—are worth more than others. Other deaths, those that do not fit a politically correct profile, are left to oblivion.

Such overtly political decisions among gay activists and their newsroom allies might well provoke a backlash, Sullivan noted. "Don't these squeamish people realize that, by helping to hush this up, they seem to confirm homophobic suspicions that this murder actually is typical of gays?"

Even those journalists who can now admit they put advocacy ahead of the neutral pursuit of facts when covering AIDS during its beginnings in the 1980s still grow very defensive about it, insisting that their approach must be evaluated within the context of the times. Because their editors were either homophobic or simply uncomfortable with the subject, these reporters say, they had no choice but to become advocates simply to get the issue of AIDS on the news agenda at all.

In the process, gay as well as straight reporters sympathetic to the cause screened out (as some of them have admitted retrospectively) those unflattering truths about AIDS and the effort to fight it which might have undercut public support and government funding. Elinor Burkett, author of *The Gravest Show on Earth,* wrote of her time as an AIDS reporter for the *Miami Herald:* "The experience reminded me how expendable the truth is when a wider agenda is being pursued.... Dozens of stories didn't make it into the paper or on the air because they might have offended the sensibilities of the pc police."

This was particularly true with respect to gay male sexual practices, such as anonymous, unprotected anal sex and sadomasochistic exotica like "fisting." Scientists studying the disease, as well as activists looking for government money, knew these gay male practices were the primary reasons for the soaring infection rate. Nevertheless, the gay community adopted the position that heterosexuals were just as much at risk as homosexuals, that AIDS was an equal opportunity killer and that "safe sex" would save us all. Journalists went along with this new orthodoxy and made the subject of gay sexual mores taboo.

Some reporters put their fear of stigmatizing gay men ahead of their journalistic obligation to disclose scientific facts about AIDS and how it spreads. This taboo against candor made it very difficult to write about what was really driving the disease or to pierce public hysteria fed by the "everyone is at risk" line. Frank Bruni, who covered the AIDS beat for several different newspapers, told Elinor Burkett, "It is considered unseemly to ask people what their risk factors are and how many partners they had. If you do you are accused of playing the blame game."

The strength of the taboo was underscored in 1990 when Michael Fumento published *The Myth of Heterosexual AIDS.* Citing convincing statistical data, Fumento insisted that AIDS was not a generalized disease. Accordingly, he argued that it was wrong to spread the hysteria of a possible heterosexual "breakout" and to waste scarce resources trying to prevent infections in the heterosexual community that would never occur. As Burkett described it, Fumento had scientific fact on his side, "but since it wasn't part of the party line, no one wanted to listen."

Showing just how little they wanted to listen, AIDS activists at that time condemned both Fumento and his book, sometimes violently, and were able to force his publisher to let *The Myth of Heterosexual AIDS* die on the vine. Fumento, working at that point as an editorial writer at the *Rocky Mountain News*, found it difficult afterwards to write for anything but conservative publications.

Wedded to the insistence that AIDS was everyone's problem, reporters for years danced around the stark reality of disproportionate rates of infection among blacks and Latinos and the cultural dynamics behind those statistics. In the mid-1990s, black men were three times as likely to be infected by AIDS as white men, and black women had an infection rate ten times that of white women. Infection rates in the Latino community roughly followed the same disproportion. Worse, while prevention and education efforts were paying off in terms of a decline in the white HIV infection rate, the rate in minority communities continued to swell throughout the 1990s.

Poverty and drug abuse within minority communities played a part in the high rate of infection, to be sure. But according to public health researchers, black and Latino men are also twice as likely as white men to be bisexual. Female infection rates for these nonwhite communities showed just how dangerous was this bisexuality that dared not speak its name. At one point in the late 1980s, 84 percent of the women with AIDS were black and Latino. Compounding the problem was the profound denial within these groups, a reflection of the deep strains of homophobia that made it difficult to mount a communal response.

In all, this subject cried out for thorough reporting and even more careful presentation. Yet for most of the AIDS years, the surging racial and ethnic imbalance in infection rates, and the cultural issues underlying it, were rarely addressed by the mainstream media. When the subject did finally get the attention it deserved in mid-1998, in the form of a front-page *New York Times* piece describing the denial of the black community and its leadership, it was many years overdue, and many thousands had meanwhile died.

Wary of challenging pieties about what was causing AIDS, journalists were also reluctant to challenge the radical gay party line on how best to fight it. While the origins of the disease were still a mystery in the early stages of the epidemic, the means to prevent its spread were not. What had worked to contain syphilis, gonorrhea and other sexually transmitted diseases—testing, contact tracing and public education—were exactly the methods that most public health officials believed would work for AIDS, too. Yet insisting that these "sex negative" procedures would stigmatize gay men, activists were able to make AIDS the exception to standard public health measures. Turning a disease into a political issue, the AIDS community insisted that testing had to be strictly voluntary and completely confidential. It was left up to infected gay men to warn potential partners, if they so chose. It was an approach that was not only ineffective but deadly.

Ignoring those public health officials who regarded the politicization of this disease as irresponsible, many AIDS reporters helped to vilify those who stood up to the gay community by insisting that AIDS was most effectively fought with traditional public health methods. As a result, many officials who knew they would be attacked by the press as well as in community meetings simply refused to go out on a limb.

Worries of offending gay activists also discouraged journalistic scrutiny of AIDS education and awareness programs. Thus when the Centers for Disease Control and Prevention (CDC) began an ambitious campaign to broaden public support for the fight against AIDS by suggesting that it was an equal-opportunity killer, reporters failed to examine these claims. According to the campaign's broadcast ads, the disease started in the homosexual population but was now infecting suburban housewives, college students, doctors, dentists and other middle-class heterosexuals. Yet as CDC officials and the activists collaborating with them knew at the time, this "breakout" into the heterosexual community was both a myth and a strategy.

Such a campaign represented not only a deliberate manipulation of the public trust, but a misapplication of public funds. As the *Wall Street Journal* pointed out nearly ten years after the fact, public service advertising like the CDC campaign was as inefficient as it was expensive. The emphasis on communities not at risk for the disease ensured that communities in desperate danger—IV drug users, gay men—did not get the starkly focused message they needed about dangerous behaviors, and prevention money for testing and counseling was wastefully channeled into large sectors of society (e.g., heterosexual college students) not facing any real threat. At the time, some of the journalists covering the AIDS beat knew the CDC campaign was built on a lie. Yet no one revealed the truth. The party line that AIDS was "everyone's problem" for the most part went unchallenged.

Matching this deference to the sensitivities of the gay community was journalistic indulgence toward the tactics and strategies of the AIDS community's leading organizational instrument, Act Up. Several prominent journalists on its media advisory board, including Michelangelo Signorile, succeeded in generating favorable coverage for the organization. Impressed with its passion, its daring, iconoclastic tactics and its leaders' ability to provide good quotes on tight deadlines, some reporters on the AIDS beat, according to Elinor Burkett and others, did not see that Act Up's confrontational tactics were actually diminishing public sympathy for their cause. They were also blind to how Act Up had become "a quagmire of backbiting, ego tripping and political infighting." But most important, they missed the unresolved contradiction at the heart of the group's mission: its twin goals of limiting gay men's suffering and winning legitimacy for the sexual mores of the gay lifestyle.

By the mid-1990s an emphasis on safe sex, along with the introduction of protease inhibitors, produced a remarkable decline in the HIV infection rate, lowering it to practically negligible levels. At the same time, however, a rising generation of younger gay men who had not seen their friends and lovers die began to flout the new safe-sex conventions. Surveys indicated that despite aggressive campaigns to promote condom use, roughly one-third of gay men continued to have unprotected anal intercourse. Much of this was taking place in the same baths, bars and clubs where the disease had incubated in the first place, as well as in the so-called "circuit parties"—events held in cities around the country and around the world that began as AIDS fundraisers but evolved into drug-, alcohol- and sex-soaked bacchanals.

For many reporters who had covered AIDS, this "second wave" or "relapse" story was appalling. Although they had once been scourges of anyone daring to cross the gay party line on AIDS, figures like Michelangelo Signorile of *Outweek* magazine and *Newsday* columnist Gabriel Rotello began to argue that gay men, in light of the resurgent infection rate, had to take more responsibility for the consequences of unsafe sex. How could the gay community continue to point fingers at the media, the government and an uncaring public when many members of that very community were acting so irresponsibly? they wanted to know.

Along with other journalists who were alarmed at the second wave of AIDS, these two also began to question publicly the role that politically correct journalism had played in allowing the plague to spread. At the 1995 convention of the National Lesbian and Gay Journalists Association, for instance, Signorile and Rotello took part in a panel discussion moderated by Elinor Burkett, titled "Why We Don't Get the Truth about AIDS." Amid second thoughts, self-incrimination and the moderator's pleas for civility, the predominantly gay journalists assembled that day were in essence saying that the reason why the gay community wasn't getting the truth about AIDS was because journalists sympathetic to the cause of gay rights had been too long reluctant to report it.

Yet reporters tackling the "Return of Unsafe Sex" story were often subjected to the worst kind of abuse and denunciation. "Leave the baths alone; they are none of your business," one Dade County AIDS activist told *Miami Herald* reporter Elinor Burkett when she investigated a number of clubs where irresponsible sex was taking place, some of them owned by a major Democratic Party donor and hence all the more newsworthy. Another activist was even blunter: "You homophobic bitch. You just don't want gay men to have sex." Many in the gay community simply did not want to hear the bad news. A group of academics and journalists formed a group called Sex Panic and attacked those like Rotello and Signorile who dared to criticize promiscuous sex as neoconservative "turdz" who were no longer welcome in the community they once led.

Of course, many reporters were able to surmount the hostility and turn in fine reporting. But for others, the pressure to uphold the party line proved too much. Seeing his editor's eyes light up when he pitched the relapse story, Frank Bruni, then a *Detroit News* reporter (now a top Washington correspondent for the *New York Times*), knew he could have gotten the time and travel budget to do it in a serious, in-depth way. "But I never pursued it," he confessed. "I was hesitant to do a story that would give comfort to our enemies. That would immediately be hated by my friends, that would be questioned every time I went to a gay event. On balance I made the wrong decision. I chose to protect the community from critics, rather then holding gay men's feet to the fire."

The issue of gays in the military, which has been the object of ongoing press attention since late 1992, provides another instance of partisanship trumping professional detachment. The national press corps' support for the president's controversial proposal to lift the ban on open gay military service was apparent right from the start. Candidate Bill Clinton had first pledged to rescind the ban before gay supporters in October 1991. Although there were exceptions, such as Ronald

Brownstein of the *Los Angeles Times,* who reported the pledge and its significance, for the most part the rest of the media merely reported that Clinton held "pro-gay" positions. Reporters thus failed to convey the depth of the opposition waiting in the wings and did not consult opponents, such as retired military officers and socially conservative political figures like Sam Nunn, the Senate Armed Services committee chairman. Nor did they feature in any significant way a resolution passed by the Veterans of Foreign Wars at its summer 1992 annual convention, which called on Clinton to keep the ban in place.

"This most fascinating failure of modern campaign reporting," as *Baltimore Sun* reporter Carl Cannon called it, seemed to be less a function of news judgment than of political attitudes and assumptions. Explaining why she thought editors like herself did not pay more attention to Clinton's pledge when it was first made, *Baltimore Sun* editor Vicki Gowler said, "We're liberal. When Clinton says he'll fight for gay rights or rescind the ban, then we're hearing something that doesn't sound outlandish to us. In fact it sounded reasonable. It sounded fair."

The same ideological insularity proved troublesome in the coverage of Clinton's effort to make good on his campaign pledge once he took office. While almost all the nation's elite news organizations followed the pro-gay line in both editorials and news coverage, at the *New York Times* the cause of gays in the military was defended with particular insistence, while traditional concerns over conflicts of interest, which might have disqualified certain reporters from covering the story, were waived. The *Times* saw only one way to think about the issue. Those who differed were both morally wrong and historically retrograde.

To the many experienced military officers who said that openly gay behavior was incompatible with an effective military force, one *Times* editorial replied, "The only thing homosexuality is incompatible with is bigotry and timidity." Anna Quindlen invoked the memories of slavery, segregation and suffragism, intoning: "Fashions in bigotry come and go. The right thing lasts." Quindlen's op-ed page colleague Anthony Lewis said that the central issue was civil rights: "All the rest of the noise around the issue—the talk about service morale, and fighting effectiveness, the shrilling on talk shows—is demonstrable humbug—and bigotry."

Having dismissed the possibility of honorable or informed opposition, the *New York Times* disparaged those leading the fight against Clinton's plan to lift the ban. The paper targeted, in particular, the Joint Chiefs of Staff and the chairman of the Senate Armed Services

Committee, Sam Nunn. A front-page story allowed anonymous Pentagon aides to charge that the Joint Chiefs' opposition to Clinton's
initiative verged on "insubordination," an accusation repeated in a subsequent *Times* editorial that criticized the Joint Chiefs for their
"encrusted leadership." The *Times* also used anonymous congressional
sources—a Democratic senator and a former Democratic Senate aide—
to assert that Sam Nunn was opposing the lifting of the ban out of
small-minded pique at Clinton for his lack of deference to the senator
during the presidential transition.

By contrast, the celebrities of the pro-gay movement were cheered
in the *Times,* especially those serving in the military who had come out
of the closet. Joseph Steffan, a former midshipman who was kicked out
of Annapolis shortly before graduation for revealing he was gay, was
"every mother's dream for their daughter," wrote Jeffrey Schmaltz in a
Style section profile: "Handsome as can be with a principled intelligence and a diffident way." Also lauded was Scott Peck, the gay son of
the distinguished Marine colonel, who was described in an editorial as
"All American."

Heterosexual men who worried about gay soldiers "have an
annoying habit of overestimating their attractiveness," said Joseph Steffan in the Style profile. Those who objected strongly to gays might be
demonstrating anxiety about "their own reaction and the prospect they
might respond sexually," noted Catherine Manegold, a pro-gay *New
York Times* reporter, in a Week in Review piece. For decades, psycholo-
gists have said that at the core of homophobia is repressed fear and
latent homosexuality, she explained, bolstering her analysis with the
insights of a psychiatrist who had written on the *Times'* op-ed page:
"Hatred of gay men is based on fear of the self, not of the alien other."

Reservations about the impact of gay soldiers and their sexuality
on small unit morale were airily dismissed as homophobic fantasies.
Existing rules prohibiting demonstrations of affection between male
and female service personnel would work for gay relations too, the
*Times* reported in a piece by Jane Gross. In endorsing the status quo in
military life, however, Gross ignored what many feminists said was
the military's rampant problem of sexual harassment, as well as the
embarrassing epidemic of pregnancies that occurred among servicewomen on duty in the Gulf War. She also ignored a statistic that the
*Times* itself had reported earlier: that in 1992, more than 10 percent of
the 360 sodomy investigations by the Army involved rape.

Another apparently sensitive topic at the *New York Times* was the
Joint Chiefs' fears that open homosexuality in the services could spread

AIDS to heterosexuals through battlefield blood transfusions. In dealing with this problem, the *Times* relied on the assertions of the gay lobby that semiannual and annual HIV testing procedures would bar that from happening.

The reporting and commentary of the *New York Times* also tended to disparage the opponents of the new policy. When rank-and-file servicepeople who objected to Clinton's proposals were quoted, it was in a way that often made them sound silly, shrill or bigoted. Clearly siding with those who blamed the manipulations of right-wing radio hosts and the political activists behind them for the wave of pro-ban phone calls inundating Congress, *Times* reporter Elizabeth Kolbert's analysis was headlined "The People Are Heard, At Least Those Who Call Talk Radio." Making that insinuation explicit, Anna Quindlen said that "the outbreak of phonathon democracy in our nation's capital" was "a sorry exhibition of government in action." Such a wave of public protest, she thought, was to public opinion "what David Duke's ascendancy was to the national ethos."

The biased reporting became especially fervid in April 1993, as hundreds of thousands of gays marched on Washington. "Tomorrow's march can be helpful," declared the *New York Times* editorial page the day before, if it held up "a mirror for the nation to see its own reflection."

The day of the march, news reports made sure that this was exactly what happened—about as glaring an illustration of editorial policy leading news reporting as one could find. Claiming, as the *New York Times'* Jeffrey Schmaltz did, that the march was "remarkably restrained," most news organizations focused on the feelings of gay pride and solidarity among the marchers. The *Times* editorial page invoked images of Ozzie and Harriet, insisting that " 'ordinary' and 'the people next door' were mantras of the weekend." But anyone who happened to be watching C-Span saw a somewhat different story. In additional to conventional couples, the march was filled with topless lesbians, men in leather harnesses and flagrant cross-dressers. A lesbian comedian at the microphone said she wanted to "fuck" Hillary Clinton, and another speaker said she "wanted to get it on with Anita Hill."

News organizations were correct, of course, in not letting the excesses of a few characterize the whole. But neither should they have trimmed and sanitized unflattering aspects of the march in ways that denied the obvious in order to establish a politically desirable image of wholesomeness. Making note of the gay lobby's anxiety about its tawdry public image, *Washington Post* media critic Howard Kurtz wrote that media self-censorship reflected an ethic of "When in doubt, leave it out"—an ethic which consigned crucial information "to the cutting room floor."

As for the "Don't Ask, Don't Tell" compromise eventually reached by the Clinton administration, one *New York Times* editorial called it "a benighted retreat from principle" that was "driven by prejudice and politics." Another said that rather than representing an advance for gays in the services, the decision would entrench "the archaic and homophobic ban on gay soldiers more firmly than ever." The president's loss of nerve, thundered the *Times*, "has simply allowed the bigots to tighten their grip."

Since then, ongoing coverage of the 1994 "Don't Ask, Don't Tell" reform has largely accepted the spin of gay organizations. According to these groups, the policy not only has not lessened the witch hunt atmosphere in the military, it has also increased the number of gay-related discharges and fed an alarming attrition rate of talented gay servicepeople, thus adversely affecting the strength and readiness of the armed forces.

In April 1998, for example, the *New York Times* ran a piece describing the 67 percent increase in discharges of gay and lesbian servicepeople since the "Don't Ask, Don't Tell" policy was instituted. According to the story, which cited Pentagon statistics, a total of 997 military personnel were discharged in 1997 compared with 597 in 1994. The article noted the Pentagon's contention that the policy was being exploited by some personnel looking for cover to get out of military service by claiming to be homosexuals, but seemed to lean in favor of darker explanations favored by pro-gay groups, which insisted that many officers in the field were still persecuting gays simply for *being* homosexual.

To back up these contentions, the *Times* article cited the case of Navy Chief Petty Officer Timothy McVeigh (no relation to the Oklahoma City bomber). According to reporter Tim Wiener, McVeigh was a seventeen-year veteran sailor with a sterling record who had been discharged for violating the "Don't Ask, Don't Tell" policy. Clearly echoing those who felt McVeigh had been victimized, Wiener maintained that the Navy had even pried his e-mail messages out of his America Online (AOL) account. Wiener noted that federal judge Stanley Sporkin, who ruled in the sailor's favor when he challenged his discharge, contended that the Navy had gone too far and had "impermissibly embarked on a search and outing mission against the sailor."

Navy investigators had in fact gone into McVeigh's AOL account, and the online service had provided them with access to it, against the company's stated standard policy. But what Wiener elided from his account was that McVeigh had corresponded anonymously with the wife of one of the sailors on his submarine and made inquiries into the ages of their children under the screen name "BOYSRCH." It was in these e-mail exchanges that McVeigh had confessed that his favorite hobby was "boy watching and collecting pictures of other young studs." This prompted the woman to go to the Navy with the information BOYSRCH had sent her, which in turn moved the Navy to throw McVeigh out—a not entirely unjustifiable or mystifying response, according to many military authorities.

As for reportage favoring the insistence that the "Don't Ask" policy was encouraging many talented, and expensively trained gay servicepeople to leave the armed forces altogether, there was a piece in a March 2000 *Newsweek* cover package detailing the story of "Reggie and Billy." These pseudonymous U.S. Army paratroopers had exemplary records in one of the Army's most elite and demanding units, only to be discharged when their homosexual romance was discovered. When rumors of gays in the ranks swept through their unit and one of them was abruptly reassigned, *Newsweek* reported, both men panicked and went AWOL for two weeks out of fear for their physical safety, hiding out together in an abandoned house in the Italian countryside. Finally returning to the base, the two paratroopers were soon headed home. One left with an honorable discharge, courtesy of a sympathetic commanding officer; the other, not so lucky, was discharged without honor.

The fact that "Reggie and Billy" had gone AWOL alone would have made them eligible for dishonorable discharge, if not court-martial on desertion charges; yet the *Newsweek* piece made their expulsion from the army seem to be entirely a function of their homosexuality. "Throw homosexuality into the equation and all of my talent and experience becomes tainted as far as Uncle Sam is concerned," the soldier called "Reggie" was reported as saying, with *Newsweek* supplying no legal context or contradictory information that might have opened other possible interpretations of the episode.

Accusations of bigotry and intolerance, made in partisan support for the positions of the organized gay lobby, dominated the coverage of efforts to include an openly gay contingent in New York's annual St. Patrick's Day Parade through most of the 1990s. The controversy first erupted in 1991, when a group called the Irish Lesbian and Gay

Organization (ILGO) first sought permission to march in the famed celebration of Irish ethnicity and the Roman Catholic faith. Barred in 1991, ILGO has continued to challenge the parade's organizers, its annual court actions becoming a tradition of their own.

To the Irish Lesbian and Gay Organization, the ban represents classic anti-gay discrimination, a denial of their rights to affirm their identity in public and to have the parade reflect the true diversity of the Irish in America. St. Patrick's Day Parade, ILGO has argued, is a public event—a public accommodation, to be legally specific—so barring gay marchers is just like barring them from any other public accommodation, like a hotel or a ball game. To the Ancient Order of Hibernians, the organization that has sponsored the parade for almost 150 years, however, it is a private affair, and their right to control it is guaranteed by constitutionally protected rights to free assembly. Thus the organization has a right to exclude any group it wishes, especially one like ILGO, which flouts the traditional moral teachings of Catholicism. The Hibernians have asserted that ILGO may not march as a group, but its members could march as individuals within other parade contingents.

In 1992, a judge for the New York City Human Rights Commission decided in the Hibernians' favor, ruling that the parade was indeed a private affair that was in character "Irish and Roman Catholic." Forcing the parade's organizers to accept a group espousing anti-Catholic teaching, the judge decided, would in fact be, as the Hibernians had argued, a violation of their First Amendment freedoms. A year later, when ILGO filed yet another court case, once again backed by the city's liberal political establishment, a federal court judge was even more emphatic in ruling in favor of the Hibernians.

Noted First Amendment attorney Floyd Abrams called the ruling sound, declaring that there is a "powerful First Amendment right for people to associate with whom they choose to associate." Norman Siegel of the New York Civil Liberties Union (NYCLU) pointed out that political correctness cannot nullify the right of association under the U.S. Constitution. Within the city's journalistic precincts, on the other hand, the ban on the gay marchers and the rulings that sustained it elicited contempt. Repeating the pattern that had governed its reaction to the controversy over gays in the military, the *New York Times* responded with reporting and editorials that painted the stance of the Hibernians as rank bigotry. The paper clearly felt it had a mission to force-feed "diversity" to those whose faith and traditions led them to see homosexuality as morally unacceptable. The pursuit of this goal justified treating Catholics and Irish with exactly the kind of insensitivity to cultural and religious issues that the *Times* opposed when it came to gays.

In 1993, for example, the *Times* editorial page, notably short of Irish Catholics in its ranks, said the Hibernians' position was "an embarrassment to the traditions of the Irish people and to a city that stands for tolerance." Another editorial called on the public to ignore what it said was the parade's "bigoted message," urging, in effect, a public boycott. Still another editorial called the event a matter of "parading bigotry."

The paper's columnists piled on. Ignoring the religious dimension of the conflict, Anna Quindlen said that everything the Hibernians had done "stinks of the stereotype of the small minded Irishman.... For all of us who know that stereotypes exist to reduce understanding, not to enlarge it, I say they should be ashamed of themselves." Francis Clines, in a Sunday Metro section column, called the Irish "writ-ensconced and wary of their perceived identity," and urged them to take a leaf from Third World newcomers who were not so hung up on sexuality. And in an op-ed piece, Harvard sociologist Orlando Patterson called the smiling eyes of the lucky Irish the very "face of American racism."

Granted, columnists and editorial writers may say what they want. Yet it was surprising that a paper placing so much emphasis on diversity could not find at least one voice to defend the parade sponsors. Even more striking were the news stories riddled with snide innuendo, sketchy facts, and what seemed to be willful blind spots, giving readers a distorted picture not only of the Hibernians but also of the political establishment that had mounted such a united front against them.

"One thing to remember," a *Times* reporter quoted one political scientist as saying in 1993, "is that there are almost no Irish left in the city.... There are probably almost as many gay Irish as there are straight Irish in this town."

Another dimension to the story that the *Times* never got around to exploring was the longstanding bitterness between the Catholic Church and the organized gay community, particularly groups like Act Up, which had interrupted a mass at St. Patrick's Cathedral in an infamous 1989 incident, with one protester taking Holy Communion and spitting the host on the floor. Such blasphemy rankled still, as did years of gay pride marchers spouting profanities, openly masturbating and simulating anal sex as they passed by St. Patrick's.

Perhaps the most biased part of the *New York Times'* coverage came in the paper's profiles of ILGO and its members, portraying them as apolitical, more interested in expressing their Irish heritage than in making any grand statement on homosexuality. *Times* reporters showed ILGO members as warm and cuddly, full of Irish mirth and devilishness, the wronged victims of intolerance with absolutely no political agenda behind them.

Yet one of ILGO's leaders, Anne Maguire, belied the apolitical posture with an essay published in an Irish magazine in 1996, expanding on the organization's quest to gain a spot in the parade. "What is clear about ILGO and the St. Patrick's Day Parade," she wrote, "is that most ILGO people, particularly those who are most actively involved, had no inclination to be *associated*, never mind *march* in the parade [italics mine]." The protest, she continued, "very simply is where our coming out took place."

This was an open admission of something the Hibernians themselves had been saying for years: that ILGO members were more interested in validating a gay lifestyle than in venerating Ireland's patron saint. But Maguire's admission never made its way into the *New York Times*, leaving it once again to the less "authoritative" tabloids to fill in the blanks.


Even the furor over St. Patrick's Day is relatively tame compared with the passionate way gay marriage and the related issue of gay adoption are treated. Taking cues from activists—at the 1995 National Lesbian and Gay Journalists Association meeting in Washington, for example, reporters brainstormed with prominent political organizers on how best to "shape" the gay marriage and benefits story—the coverage of gay marriage and adoption has been skewed and one-sided, burdened by cant and questionable factuality.

On the fringes of the media radar for several years, gay marriage became a full-blown controversy in 1995, when the Hawaii Supreme Court affirmed the right of gay couples to marry. Gay rights activists tried to portray the issue as one involving basic civil rights, one that would allow gays the same protections and prerogatives as heterosexuals, such as the right to inherit a partner's property and receive medical benefits. The right to marry, activists said, would also provide help in dispelling stereotypes of gay sexual promiscuity, proving that gays were just as capable of monogamy and loyalty as everybody else. But to its opponents, gay marriage was an affront both to traditional religious teachings and to fundamental ideas about society's most basic social institutions, which have lasted thousands of years.

Occupying a complicated emotional and legal terrain, gay marriage was one of those inflammatory social issues crying out for sober, balanced commentary and reporting rooted in a receptivity to all points of view. Balance, sobriety and respect, however, were not what the media provided. Despite the colossal challenge gay marriage represented to most of American society, there was almost no real debate about it in most of the mainstream press.

Implicitly putting gay marriage in the context of the Civil Rights Movement, the *New York Times* editorial page said that arguments invoking family values and religious traditions were uncomfortably similar to those raised in resistance to repealing miscegenation laws a few decades earlier. Much of the resistance underlying the public dialogue, the *Times* insisted, reflected "entrenched anti-gay bigotry" and "social intolerance."

Network television, particularly ABC News, demonstrated an even sharper partisan edge. In a segment on the Hawaii case, the magazine show *Day One* (now defunct) portrayed the couples involved as "pioneers" who were "just trying to secure our future and a future for all other same-sex couples." The show presented critics of the court ruling in a buffoonishly bigoted light. "Screw those queers," one "man on the beach" said to the cameras. "That's what's wrong in this world is these faggots."

Another ABC News effort, *Turning Point*'s "For Better or Worse: Same-Sex Marriage," presented the issue even more unfairly. Tracing the lives of four same-sex couples as they made the decision to get "married"—one of the individuals a freelance producer who often did work for *Turning Point*—the show was a bit of a cartoon, leaving no ambiguity about what it thought the "right" position was. Although Diane Sawyer mentioned in the show's introduction that the issue of gay marriage had provoked a division "as wide as the Grand Canyon," the show did not present the opposition in such a way as to make its objections comprehensible. It focused on the sister of one of the lesbians getting married, a radical Christian fundamentalist whose religious inflexibility and biblical paranoia—she said at one point that the cities of Sodom and Gomorrah were destroyed by God because of homosexuality—made all opposition to gay marriage, in an instance of guilt by association, seem irrational. Toward the end of the show, the father of one of the newly wed gay men stood up and said, "Twenty years from now, we'll look back at this and say, 'What was all the fuss about?' "

This tone of advocacy marked the *New York Times*' coverage of efforts to pass a gay civil union law in Vermont in 2000, as well as a

California bid to ban the right to gay marriage that same year. *Times* reports that were mostly even-handed still tipped their hand in their final quotations. Closing one such piece about the situation in Vermont, a high school teacher was quoted as saying that her hope "is that my students, when they're old enough to be married, will be able to marry whoever they want." Another piece had a seventy-eight-year-old woman with eight children, one of whom was gay, close by explaining, "He knew and we know that he was just plain born gay. I can only say, God blessed us with eight children and my God made no mistake when he blessed us with homosexuals and when he gave us our gay son." In a report about the California ban, one young lesbian complained, "What I don't understand, is what are people scared of." The *Times* was barely able to restrain its enthusiasm when the Vermont Supreme Court decided that gays and lesbians were due the same legal rights and protections enjoyed by heterosexual married couples. A profile of Chief Justice David Amestoy was fulsome in its praise for the judge's "moderation," even as the editorial page, implicitly acknowledging the decision's radical nature, championed a "momentous ruling" that was "a breakthrough for fairness" and represented the "biggest victory so far in the struggle to achieve legal recognition and acceptance for same-sex marriages."

Coverage of gay adoption—an even more complicated and volatile issue than gay marriage itself—was one-sided too, though the psychological complexity of this issue made even supporters of gay marriage uncomfortable. According to some studies, including a few organized by gay researchers, children raised by gay parents turn out just as well as those raised in traditional heterosexual families. But other research indicates that the experience of growing up in a gay-parented household is not all that healthy, and children who have such backgrounds suffered later in life from resentment, hostility, and confusion.

Instead of acknowledging all of this research, much of the press coverage has tended either to duck the issue entirely, or to cite only the findings that affirm gay adoption. Dismissing arguments calling for more conclusive research before gay couples are given the same consideration for adoption as heterosexuals, the press has put the civil rights of prospective adoptive gay parents ahead of what might be the best interests of the children. A *Seattle Times* editorial in 1995 asserted that opposition to gay adoption was "motivated by blind prejudice." Implying that opponents of gay adoption were animated only by homophobia, the *Washington Post*'s William Raspberry asked, "What are we afraid of? "

A May 1996 *New York Times* report on homosexual couples raising children in suburbia made absolutely no mention of the possible
psychological consequences of the arrangement. Ignoring research to
the contrary, an ABC *Turning Point* special gave a platform for one of the
lesbians it showed getting married to say, "there's no studies that find
someone who's raised by a single mother or two men are any worse
off than anyone else." Likewise, *Newsweek*'s November 1996 cover story
on gay parenting (featuring rock star Melissa Etheridge and her pregnant lesbian lover on the cover) asserted that it is the "quality of the
parents, not the parents' lifestyle that matters most to kids."

The same monochromatic view dominated reporters' response to
the Hawaii court decision. According to the *New York Times*' Carey
Goldberg, the judge's decision, in this case in favor of gay marriage,
was partly based on favorable studies on the children of same-sex parents which "have become increasingly broad and authoritative in recent
years."

Another *Newsweek* cover story, "Two Kids and Two Moms" in
March 2000, repeated this blithe dismissal of the psychological
ramifications of gay parenting. The two lesbians in question "make no
particular arrangements to have the boys spend time with men, and
there is no special man in their lives," the report explained. "It sounds
so trite but what children really need is love and security, an understanding that someone is there for them and will play sports with them
and read with them or whatever they want to do," one of the moms
declared.

As Maggie Gallagher, author of *The Case for Marriage*, wrote in
2000, "The technical flaws of [gay parenting research] are numerous
and obvious even to lay eyes: small sample sizes, only a small number
of outcomes measured, samples that are not nationally representative,
lack of controls for confounding variables (children of lesbian mothers
with Ph.D.'s compared to single mothers with mostly high school diplo-
mas, for example), no comparison groups." Advocacy for same-sex
unions and gay parenting bore a striking resemblance to the rush to
deny any adverse psychological impact that divorce might have on children, Gallagher observed in another column: "In the 70s adults
suddenly insisted divorce was no problem at all for kids. It took twenty
years when children of divorce grew up and told us first-hand about the
traumas of fatherlessness, for us to begin to change our minds."

The ideologically tinged journalistic support for research bolstering the case for gay parenting and adoption seemed to undergo a bit of
a reassessment in the wake of a controversial *American Sociological*

*Review* article in 2001. Authored by University of Southern California scholars Judith Stacey and Timothy Biblarz, the article that found many of the studies in the field claiming to show no differences in effects on kids actually contained data that did show differences, and that these differences had been downplayed by researchers for fear that "the findings would be misused," as a *New York Times* article by Erica Goode in mid-July 2001 explained.

According to the article, the researchers found that the studies they examined had data suggesting that "both the experience of having two parents of the same sex and of growing up in a house where homosexuality is accepted influence children's behavior, self-image and life goals." The seemingly intentional suppression of evidence of these differences, one of the sociologists told the *Times,* stemmed from "not so much political correctness but political anxiety."

Yet even in reporting this news that past scholarly research had been colored by political exigency, the *Times* performed its own tint-job.

One of the more controversial findings of Stacey and Biblarz was that, contrary to most published studies, data did show that children of same-sex parents were more likely to engage in homosexual activity than were children of heterosexual couples. This assertion was made to seem very brave; the sociologists interviewed by the *Times* reporter said, "We recognize the political dangers of pointing out that recent studies indicate that a higher proportion of children with lesbigay parents are themselves apt to engage in homosexual activity. Nonetheless we believe that denying this probability is apt to prove counterproductive in the long run." The *Times* also reported the reaction of Lynn Wardle, a law professor at Brigham Young University who is an outspoken critic of gay parenting. "I was quite pleased to see the writers actually saying, 'Yeah, the studies just don't show what they purport to show,' " Wardle told *Times* reporter Goode. "The science that has been done is simply unreliable."

But in reporting this provocative candor, Goode neglected to note that the percentage of children of gay parents who engaged in gay activity themselves was not small: according to Wardle, studies have shown between 10 and 25 percent of children raised by gay or lesbian parents have some same-sex attraction, interest, identity or experience, which is significant in light of research showing that the proportion of kids with straight parents reporting homosexual activity or relationships is approximately 3 percent, about the same as the population at large. The *Times* article also spent a great deal of space reporting only positive differences between children of gays and children of straights, describing attributes of the former, such as open-mindedness toward same-sex activity, ideas about the fluidity of sexual roles, and strength of character—all of which seemed to imply that same-sex parenting made for better kids.

To Lynn Wardle, the *Times* story seemed to reveal that the sociologists wanted to have it both ways, to be seen as having scholarly rigor without undercutting pro-gay conclusions—something the *Times* apparently wanted as well. The *Times* story also seemed to show that the paper was intent on putting a pro-gay spin on what was "a tenuous and minor point in the article itself, chiefly that children of gay parents are better off and have advantages other children don't." To Wardle, the most important factor driving the *Times* reporting was the paper's ideological agenda. "If anything, they give my [usually anti–gay parenting] arguments token play," he told me. "I'm there for window dressing—as a sop to the notion that you should hear both sides."

Skewed coverage of the effort to force the Boy Scouts of America to accept openly gay members and leaders is another area in which the press has collaborated with the gay lobby's bid to "reform" yet another traditional American institution. Most of this skewed coverage centered on a lawsuit brought against the Boy Scouts by former Scout leader James Dale, which worked its way through the New Jersey court system toward a state supreme court decision in June 2000. At eight years old, Dale had become a Cub Scout, rising to the rank of Eagle Scout as a teenager. He stayed on in scouting as an assistant troop leader, but was forced to leave in 1990 when his photo appeared in a local newspaper identifying him as a student leader of a Rutgers University gay and lesbian organization.

According to Dale's suit, the Boy Scouts were guilty of bias and discrimination, having forced him out of the organization, which recruits widely with no formal membership criteria, simply because he was gay. With so many Scout troops using public facilities such as schools for recruitment and meetings, the Scouts were a public accommodation, Dale's attorneys argued, making them subject to the same anti-bias laws that applied to schools, libraries, theaters, restaurants and hotels.

To the Boy Scouts, however, forcing them to accept gay leaders and members was a violation of their right to free assembly, and their right to set the standards for membership as they saw fit. The Boy Scouts also held to the position that accepting gays would discourage some parents from letting their boys join the organization, out of fear—justified or not—that their sons would be exposed to unwanted influences.

The case was legally complicated, touching on many of the most important constitutional protections we as a society hold dear. It was also complicated socially, coming to rest at a crossroads where social ideals—openness to diversity—intersect with social realities—issues of parental confidence and institutional traditions. But with exceptions only at the margins, most news organizations had trouble seeing the shades of gray, coloring their reporting with righteous indignation.

According to the *New York Times*, the Scouts' resistance to Dale was a throwback to the days when homosexuals were considered "sinfully, criminally and mentally flawed." When the New Jersey Supreme Court sided with Dale in August 1999, the story made the front page, and the editorial page again weighed in. "As a group with an important role in the civic life of communities, [the Boy Scouts] cannot be allowed to operate outside of laws designed to eradicate bigotry," the editorial said, cheering the court for "showing wisdom" in siding with Dale's position. "The organization would serve its mission better by ending its ugly prejudice against homosexuals and adding to its list of Boy Scout qualities the virtue of tolerance."

In the wake of the U.S. Supreme Court decision affirming the Scouts' position in June 2000, gay activists pressured organizations hitherto supportive of the Scouts to back away from the group. But the reporting on the impact such pressure had was wildly exaggerated, offering up some embarrassing, high-profile inaccuracies.

A front-page *New York Times* piece on August 29, 2000, detailed what its headline said was a significant "loss of support" that followed the Scouts' "successful ban on gays." In the two months since the Supreme Court ruling, the first paragraph said, "corporate and governmental support for the organization had slipped markedly." Cities including Chicago, San Francisco and San Jose had told local Scout troops that they can no longer use parks, schools and other municipal sites, the *Times* correspondent, Kate Zernike, reported. Companies like Chase Manhattan Bank, Merrill Lynch and Textron had withdrawn hundreds of thousands of dollars in support to local and national scouting groups nationwide. Dozens of United Ways from Massachusetts to San Francisco had cut off money amounting to millions of dollars each year.

The piece admitted that cutting off money or access to one private group raised troubling questions for other organizations that had similar policies. "Do states stop allowing Roman Catholic youth groups to use public campgrounds or school meeting rooms because the church does not ordain gays?" Zernike asked. The piece closed with the implication that not everyone associated with the Boy Scouts approved of current policy and that a grassroots rebellion, particularly among more open-minded parents, could be in the offing. "It's time now for parents to speak up and say, I don't agree with it. It's time for people to start fighting from within," Zernike quoted a Connecticut father as saying.

Not a week later, though, the *Times* was forced to run a mortifying, five-paragraph correction undercutting almost every one of Zernike's contentions. Chicago still let the Boy Scouts use parks, city buildings and schools, but *charged* them, the paper now said; and the public schools of San Francisco no longer sponsored Scout recruitment drives or other programs *during school hours.* Further, these restrictions *did not* come in response to the Supreme Court decision but in fact predated it. And San Jose did not restrict the Scouts' access to its public schools for recruitment purposes because of the policy on gays, but because letting the Scouts recruit impinged upon the time reserved for instruction. There were not *dozens*, but only *about a dozen* United Ways that had cut off funding. The reporter had also been wrong about the Roman Catholic Church policy on ordination—which requires a promise to lead a celibate life—as it pertains to gays. "While the church condemns homosexual activity, it does not have a policy on ordaining gay men," the correction said.

In the days following, other news organizations found even more mistakes. References to Chase Manhattan Bank's discontinuation of funding were mischaracterizations, the *Wall Street Journal*'s editorial page noted. In fact, Chase and Merrill Lynch both said they would continue to fund Scout programs. And far from large numbers of parents disagreeing with the official Scouts policy, as Zernike implied, most endorsed it, as columnist Michael Kelly noted in the *New York Post*, citing a Princeton Survey Research Associates poll in which 56 percent of registered voters said they agreed with the Scouts' position as opposed to 36 percent who disagreed. "How many errors can one reporter pack into a single story?" asked *New York Observer* columnist Nicholas Von Hoffman. "The byline belongs to one Kate Zernike," Hoffman continued, "about whom the *Times* correction has naught to say. Is she a summer intern? An affirmative action hire? An asshole? Whatever or whoever she may be, there was a time when the newspaper wouldn't have let a reporter who displayed such talents cover a fender-bender on the Major Deegan." Another *Observer* columnist, Richard Brookhiser, said the incident "was no surprise from the paper which might as well rename itself *Gays in the News.*"

The equally controversial question of Christian groups' reaction to issues of gay identity has also generated fierce partisanship in the press. This issue burst into the news in late 1997 and 1998 when Christian conservatives mounted a nationwide campaign to advance the idea that homosexuals could be "saved" from their sinful lifestyles and brought back into heterosexuality through prayer, will power, psychological counseling and denial. However antithetical to liberal orthodoxy, such a view at least deserved a fair public examination. Yet when gay activists demonized these Christian organizations, they were for the most part backed by news organizations, with the handful of journalists who defended the right of the Christian groups to publicize their point of view often the object of scorn.

In Boston, for instance, pro-gay students at Harvard tried to block a Christian student group from holding a public discussion of whether homosexuality was genetically determined or a lifestyle choice, ripping down the group's posters before the meeting and then heckling the participants when the forum finally took place. These actions caught the attention of *Boston Globe* columnist Jeff Jacoby, who took the students to task for their thuggish behavior and their strident rhetoric. "Dare to suggest that homosexuality may not be something to celebrate," Jacoby wrote, "and instantly you are a Nazi, a hatemonger, a gas chamber operator." Closing his piece, Jacoby asked, "What does it say about gay advocates, who so loudly champion tolerance and freedom of sexual choice, that they are so poisonously intolerant of people who make a choice different from theirs?"

The column triggered loud complaint in Boston's vocal gay community and among outraged gay staff members at Jacoby's own paper. This was the second time that he had run afoul of the *Globe*'s gay lobby. A 1994 column in which Jacoby had written that gay protest marchers were unified by "carnal desires" and the demands of their bodies had resulted in a letter of protest from fifteen colleagues, causing the *Globe*'s top editors to put Jacoby on notice that he had to be more careful in writing about gay issues. This time, two copy editors, both of whom were identified in the *Globe*'s own accounts of the controversy as "gay activists," submitted formal complaints against Jacoby, and the paper's ombudsman raked Jacoby over the coals in print, calling the column "offensive" and "homophobic."

One of those activist/editors, Robert Hardman—who was also a founder and at the time a chairman of *Out* magazine—happened to be out of the office on the day Jacoby's copy would otherwise have come across his desk. Had he been there, Hardman insisted in an interview, he "absolutely would have tried to kill that piece." According to Hardman, the Harvard group calling for gays to abstain from same-sex activity was little different from right-wing extremists "who think that the private behavior of gay people should be criminalized." The Jacoby column, he insisted, represented little more than giving "evil doers" aid and succor since those criticizing gay sexuality were setting a stage for gay-bashing and murder to take place.

Hardman made clear his feelings about the responsibility of the media to preserve all sides of controversial issues: "It is fine to have a debate but my argument is that as an editor of the *Globe*—a paper with a leadership role in this community and in the nation—I have a responsibility to decide which things should be part of the debate and which should not. Jacoby's column edged to the latter, and I think it should have been spiked, and a newspaper that was really exercising leadership and responsibility would have done so."

The episode left Jacoby wary. "A lot of gay activists, think that any point of view different from theirs is not only wrong, but so illegitimate and beneath contempt that it doesn't even deserve to be considered," he said.

> I know up front that if I want to write about this topic, I have to be prepared to run a gauntlet and to jump a lot of hurdles—not among the readers who I think mostly agree with me, but right here in the newsroom. I don't want to pick a fight with these guys.... I need their good will and I need their trust, but I do feel a chilling effect, and I am afraid that's exactly what they want me to feel. I can assure you that on no topic—not race, not the death penalty, not multiculturalism, not welfare—are you made to endure as much fury as you have to endure if you say anything on this topic that is considered politically incorrect.

Sanitized coverage of gay issues is mirrored by a deference to the pieties of organized feminism. A willingness on the part of the media to move away from its history of male condescension and chauvinism in the coverage of women and women's issues was unquestionably necessary.* But instead of balance, there has been an equal and opposite reaction.

---

* Recall *Time* magazine's description of author Kate Millet as late as 1970 as "an unsmiling thick-eyebrowed sphinx with emerging eyebags and a laser-beam stare that could melt male testicles from 50 yards."

Feminist critics like Susan Faludi may continue to complain of media bias against women and the "backlash" against feminism it has fed. But an examination of the coverage of a variety of feminist issues—particularly abortion and gender integration in the military—reveals a sharp skew in *favor* of movement feminism and the view that American women are structurally oppressed and in need of relief from institutionalized misogyny.

The media's bias in its treatment of the abortion issue—feminism's premier cause—was borne out in a lengthy 1990 series by *Los Angeles Times* reporter David Shaw. He studied reams of reportage in eighteen major American newspapers and hours of network videotape, and interviewed reporters and editors responsible for abortion coverage. Estimating from this analysis, 80 to 90 percent of American journalists favored abortion rights. Shaw cited scores of examples showing that in content or tone, coverage was riddled with double standards against the anti-abortion camp. Many of the reporters cited in the series stated that while abortion opponents were often shrill in their complaints of media bias, they were " absolutely right," as Ethan Bonner, then of the *Boston Globe,* told Shaw. Lisa Meyers of NBC News agreed that "some of the stories I have read or seen have almost seemed like cheerleading for the pro-abortion side."

Shaw found that while reporters adopted the term pro-abortion to describe abortion rights supporters, they balked at using the anti-abortion movement's preferred "pro-life." Shaw also underscored the politics of euphemism involved in coverage, recounting Ethan Bonner's experience of censorship by the copy desk at the *Boston Globe* of a story he was doing on late-term abortion procedures. In his original draft, Bonner had described doctors "destroying" the fetus "by crushing forming skulls and bones." But his copy editor sanitized the language. "As far as I'm concerned until that thing is born it is really no different than a kidney. It's part of the woman's body," the editor said. "To talk about 'destroying it' or about 'forming bones' is really to distort the issue."

For most journalists, opposition to abortion is not a civilized position, and this view gives them the right of way to caricature pro-lifers as religious zealots, while abortion rights activists, no matter how radical and inflexible, are described with respect, and in many cases with adulation. Shaw noted that the *New York Times* referred to Fay Wattleton of Planned Parenthood as "smoothly articulate," "relentlessly high-minded," and "a stunning refutation of the clichéd 'dowdy feminist,' " while Randall Terry of Operation Rescue was described as "a former used car salesman."

According to Shaw's analysis, female print reporters quoted supporters of abortion rights three times as often as abortion opponents. (Stories filed by men were much more evenly balanced.) One news executive said, "The problem with abortion coverage is that the media is loaded with women who are pro-abortion." But the bias is also a function of pressures from feminist groups and the media strategy committees within them, who are very successful at guilt-tripping female journalists into believing that their reporting "is hurting the cause."

The fact that a mainstream news organization like the *Los Angeles Times* would assign someone of Shaw's stature to critique abortion coverage might suggest that things are not so bad. But while Shaw's series was eagerly passed around newsrooms all over the country like *samizdat*, and bolstered those who were trying to get their colleagues to see the blind spots of contemporary journalism, it had little lasting effect on the way abortion was covered. The dynamics Shaw described in 1990 could still be seen at work in the controversy over the Partial Birth Abortion Ban Act of 1997, in which journalists who should have been trying to help the public sort through a complex and deeply felt issue struck poses and insulted those they deemed to be on the wrong side.

Opponents of the ban maintained that intact dilation and extraction (the technical term for this procedure), which punctures the head of a fetus and sucks out the brain matter, is performed only a few hundred times a year and then only in the third trimester of pregnancy when the fetus is severely deformed or the mother's health is in serious jeopardy. According to those supporting the ban, however, the procedure is used thousands of times a year, mostly on healthy mothers and on viable babies. In fact, supporters of the ban claimed, most partial birth abortions are elective, sometimes for such frivolous reasons as cleft palates or sex selection.

The *New York Times* set the tone for reportage on the issue by immediately lumping the partial birth abortion bill together with a dozen or so other efforts sponsored by Christian conservatives to roll back abortion rights. A June 1995 dispatch from Washington asserted that the procedure was only "used in the latter stages of pregnancy to abort fetuses with severe abnormalities or no chance of surviving long after birth." While quoting no supporters of the legislation, the author of that dispatch, Gerry Gray, allowed abortion rights activist Kate Michelman to say that the ban on third-trimester abortion was an effort to "sensationalize" and distract from the real issue in the debate: "who should decide"—women or the government? After that piece came a salvo of *Times* editorial columns, as well as a string of pieces by op-ed page columnist Frank Rich, who stressed that the ban was a prelude to the total denial of abortion rights.

The most egregious misrepresentation of the issue, however, came from CBS News's *60 Minutes*. Favoring the language of the pro-abortion lobby, correspondent Ed Bradley quoted one doctor who called "partial birth abortion" a "propaganda term" not found in medical dictionaries. Bradley also showed his hand by choosing to highlight the case of a mother named Vicki, whose fetus's brain was growing outside its head, making no mention of how atypical—almost bizarrely so—this case was among prospective third-term abortions. By featuring this case, and in other comments he made minimizing the number of these procedures done for elective reasons, Bradley was clearly parroting the abortion lobby's insistence that partial birth abortion was largely reserved for cases of catastrophic fetal deformity. Ignoring those who claimed otherwise, Bradley gave the last word to Dr. Warren Hern, a physician who has written the standard textbook on abortion procedure and who claimed that no doctor would perform this procedure "on a healthy baby in the last trimester."

When the press finally did make an effort to get the facts about partial birth abortions, it was a case of too little, too late. Coming fourteen months into the story, the tardy revelation that the abortion lobby might be playing fast and loose with the truth failed to find lasting purchase among reporters or politicians.

Using old-fashioned legwork and basic mathematics, Ruth Padawar, a reporter at the *Bergen (New Jersey) Record*, called around to physicians in New Jersey who performed the procedure and asked them about the frequency and circumstances under which they performed it. Contrary to claims by the pro-abortion lobby that there were at most 500 partial birth abortions performed nationally in any year, Padawer calculated that more than 1500 of the procedures took place in New Jersey alone. Padawer also found that contrary to claims that almost all of the procedures are done only in cases "where the woman's life is in danger or in cases of extreme fetal abnormality," only a miniscule number had been performed "for medical reasons."

Echoing these findings, *Washington Post* medical reporter David Brown took a look at the issue on a national scale in a piece that ran under the headline "Late Term Abortions: Who Gets Them and Why." According to Brown, most of the women receiving the abortions were not having them for medical reasons and most of the fetuses were not deformed at all, but healthy. Brown also laid to rest yet another fallacy:

that the fetus felt no pain. According to researchers he talked to, in fact the fetus did feel pain, since the anesthesia used to sedate the mother does not render it unconscious.

Yet apart from mentions by conservative columnists and the *Wall Street Journal's* editorial page, most of the national media ignored these revelations. Worse, many continued to characterize the controversy in the terms established by the pro-abortion camp. Through the New Year of 1997, major newspapers continued to describe the procedure as restricted to situations in which the woman's life is endangered or the fetus is determined to be suffering from severe physical anomalies. On the eve of the Senate vote to override Clinton's veto of the ban, the *New York Times* endorsed partial birth abortions in an editorial that failed to acknowledge the newly reported numbers. "The bill banning the procedure was not a serious effort to confront the moral issues raised by late term abortions," wrote the *Times*. "Rather it is a first shot in a campaign by anti-abortion forces to erode access to abortion by nabbing one procedure after another."

In February of 1997, Ron Fitzsimmons, an official with the National League of Abortion Providers, admitted that he had "lied through his teeth" to interviewers from *Nightline* when he said that the procedure was done only five hundred times a year and only on unhealthy mothers and fetuses. In a subsequent interview with David Brown of the *Washington Post*, Fitzsimmons said he "just went out there and spouted the party line." It was a stunning admission. Yet even as most of the media were reporting Fitzsimmons' lie, they continued to shy away from the clear implication that the abortion lobby, which had based much of its case on his figures, was lying too, and that it had duped the press into swallowing vastly understated numbers of partial birth abortions and misleading statements about the conditions under which they were performed.

In the last week of February, at least two weeks after Fitzsimmons' admission, National Public Radio did a piece on the controversy in which it still maintained that most of the partial birth abortions performed in the United States involved unhealthy mothers or unhealthy babies. *New York Times* columnist Frank Rich said that there was "nothing new" in what Fitzsimmons had to say, and added once again that the ban on the procedure "begins the end run process of gutting Roe vs. Wade a few procedures at a time."

With the myth of the practice's "infrequency" having been demolished, the *Times* established a new fallback position: that "a ban on the procedure is still an unacceptable political invasion of private medical decisions." Quoting a doctor who performed the procedure and found it "bizarre" that Congress wanted to ban it, Deborah Sontag closed a March 21 piece with the doctor complaining about politicians meddling where they shouldn't. "In my view," he told Sontag, "it's as if they were to forbid me to use a certain kind of suture."

The press was so easily misled on the third-trimester abortion story partly because it was difficult to get reliable statistics on this contentious subject. Yet there seemed to be something much deeper going on that could only be explained by ideological bias. As John Leo of *U.S. News & World Report* asked, "If anti-abortion activists were making the sort of dubious and clearly false statements that [were] coming out of the National Abortion Rights Action League the media would do some hard investigating. Why can't more reporters bring themselves to do it now?" *Newsweek's* Jonathan Alter admitted, "Journalists are more disproportionately liberal on this issue, so they are more likely to rely on, whether consciously or unconsciously, the information they get from the pro-abortion side."

Though perhaps lacking the passion of the abortion debate, gender integration of the military is another issue where the coverage is demonstrably in thrall to "progressive" dogma.

With the military on the defensive for most of the decade since the Tailhook scandal of 1991, feminists have been able to get the armed services to roll back prohibitions against women serving at sea, in combat aircraft and in forward fighting units. Even though bans on front-line combat are still in place, the relaxation of the old rules represents a profound transformation of military culture, and this has not happened without debates as heated as those surrounding gays in the military.

On one side are those who claim that opening up combat roles to women will adversely affect cohesion, discipline and military readiness. On the other side are those arguing that equal opportunity for women will not diminish military preparedness. If women are to achieve ultimate power and status in American society, these integrationists say, then one of the arenas where society has traditionally issued those credentials—the military—must be opened to them without restriction.

The issue is a complicated one, involving a strange mix of gender, family, masculinity, femininity, biology, anatomy, preferential policies and diversity. Yet reporters, editorial writers and columnists have simplified this complex culture clash into a contest between the forces of progress and the forces of reaction. For the most part, the reporting and commentary have echoed the feminist position, which views any opposition to full gender integration in the military as simple misogyny. An acknowledgment of the harder realities of war and the preparation needed to win it has been conspicuously absent from the pages of our leading newspapers and the broadcasts of our new networks.

One of the core problems journalists have virtually ignored is that of lowered physical standards. Because women are, on average, five inches shorter than men, with half the upper-body strength, lower aerobic capacity, 37 percent less muscle mass and significantly less tolerance for the pull of G forces in fast-flying aircraft, the services have lowered, eliminated or "gender-normed" physical conditioning requirements. In addition to institutionalizing double standards, the armed forces have accommodated women by revising requirements for what they call Military Occupational Specialties (MOS), retooling their procedures and equipment for everything from KP duty to loading missiles on fighter jets.

The result is a two-tiered system riddled with inequity. Gender-normed fitness standards are so low that many women, even those who smoke and are overweight, easily pass their requirement, while even physically fit men find they have to sweat to meet theirs. The product of this disparity is sharp and widespread resentment. And even since the forces revised the MOS, women have had a hard time meeting the requirements for over 70 percent of the specialties. Although the services say they have devised ways to compensate for women's lack of raw physical power, many commanders in the field fret that the lifts, pulleys and other aids that have been introduced into the fitness regimen won't be there when they are needed in a combat situation, which could lead to tragedy.

Granted, the intricacies and arcana of MOS and gender-normed basic training standards don't exactly make hot copy. But even when journalists have had the pegs on which to hang the story of diminished physical standards and their deleterious effects on readiness and morale, they have shown little interest. In 1997, for instance, West Point appointed a female lieutenant colonel to be "Master of the Sword," a coveted position that made her the head of the Office of Physical Education—an ideal news peg for reporting on gender-norming of conditioning and strength exercises. Yet that aspect of the story was ignored. Similarly, 1996 marked the twentieth anniversary of women being allowed into the service academies. Although this too would have been a fine chance to explore gender-norming and its impact on academy morale and cohesion, reporters like NPR's Martha Radditz chose to focus instead on the bias which, she alleged, women still had to reckon with.

That there are real consequences of these "progressive" ideas about gender in the military was shown dramatically by the story of Lieutenant Kara Hultgreen, the Navy's first female pilot assigned to combat duty aboard an aircraft carrier. In October 1994, Hultgreen died in a training accident while trying to land her plane aboard the USS *Abraham Lincoln.* Sensitive to charges that it had lowered training requirements so it could open up combat aviation to women, the Navy was quick to blame the pilot's death on engine failure, issuing a public report citing the plane's inability to restart after the engine flamed out on approach to the carrier. But many of her fellow fliers in Air Wing 11 believed that this tragedy was the bitter product of the special treatment the Navy had given Hultgreen and her female colleagues. More tragedy would come, they said, unless the Navy reversed course and measured all its fliers by the same yardstick.

Conditioned by its experience during Vietnam, most of the national media reflexively distrusts the military, yet here they were quick to echo the Navy's official line. They were just as quick to disparage those who were alleging that Hultgreen was incompetent, had been rushed into a combat role for political reasons, had failed to handle the flame-out properly and had been given below-average grades in flight school. Echoing Navy investigators' *public* statements about the accident, the *New York Times* editorial page spoke of "a gender neutral tragedy" and said, "When the next servicewoman dies in the line of duty let the reaction be gender neutral too."

In fact, though, the Navy's official pronouncements contradicted its own internal findings. According to the Mishap Investigation Report—which is by nature much more exhaustive and candid than what the Navy generally releases for public consumption—engine failure was indeed involved to some degree in the accident. But the report made clear that pilot errors, very similar to those that Hultgreen had consistently made at earlier stages of her training, were the principal force behind the accident. The internal report also blamed Hultgreen for failing to make a timely ejection, a mistake that ultimately killed her when she hit the water straight down from a height of less than sixty feet.

The Navy does not release Mishap Investigation Reports. But uniformed sources close to the investigation, alarmed at the disparity between the Navy's public statements and what they knew to be true, leaked this one to Robert Caldwell, the editor of Insight, the *San Diego Union-Tribune*'s Sunday opinion section. Running its analysis of the report in March 1995, the *Union-Tribune* highlighted the disparity between the two reports, vindicating those within the Navy who had been tarred as misogynists for raising questions about special treatment and threats to safety, competency and readiness posed by the movement to integrate women into combat aviation. Hitting hard, Caldwell wrote: "Presumably the Navy feared that acknowledging Hultgreen's mistakes might have raised embarrassing questions about her qualifications and about preferential treatment for female aviators in the newly gender sensitive Navy." The *Union-Tribune*'s report received little bounce in the rest of the media, however. The original interpretation—i.e., that Kara Hultgreen was a victim of mechanical failure—was allowed to stand uncorrected, preserving her status as a feminist icon.

Like the threats to safety and readiness, the threats of gender integration to unit cohesion, discipline and morale are very real as well, and are just as much the focus of journalistic denial. Most of the services bar fraternization between officers and enlisted personnel and ban troops within the same units from having sex on overseas deployment or in battlefield operations, including peacekeeping missions. They do so because sexual relationships on any level, but particularly those involving members of the same unit, can be enormously disruptive, poisoning unit cohesion and morale. In addition to raising questions of whether an officer may be selecting one subordinate for a particularly dangerous mission to avoid assigning it to a lover, for example, there is also the risk of pregnancy and the damaging effects it has on unit strength and the morale of those left to do the more demanding chores that military policies forbid pregnant soldiers from undertaking.

In the new military, however, sex between males and females is rampant. According to a 1992 survey of veterans from the Gulf War, more than half of the men and three-quarters of the women said that troops in their units had sex in Saudi Arabia as much or more than at home. And according to reports in the Army's semi-official newspaper, the *Stars and Stripes*, sex within the ranks among Bosnian peacekeepers, where women represented 10 percent of the American force, was widespread. Condoms were big sellers at local PXs, *Stars and Stripes* reports, and medical units had trouble keeping birth control pills in stock. The paper also reported that soldiers admitted to having sex everywhere: in showers, the back of Humvees, and other covert locations. "They've locked us down," an Army captain told the *Stars and Stripes* in July 1996, referring to orders restricting the troops to their bases, "so what else is there to do?"

Yet the press has been lackadaisical about bringing the problem to light. Although the Gulf War survey finally received attention in 1996 and 1997 when the issue of women in the military broke wide open, it was either ignored altogether or given only the most cursory attention when it was first released in 1992. Even when journalists get close to the story, they have shown a marked reluctance to draw out the implications of the facts they report.

An "exclusive" *Time* magazine report about life aboard the USS *Eisenhower* during its historic first co-ed cruise in April 1995, for example, made note of the female crew member who falsely claimed she was sexually assaulted, the fifteen women who had to be evacuated because of pregnancy and the extensive fraternization that secretly went on during the six months at sea. The report also noted that male and female crew members had videotaped themselves having sex in a ship's compartment, and quoted one junior officer who said the "Ike" had become a PC "showboat" of doubtful readiness. Yet in language that could have been written by a Pentagon public affairs officer, it nevertheless concluded that "the mission was a resounding success" and that naysayers "would be sorely disappointed" when they heard about it. Throughout the cruise, the ship performed "as well if not better than before women were aboard," as the ship's executive officer maintained, adding, "If you took women off right now it wouldn't feel right."

Coverage of the problems posed by pregnancy, much of it the fruit of illicit, against-the-regulations sex, has been equally deficient. During the Gulf War, for instance, 36 women out of a female crew of 160 aboard the USS *Acadia* had to be evacuated because of pregnancy during the ship's deployment. Some had become pregnant before the ship got underway, some from sex on liberty calls. But others were surely pregnant from sex that occurred while the ship was at sea. In some media, the story was picked up quickly and the *Acadia* became know as "the love boat." In most of the mainstream press, though, the story was barely mentioned.

Information about pregnancy rates among female soldiers assigned to the U.S. peacekeeping mission in Bosnia has been met with similar denial and avoidance. According to reports in the *Stars and Stripes*, women are showing up pregnant at a rate of one every three days, representing an 8 percent pregnancy rate, which is a disability rate nearly twice that of men. Yet aside from the conservative press, the news went unnoted in most national media, which chose to highlight the co-ed deployment in Bosnia as an example of successful gender integration.

Even when an important story crops up, such as the sex scandals at the Army's Aberdeen Training Grounds, the media is reluctant to grasp the larger implications for gender integration. Filled with shocking tales of sexual abuse and sexual favoritism between enlisted female trainees and their drill sergeants, the Aberdeen scandals culminated in a series of wrenching courts-martial in 1997 as lurid details of sex run amok made front-page headlines throughout the country. According to reports, Aberdeen was a base out of control, where all-powerful drill sergeants used their authority to engage in sex with trainees, some of it consensual but much of it coerced.

In some accounts, drill sergeants were said to have established a game in which they competed with each other to have sex with as many trainees as possible, often referring potential partners to one another. In the cases where the sex was consensual, female trainees submitted either out of romantic infatuation with their superiors or to gain preferential treatment, a complete corruption of traditional notions of military order, hierarchy and discipline. One trainee who became pregnant by a sergeant bragged that because of her widely known sexual relationship with the superior, she could talk back to instructors and refuse their orders. "If I didn't feel like cleaning the barracks, who was going to make me do it. It kind of turned to my advantage. I could tell people above me to shove it."

Aberdeen was a source of deep consternation and disgust to many, but to supporters of aggressive gender integration, the scandals represented a military culture deeply alien to women, one in which protections against sexual harassment were weak and ineffective, and where the exclusion of women from important combat-related positions left them in a second-class status.

Some commentators raised the possibility that gender integration needed to be re-thought altogether. Calling the military "the most politically correct institution in the country," *Washington Post* columnist Richard Cohen, one of the few journalists to write on the subject who actually had military experience, said that it was indeed possible that Aberdeen was a "sordid anomaly." But it was "also possible that the scandal is a warning to both the brass and the civilian leadership that they are attempting the impossible." The fight, Cohen said, "was not against a few bad men but against a more formidable foe: human nature." Cohen saw something else that had eluded many newspeople, all too anxious to use Harry Truman's racial desegregation of the military in 1948 as an analogy to advance larger civil rights goals: The military's primary purpose was to win wars. It was not the place "where an ideology, no matter how worthy, should be imposed so that the rest of society should follow."

Yet the overwhelming bulk of the reporting and commentary failed to pursue obvious questions raised by the case and to take stock of how gender integration was actually working in the real world. Instead, it embraced the story line of systemic dysfunction, affirming the position of feminists and civilian political appointees in the defense community who shared the view that what had taken place at Aberdeen should not become an excuse for a reevaluation of policy. The problem was not the inherently disrupting presence of women in the military and the way sexual attraction eroded discipline and order, most news reporters and commentators maintained, but rather the military's structural bias against women and the exploitation it encouraged in the ranks.

Typical of the one-sided interpretation were reports filed by ABC News's John McQwethy from the trial of Delmar Simpson, an Aberdeen drill sergeant charged with nineteen counts of rape and thirty-nine other sex-related charges. Though this was a criminal case against one soldier at Aberdeen, McQwethy noted, "the entire army is also on trial, about how it treats women and how quickly it can change the attitude of men who seem to have tolerated what was happening here." At the time of the trial, several conservative congressmen were readying legislation to ban co-ed basic training. Yet McQwethy failed to mention them or their proposal. Instead he allowed Senator Olympia Snowe, an outspoken feminist critic of the military (although a Republican), to be the voice that framed the issue. "Women right now in the military do not feel assured that if they report a case of sexual harassment or sexual misconduct that they are going to have their charges treated seriously," Snowe maintained. The fact that the trial itself and the attendant publicity seemed to undercut that contention was not something McQwethy bothered to note.

In direct response to its conservative critics, the armed services went on a broad public relations offensive in support of gender integration, inviting reporters on deployments and into training facilities to bolster the sense that the effort was working and that cases like Aberdeen were an aberration. These visits could have been an opportunity for reporters to ask questions long left unasked and to pierce the public relations front the military had taken pains to construct. But the reporters involved came home essentially parroting the official line.

In May 1997, for instance, NPR's Martha Radditz (now with ABC

News) filed a story from Bosnia that purported to examine the realities of women in the peacekeeping mission there. Deployed as military police, Radditz explained, the women were confronting conditions that were equivalent to what they would face if sent into actual combat. Implying that if women could make it there they could make it anywhere, Radditz's reporting left out significant facts, such as the 10 percent pregnancy evacuation rate and the reports carried in the *Stars and Stripes* about rampant sex in the ranks.

While Radditz noted complaints from men that women were not pulling their own weight because of inferior upper-body strength, she let the issue slide with a feminist dismissal: "What is astonishing about the females deployed in Bosnia is that they don't seem too worried about what their male colleagues or anyone else seems to think." Quoting one female soldier who disparaged the macho attitude of male colleagues, and made a self-congratulatory reference to the "extra caring" and sensitivity women brought to the mission, Radditz acknowledged that to a Vietnam-era veteran this would sound odd. "But touchy feely or no," Radditz concluded, the women deployed in Bosnia "insist that gender integration is working." Calling it "the future of the U.S. military," Radditz closed the report by saying, "It will be only a matter of time…that men will not even remember what it was like to work without women at their side."

Dana Priest of the *Washington Post* turned in another one-sided report on the Bosnia deployment. Unlike Radditz, Priest found the women she talked to that same week "just as stereotypically macho as their male counterparts." But like her colleague at NPR, Priest declared that the disruptive sexual tension found stateside was "not the reality on the ground for the troops of the 720th MP Battalion." Priest also seemed to suggest that the successful integration of women into a peacekeeping mission like Bosnia argued for the enlargement of combat roles—failing to see the difference between duty as military policemen and the bloody rough-and-tumble of actual combat. And like Radditz, Priest minimized the amount of sexual activity in the ranks, activity that certainly posed at least the *risk* of compromising unit cohesion and performance. She flippantly quoted one soldier who said, "What's the big deal? We're not *sleeping* together, just sleeping together."

A late 1997 NBC *Dateline* account of female trainees negotiating "the crucible"—a physically punishing two-and-a-half-day ordeal that recruits must complete to graduate from boot camp—was another meretricious treatment of the debate over gender integration. Claiming that the ordeal was "exactly" the same for women as it was for men,

*Dateline* misrepresented the reality of what they were actually show-ing, which was a heavily gender-normed event a world apart from what women in combat would actually experience.

In keeping with Marine tradition of never leaving a fellow Marine behind, both women and men were required to "rescue" wounded comrades from the battlefield. Yet in the exercise, women got to carry only other women—a courtesy that actual battle conditions would not always extend, although *Dateline* did not point this out. The segment also failed to note the disparity involved in the hand-to-hand combat portion of the test; like the rescue simulation, women hit women and men hit men, affording the female recruits an insulation from reality that actual combat would certainly not provide. Recruit Vanessa Jenk-ins, who was allowed the last word, summarized the intellectual vacuity of the reporting. "A woman can do anything a man can do," she insisted, "and lots of times a whole lot better."

If journalists have been reluctant to acknowledge that gender inte-gration has encouraged lower standards, they have been more than ready to disparage the military when it tries to hold servicewomen to the same standards as their male counterparts, especially in the demanding, and politically high-profile, world of combat aviation. This was underlined in the Kara Hultgreen tragedy and again in the case of Lieutenant Carey Lohrenz, an F-14 pilot who was washed out of car-rier duty in Carrier Air Wing 11 not long after Hultgreen's death, while the wing was sailing to the Gulf to enforce the "no fly" zone over Iraq in June 1995. According to Lohrenz's commander, the pilot was an "unpre-dictable, undisciplined and unresponsive aviator" whose continued flying was a threat to safety aboard the ship. After assigning her to extra practice, the commander recommended that she be grounded, a deci-sion with which several mixed-gender investigative panels concurred, citing documented evidence of substandard performance as well as atti-tude problems.

According to Lohrenz, however, the commander had singled her out because she was a woman and had let male aviators with equally poor flying records go forward without being assigned extra practice. Lohrenz broke the chain of command to appeal her case to the top lev-els of the Navy. She also filed a lawsuit against an organization called the Center for Military Readiness (CMR), a watchdog group that has taken a hard line against lowered standards in the pursuit of gender integration. Her suit charged that a cabal of anti-female naval aviators had stolen her training records and given them to CMR, which in turn circulated them to the media. With her identity clear even though the

CMR identified her as "Pilot B," Lohrenz contended that the publicity undermined her confidence, resulting in a further deterioration of her performance on the carrier.

According to the CMR's analysis, Lohrenz's record was substandard, marred by numerous and serious examples of unsatisfactory flying. According to CMR director Elaine Donnelly, the Navy was compromising training standards and risking lives in a politically driven effort to produce female fighter pilots. The report cited chronically low scores, repeated failed exercises, unsafe flying tendencies, and a failure to improve despite multiple opportunities to do so, all of which should have blocked Lohrenz from being sent out to the fleet in the first place. This interpretation of her training records was echoed by five retired aviators consulted by the *San Diego Union-Tribune,* who were asked to sort through the technical data and describe what they saw in layman's terms. One of the retired aviators said he was "astonished" at the number of failed training exercises Lohrenz was permitted without being dropped from the program or at least called before a formal review board. Another called Lohrenz's records "the worst flight records I have ever seen."

The case of Carey Lohrenz was a complicated one indeed, filled with the kind of accusations and technical arcana, not to speak of personality questions, that can drive responsible and fair-minded reporters crazy, especially if much of the detail is shrouded by official noncooperation and policies preventing release of personnel records. Nevertheless, the story line embraced by much of the press was as simplistic as it had been in the case of Kara Hultgren. Virtually absent from the coverage, as Robert Caldwell of the *Union-Tribune* almost alone emphasized, was the Navy's need to enforce a single standard for aviators of both genders.

More concerned with the "theft" of her training records than the lowered standards those records reflected, the press portrayed Lohrenz as a feminist hero fighting the forces of male domination. One of the more demonstrably one-sided treatments was NBC *Dateline*'s July 1996 report by correspondent Gary Matsumoto, who repeated the feminist line that there was a double standard in the Navy cutting against pioneer female fliers like Lohrenz. Matsumoto allowed the accusation that her commander had lied about her flying record to stand without substantive proof, and presented the commander's executive decisions regarding Lohrenz in such an invidious way as to make the conclusion of anti-female bias almost inescapable. Facts that made such conclusions seem pat and simplistic were slighted or ignored by him altogether.

If, as he claimed, the commander found evidence of preferential treatment in reviewing the female aviator's training, he would have been more than justified in assigning extra practice. It was, after all, his responsibility to make sure that the ship and its crew were safe from unnecessary danger. In fact, there was considerable evidence that Lohrenz had been cut a lot of slack, allowed to repeat training tasks at which male aviators had one shot.

Meanwhile, Matsumoto went hard on everybody associated with the campaign against double standards in combat aviation. He cast Elaine Donnelly and the Center for Military Readiness in the worst possible light, and made the act of leaking documents, which the press usually regards as a courageous act of whistle blowing, into part of a sinister conspiracy to smear Lohrenz. Matsumoto did not report that in Lohrenz's particular case, six separate panels had upheld the decision to ground her. He also failed to note that the "special considerations" she was given were not minor.

Equally one-sided were the reports of NPR's Pentagon reporter Martha Radditz, who gave Lohrenz a platform to say that those opposed to her flying because of lowered standards were individuals "whose sole purpose is not to have women in the military or women in combat aviation." Implying male bias was at the root of the whole episode, Radditz closed the piece with a note about an internal survey in a Florida air squadron in which "a large number of aviators still do not believe women should be flying."

A lengthy *Newsweek* report in the middle of March portrayed Lohrenz as the target of a cruel and heartless campaign of humiliation and ostracism from porn-watching fellow pilots who made her feel like a "leper." The piece chose to highlight confidential internal reports that questioned whether the women in Air Wing 11 were given the support they needed from their male comrades, while ignoring information contained in the same reports which documented Lohrenz's lapses in performance. It dismissed the material leaked to the CMR as a "selective and doctored" version of the aviator's records, unfairly impugning their accuracy. *Newsweek* concluded that "deep prejudices will have to be overcome before women can be accepted as top guns."

In June 1997, the Navy finally released a comprehensive report on the Lohrenz affair. Determining that there had been no gender discrimination in the case, the author of the report, the much-revered Rear Admiral Lyle Bien, said that Lohrenz's commanders were acting properly when they relieved her of her ability to fly carrier-based aircraft. Indeed, contrary to the charges of gender bias, the report painted a picture of Lohrenz's performance as more than justifying the commander's assessment of her as an "unsafe, undisciplined and unpredictable" aviator.

According to the report, far from ganging up on the aviator, many of Lohrenz's superiors were concerned about her erratic and undependable flying habits, but reluctant to ground her because no one wanted to appear to block the integration of women into the fleet. Meanwhile many of the pilots and flight officers aboard the *Abraham Lincoln* believed that "the fix" was in—that the chain of command, having already engaged in what one flight officer called "intentional deception" in the death of Kara Hultgreen, was playing politics with Lohrenz, too. According to testimony provided by three officers, the commander of the training wing told a group of instructors who had expressed reservations about the competence of the female pilots that "these women will make it to the fleet, and they will make it on time, and we'll do whatever it takes to get them there." Another officer interviewed for the report told investigators that Navy public relations officers were applying pressure on the fleet in order to win " a race with the Air Force" for who could get women into combat aviation first.

The minor concession the report made to Lohrenz—that she was qualified to resume flying *land-based* aircraft, where the margin for error was greater—was clearly a bone thrown to the feminists. Yet media accounts, built almost entirely on spin provided by Lohrenz's attorney, made the decision out to be a vindication of the aviator. "Grounded Pilot Returned to Flight: Service Seen as Making Amends for Treatment," read the headline in the *Washington Post*.

The armed services have also come under media fire for attempting to hold female officers to the same code of conduct as male officers. A case in point is the coverage of the Kelly Flinn "adultery" controversy in 1997. Flinn, a second lieutenant in the Air Force, flew B-52 bombers out of Minot Air Force Base in North Dakota. At one time considered a poster girl for the Air Force's drive to allow women into combat roles, she became the center of a firestorm in February 1997 when the service announced it was planning to bring her before a court-martial.

According to the Air Force, Flinn had had a brief affair with an enlisted man during the previous summer, a violation of well-known regulations against fraternization. The Air Force also said Flinn had violated prohibitions against adultery when she began a sexual and romantic relationship with the husband of an enlisted woman not long after. But these indiscretions were really the prelude to more serious misconduct. According to the Air Force, Flinn lied under oath about her relationship with the civilian when asked about it during the course of the investigation. The Air Force also charged her with insubordination when she refused a direct order to cease and desist from all conduct with the man.

After being confronted with sworn testimony from the enlisted man she fraternized with as well as from her civilian lover, Flinn admitted to her actions. But along with her attorneys and her public relations consultant, she charged that male Air Force officers were treated far more leniently for exactly the same indiscretions. Flinn insisted that her superiors should have dealt with her administratively, by issuing a reprimand or initiating a transfer. Instead, Flinn said, they had allowed the case to proceed up the chain of command to the point where a court martial could not be avoided. Flinn demanded that she be given an honorable discharge, which would make her eligible to continue flying commercially or in the reserves.

Kelly Flinn's case was a difficult one on which to report. The military justice system is not as open as its civilian counterpart, and the culture it reflects is somewhat alien to an American public, which has grown even further estranged from it since the end of compulsory military service. Yet to most of those covering the case, it was simply another flagrant manifestation of military misogyny driving a double standard. Turning Kelly Flinn into a sort of military version of Hester Prynne, much of the press corps failed to provide the basic facts about the case necessary to understand the Air Force's actions and the unique and demanding military culture behind them. Rather, journalists accused the service of vindictiveness and puritanism.

Corrective efforts that came weeks later were at last journalistically complete and solid. The *Los Angeles Times* reported that Flinn's treatment was "consistent with those who broke military law and then lied about it," and that women in the ranks thought it was the Air Force and not Flinn that was being unfairly slammed. Other publications such as *Time* magazine published similar catch-up efforts, debunking the feminist spin and setting the record straight.

But these clarifications came only after the Air Force made strenuous efforts to draw reporters' attention to the facts—and only after lasting impressions of injustice to Flinn had already been formed. That journalists could have taken their own initiative to uncover and report the facts earlier in the process seemed to be lost. This not only cast the military in an unnecessarily bad light, it also left politicians and the public seriously misinformed.

Savvy in the ways of media relations, Flinn's family hired a PR consultant early on in her ordeal, and drafted a series of talking points they hoped the media would pick up on in order to drive home their melodramatic point that Flinn was being prosecuted "for falling in love with the wrong man." The plan was to build pressure as the court-martial date—scheduled for the end of May—drew near.

The media strategy bore quick and lasting fruit. From the earliest accounts, a media bias in favor of Flinn was clear. The *Washington Post's* Tamara Jones, who was given an exclusive on the story, completely failed to note Flinn's insubordination and lying when she referred to her as the first female bomber pilot to be court-martialed over adultery in an affair with "a civilian who has stated under oath that he lied to her when he claimed to be legally separated from his wife." Without obtaining any balancing statements from Air Force officials, Jones gave Flinn a platform to admit that she "made some mistakes in judgment" but that her actions were not federal crimes that should force her "to spend the rest of my life as a convicted felon." Jones did make note of the fraternization charge, but did so without framing it in terms of the tight order and discipline required in the service. She also allowed Flinn's lawyer, the aptly named Franklin Spinner, to transform the case into an indictment of an Air Force that was "going back to the Dark Ages."

Echoing a defense line that Flinn was being punished inordinately because she was a woman, Elaine Sciolino of the *New York Times* charged that the case "underscores the unevenness of the way the Air Force and the military as a whole handles cases of sex." This piece, headlined "From a Love Affair to Court-Martial," did at least mention the additional lying and insubordination charges. Yet it provided Flinn with plenty of opportunity to explain them away by emphasizing the pressure she was under due to a cancer scare brought by a recent checkup.

The most egregiously one-sided account of the Flinn case—and the account that most fully framed the issue as adultery and little more—was Morley Safer's *60 Minutes* report. The story had been brought to the news magazine show by a freelance producer named Harry Moses, an acquaintance of Flinn's uncle. Moses considered the case a "no brainer." "She was their poster pilot," he later told the *American Journalism Review*, "and she was being charged with adultery. That's all you need to know."

Referring to the Air Force as "a former boys' club that by tradition turned a blind eye to the off-duty behavior of its officers," Morley Safer made the case against Flinn into a puritanical crusade from the Scopes era, against "the biblical sin of adultery," meant to punish Flinn for trespassing on male turf. Lobbing leading question after leading question, Safer asked Flinn if she felt that there was a double standard involved. Flinn answered, "I don't think the investigation would have been handled in the same manner. If I had been a man, I think someone would have stepped in a little sooner."

And while Safer mentioned the insubordination and lying charges, he, like the *Times* reporter, allowed Flinn to exonerate herself. Without challenging her reply or its illogic, Safer allowed Flinn to claim that the order to sever all contact with her lover Mark Zigo was impossible to follow because by that point he had already moved into her house. The fact that she could have booted him out as soon as she got the order never seemed to occur to Safer, who nodded sympathetically as she spoke.

The insistence that the Flinn case was essentially about adultery was at the center of snide editorial punditry that framed the reporting on the case. In a *Los Angeles Times* column headlined "Scarlet *A* Stands for Absurdity," Robert Scheer insisted that in prosecuting Kelly Flinn the Air Force was leading "a return to Puritanism" and alerted readers to a "war on female adultery." Trying to wax Swiftian, Scheer said that "Civilization must have its restraints, and it is essential, in the name of all that is decent, to certify that a pilot who may be ordered to carpet bomb civilians be sexually innocent." The *Boston Globe*, urging that Flinn be grounded instead of court-martialed, joked that this would be a difficult alternative to embrace. "But what else do high-ranking white guys have to do when Cold Wars give way to baby-sitting missions?" According to the *Globe*, Flinn "had a singularly female weakness. She believed the man she loved."

Having made the issue into a drama of a sexist and hidebound military establishment out to get an exemplary performer for violating an antiquated code of sexual conduct, news organizations bored in when the Flinn case moved toward a showdown on Capitol Hill. Not exactly Congress's finest hour, it was clear that many of the representatives weighing in on the case had a view of it formed by the blinkered and selective journalism that had made Flinn into a victim of female passion and male vindictiveness. During the course of the hearings it became obvious that many of the elected representatives grilling Air Force officials about the case had no idea that there were other charges filed against Flinn besides adultery. Finally blowing his top, Air Force general Ronald Fogelman testily lectured Senator Tom Harkin that there was "this fact thing" that he just wasn't getting. Senate majority leader Trent Lott told the Air Force to "get real" about "this so-called question of fraternization" and quoted his wife who wanted to know "where was the guy who was involved in all this." (Apparently Mrs. Lott did not realize that Mark Zigo was a civilian.) This was demagoguery at its most transparent, an obvious pandering for the women's vote. Yet the news coverage and editorial commentary glorified the ill-informed and unctuous congressional reaction.

According to a *New York Times* editorial that praised "Trent Lott's Military Mind," the Air Force had bungled the case badly and Flinn was a "scapegoat deserving of mercy rather than prosecution." Lott's glib summary of the case and the call for amnesty for Flinn got still another boost in a column by Maureen Dowd, which likened the punishment meted out to Flinn to *The Scarlet Letter*. Another *Times* editorial accused Air Force General Fogelman of "blackening" Flinn's reputation.

Just how visible and disruptive the Flinn affair was finally came into focus when Gayla Zigo, wife of Flinn's lover, whom reporters somehow managed not to interview, released a letter she had written to Air Force secretary Sheila Widnell. In the letter, Zigo described Flinn as an arrogant husband stealer who was well aware that her prey was married and flaunted her rank in front of the lowly airman. According to Ms. Zigo (who, under military rules, would have to salute Flinn if their paths crossed on base), she had often arrived home after work to find Flinn, still wearing her flight suit with its officer's insignia, alone with her husband. At this point, Flinn blinked, dropping her demand for an honorable discharge when it was clear that the Air Force was serious about proceeding.

Despite the journalistic correctives that eventually helped to resolve this case, the story line of an oppressive, misogynistic military out to get a feminist icon endured. More than a week after it was reported that the Air Force had in fact tried several times to step in before the situation escalated to that of a full court-martial, only to have a willful Flinn flout their instructions, for instance, Maureen Dowd uncritically quoted Senator Olympia Snowe insisting that "the wing commander never really intervened when he could have to tell her to discontinue her behavior or else." Shortly thereafter, the *Times* editorial page railed against "the absurdity of the military's strictures against adultery," failing to mention the huge threat to order and discipline represented by an officer poaching the husband of an enlisted woman.

Most telling of the media's stubborn refusal to drop its focus on sexism in the Flinn case, however, was how they framed accusations of adultery that soon afterward surfaced against Air Force General Joseph W. Ralston, the assistant chairman of the Joint Chiefs of Staff, under consideration for the top job upon retirement of General John Sha-likashvili. Ralston's adultery had occurred with a civilian more than a dozen years prior to his nomination, during a period when he was sep-arated from his wife. It did not cause any disruption to order and discipline, and had not involved lying or insubordination. Yet, when it appeared that Secretary Cohen would continue with plans to nomi-nate him for the chairmanship, a *New York Times* editorial headlined "Double Standards, Double Talk" declared: "Now that the Air Force has drummed out Kelly Flinn for such transgressions stemming from adul-tery with a civilian, Defense Secretary William Cohen cannot suddenly change the rules."

Given the hostility arising from feminist groups and from the media when the services have held female officers to the same discipli-nary and safety standards as men, it is small wonder, then, that a pall of intimidation and fear hangs over the broader military culture. As for-mer Navy secretary James Webb wrote in the *Weekly Standard* in 1997, an officer's views on the expansion of female roles have become "a lit-mus test for [career] advancement." Webb maintained, "Those in the ranks have learned that pointing out the difficulties inherent in an undertaking as politically volatile as the assimilation of women will quickly end a career."

Yet although this is regarded as an iron reality throughout the mil-itary, and although this attitude has been fueled in large part by the press's political correctness on gender integration, the media has largely failed to acknowledge the point that to Webb and others is obvious.

# FOUR

# Reporting by the Numbers

V oters in Houston went to the polls late in 1997 to vote on a ballot measure designed to ban racial preferences in the administration of city contracts and in municipal hiring. Houston's Proposition A was modeled on California's Proposition 209. When 209 had passed the previous year, pundits called it the leading edge of a wave of similar anti-preference measures that would sweep across the nation. The outcome in Houston would tell if this was so.

During the campaign, polls showed voters were in favor of the initiative when the ballot language referred to racial preferences. The City of Houston, this early version of the ballot read, "shall not discriminate against or grant preferential treatment to, any individual or group on the basis of race, sex, color, ethnicity, or national origin in the operation of public employment and public contracting." But when the opposition forces got the Houston City Council to use its power to change the ballot language to a less specific ban on "the use of *affirmative action* [emphasis added] for women and minorities...including ending the current program and any similar program in the future," the tide turned against the measure, and it was defeated 54 percent to 46 percent.

The failure of the Houston's Proposition A earned banner attention from most national news organizations. The *New York Times*, for instance, put the news on its front page, and ran a long account about how "Houston's voters had put a surprising brake on a national movement that often seemed to have the momentum of an unstoppable freight train." The *Times* depicted the development as a sign that affirmative action was not yet dead, despite California's Proposition 209, and implied that Houston's current elected leaders, who had campaigned hard against the measure, had set an example that politicians elsewhere might emulate.

In July 1998, when a Texas state judge ruled that the change in the ballot language had been improper and ordered a new vote, the *New York Times* gave the decision six sentences on page thirteen in a Saturday edition, offering no follow-up in its big Sunday edition the next day or in the coming weeks. Other national newspapers gave it similarly slight notice. The networks did not report it at all.

One of the news organizations that should have been particularly interested in developments in Houston was the *Seattle Times*. In November 1998, a scant four months after the judge's decision in the Houston affair, voters in the state of Washington would be going to the polls to decide Initiative 200, another state-wide referendum aimed at banning racial preferences in the public sector. But until *Times* columnist Michele Malkin wrote a piece about the media performance on the judge's action in Houston—including the performance of her own paper—not a single word of the reversal appeared in the *Seattle Time* or any other newspaper in the state. "Given its exhaustive coverage of the Houston election in 1997," wrote Malkin, "the *Times'* absolute silence [on the judge's decision] is extraordinary…. Sins of omission can be as damaging to the news media's credibility as sins of commission."

Malkin's column was answered by the paper's editor, Michael Fancher. In a piece headlined *"Times* Gave Story on Houston Ballot Measure Short Shrift,"* Fancher blamed a series of accidents for the omission. The Associated Press had not included news of the Texas judge's decision in the weekend wire report it sent to Washington State, Fancher explained. Other subsequent AP reports that did reach the paper fell through the cracks, fumbled by different newsroom teams that worked Saturday and Sunday shifts. Fancher did, however, admit that Malkin was right to take the paper to task, conceding that "Failing to come back with a complete story about the Houston ruling feeds that perception [of bias]." There were no similar admissions from those national organizations that got the AP feeds and had no breakdown in weekend newsroom regimens.

The scant coverage meted out to the Houston judicial reversal story is fairly typical of the media's undependability in scrutinizing color-coded policies proposed in the name of diversity. In addition to ignoring, concealing or slighting information unflattering to the cause of racial preferences or illustrative of their unfairness, journalists also engage in active sins of commission, reporting in a way that exaggerates the social utility of preference programs or the potential damage that would occur if they were abandoned.

It is worth noting that this has not always been the case. In fact, during the heyday of the Civil Rights Movement, newspapers like the

*New York Times* and the *Washington Post* cheered loudly when politicians like JFK and Hubert Humphrey made their celebrated denunciations of quotas and other race-based programs. As the *New York Times* editorialized on July 18, 1963, "The Negro, equally with the white man, should be wary of easy solution, quick remedies that seem to promise instant success. One of these is inherently unjust and inhumane. It is the quota system." Echoing this rejection of numerically based racial solutions a year later, influential *Times* columnist Arthur Krock warned against giving the federal government power to supervise corporate hiring practices, which would make it "a senior partner with private business." But this reflexive resistance to race-conscious remedies began to change within a few years. Growing far less vocal about objecting to race-conscious remedies, the elite press soon became one of the nation's most ardent institutional champions of them.

One factor was the increasingly bureaucratic (as opposed to political) nature of the civil rights measures being enacted. Legislation like the 1963 and 1964 Civil Rights Acts and the 1965 Voting Rights Act were debated in full public view. But after that, federal civil rights action became less visible and dramatic, and more reliant on executive orders and obscure governmental bodies like the Federal Equal Employment Opportunity Commission, operating from the hidden recesses of the Department of Labor. Out of the public eye, civil rights efforts became more a matter of minutiae than memorable speeches, and the press took little interest. The lack of curiosity gave groups with a race-conscious agenda and their bureaucratic allies wide latitude to develop and pursue their objectives. An entire federal bureaucracy devoted to racial goals, timetables and quotas grew up more or less in the dark. Its operating assumptions, and its decision-making machinery were largely shielded from journalistic scrutiny.

Another factor was national apprehension over racial unrest. From 1965 to 1968, even before the nation could celebrate the achievements of the Civil Rights Movement, disturbances broke out in more than one hundred American cities, and politicians and civic leaders grew increasingly panicked over what to do. In 1968, the Kerner Commission released its famous report, along with a set of policy recommendations. Claiming that "institutional" white racism was the single most important factor behind racial unrest and racial inequality, the Commission repudiated the anti-quota philosophy of the past and endorsed the philosophy of racial preference. The Kerner Commission's embrace of a race-concious social policy became the new journalistic orthodoxy. It laid the groundwork for the even more explicitly proportionalist vision that would eventually dominate the diversity agenda when it eventually took hold and flourished in U.S. civic institutions in the late 1980s and 1990s.

Like federal judges, Harvard professors and "wise men" such as McGeorge Bundy—the former JFK aide, who as president of the Ford Foundation had more power to determine social outcomes than he ever did in government—most of the journalistic establishment had now begun to favor the view that racism in American life was "systemic" and that in order "to get beyond race, we have to take race into account," as Supreme Court justice Harry Blackmun famously said. Although affirmative action led to inequities, they said, the virulence of white racism left the country no choice but to embrace such a remedy in the short term to "level the playing field." In their support for affirmative action, journalists and the policymaking elite also displayed a sense of moral superiority and self-congratulation that could be quite striking. A *Boston Globe* editor quoted by J. Anthony Lukas in his landmark study on race, *Common Ground*, summarized that newsroom arrogance toward the city's Boston Irish community, who objected to forced busing in the late 1970s: "If they don't like integration," the editor would say, "we'll shove it down their throats."

The new journalistic orthodoxy was explicit in the declarations of support that preference programs got on editorial pages and in the work of influential columnists. But even more important was what did not get written. Affirmative action became a given, immune from the inspection normally given to any controversial social policy. As Frederick Lynch, a political scientist at the Claremont Graduate Center, has written, "The mass media has created a reality in which the issue and its attendant problems do not exist."

Aside from coverage of the controversial Supreme Court case of *Bakke v. University of California* in 1978, the issue received little print or broadcast news attention. This was true even as race-conscious policies were spreading into almost every corner of American public life, and the rationale justifying them mutated from the original intention of racial compensation, to diversity for diversity's sake. Until very recently, the triumph of affirmative action in our national life became the greatest story never told. To the degree that it was done at all, reporting appeared after the fact, in response to court decisions. There were few enterprise stories or investigative pieces exploring the claims of alleged victims of the policies, or examining the growing divide between how affirmative action programs worked in theory and their actual everyday impact on real people in the real world.

Asked why she had been gun-shy about challenging controversial affirmative action policies, for instance, one white *San Francisco Chronicle* reporter, who would talk to me only on the telephone from her home and not from her newsroom, said," The standards for stories on affirmative action are much higher, especially if the story is critical, or if the conclusions could be read as negative about a minority group. We have affirmative action inside [the newsroom] too, and though it is hard to pinpoint the connection, it is just generally hard to question something that we ourselves do." A Latina colleague agreed:

> It is taboo for someone to get up in the newsroom and ask questions about racial preferences. Anyone who did would take a lot of heat—from activists and from colleagues. I personally believe you have to work in an environment where all sorts of ideas can be pursued. You just simply can't do good journalism in an environment where you have a lot of taboos. But the fact is we do work in an environment where people are afraid. There are tensions, real tensions; it gets under people's skin, and people have a very hard time talking about it.

One public-sector preference program where press coverage has been most one-sided is the diversity movement in big-city police departments. According to its supporters, police diversity is necessary to give law enforcement legitimacy in the eyes of an increasingly diverse urban population, much of which is suspicious of predominantly white police forces, seeing them as an "occupying army" of uncaring and bigoted suburbanites.

Although there is very little compelling research to back up claims that a more diverse police force is necessarily a more effective force, or even that inner-city neighborhoods are better served by minority officers, news reporters and editorialists almost always cite this linkage, ignoring significant contradictory evidence. Though news organizations nationwide have made much of the Los Angeles Police Department's alleged "culture of brutality," for instance, they don't say much about its almost perfect proportional representation—the best diversity record in the nation. Nor are they inclined to examine the high brutality rates in departments such as Washington, D.C., Detroit and Houston—all big-city police departments with a majority of black officers, where increasing the match between the complexion of the force and that of the citizenry has not translated into smoother relations.

Most of the efforts to increase ethnic and racial diversity in urban police departments have centered on expanding the pool of minority

applicants, largely by overhauling the civil service exams used for hiring and promotion and the psychological screening procedures, both
of which minority candidates have a history of failing at higher rates
than whites. Supporters of these tests say they are race-neutral bul-
warks against group favoritism and patronage and that they measure
the cognitive abilities, literacy skills and command of criminal procedure needed to do police work. But their critics, who embrace the logic
of proportional representation, argue that the disproportionate minority failure rate means that the tests are skewed to favor white candidates
and that if they are to be used, they must be carefully purged of bias,
usually under court supervision.

As a result, vast sums of money have been spent on overhauling
the tests so that nonwhites can pass at acceptable rates. In some places,
hiring and promotion tests have been scored on a racial curve, sometimes giving minority candidates a sizable edge simply by virtue of skin
color. Reforms have also focused on overhauling psychological screening procedures, which many minority activists say disproportionately
disqualify black and Latino candidates due to the biases white psy-
chologists bring to the table.

Charges of anti-black bias on tests, for instance, are almost never
challenged or dissected with professional skepticism, even when the
charges come in the most absurd and racist form—that written tests
*inherently* discriminate against blacks. Reporters covering the story have
rarely conveyed just how these tests have been dumbed down, particularly the hiring exams. In New York City, for example, the tests have
gotten so easy that testing officials have said off the record that "cultural
illiterates" could pass them.

Reporters have also turned a blind eye to the impact of "race-
norming" on the tests, which has allowed minorities to "pass" with
scores substantially lower than their white counterparts. Nor has much
real attention been devoted to the well of resentment and division these
disparities have created. The overall attitude was summed up by the
*Chicago Tribune*, which editorialized in favor of a proposal to abandon
civil service exams as promotion tools. According to the *Tribune*, the
sergeant's exam in question "was only a test" and officials anxious to
increase the ranks of minority sergeants should look to other criteria.

The linkage between lowered hiring and promotion standards
and police corruption is one that the press has been particularly reluctant to examine. The vast majority of police corruption cases involve
white officers, yet increasingly, minority officers have been involved at
significantly disproportionate rates. Experts examining the problem see

a troubling link between lowered standards allowed in pursuit of diversity and the hiring of cops prone to going bad.

In 1990, for example, investigators arrested five Buffalo police officers, charging them with involvement in narcotics trafficking. All five were black and had been hired as part of an affirmative action program several years before. For a city the size of Buffalo, the revelation was a bombshell, and was bannered on the front page of the leading newspaper, the *Buffalo News.*

But instead of putting photos of the officers on the front page or inside after the jump, as was the paper's policy, editors ultimately decided not to run photos at all. This was a decision that editor Murray Light freely admitted was calculated to calm public apprehensions about the controversial preference program that had brought the officers onto the force—a program that the paper had editorialized in favor of quite heavily, and that the police union had protested against. Considering the "commanding need" for black role models, Light explained, putting the mug shots of the five officers on the front page would have been "devastating." As he said later on, "I was practicing discrimination by not running those pictures and I wasn't happy about it. But it was the right decision at the time, and I want to stress I was never sorry."

An even more serious example of calculated concealment involved the *Washington Post's* reporting on corruption problems associated with an aggressive minority-hiring plan in the Metropolitan Police Department of Washington, D.C. Trying to boost its minority representation, the department lowered its hiring standards in 1989 and 1990, administering a written exam that "a third-grader could pass," as one training instructor at the police academy admitted. It also practically abandoned the criminal background checks that are standard in the world of law enforcement.

Job performance suffered. Semiliterate rookies simply could not complete complicated arrest reports; many lacked the basic skills necessary to serve as competent witnesses in court. Thousands of cases, including many murder cases, were thrown out of court, contributing to the runaway crime rate in D.C. that for almost a decade has been the worst in the nation.

The most serious consequence of the relaxation of hiring standards, however, was to make becoming a cop an appealing career move for many criminals. The effective suspension of the background checks allowed those with convictions for drug trafficking, armed robbery and other felonies onto the force. Eventually the U.S. Attorney's Office in Washington had a list of three hundred officers it would not allow to testify at trial because their tainted backgrounds and records of dubious professional conduct exposed them too readily to impeachment from defense attorneys.

By 1993, the corruption problem had gotten so bad that the FBI had formed its own special internal unit to police the D.C. police. Seventy-seven cops on the force, almost all of them black, had been indicted for serious felonies ranging from drug dealing to murder, some charged by local prosecutors and some by federal authorities. Among those were twelve black officers arrested in late December of that year in Operation Broken Faith, a federal sting operation in which the police officers were caught making deals to protect undercover FBI agents posing as drug kingpins. (Nine of the twelve pled guilty in early plea-bargaining arrangements and the other three were convicted at trial. In taped conversations, the cops boasted to agents of their "credentials" for the job, bragging that they had worked for drug gangs before joining the force.

In 1993, a front-page *Washington Post* piece by reporter Keith Harriston, headlined "City Paying Dearly for Its 1989–90 Rush to Hire," explained that 43 of the 77 officers under indictment had been hired in that initial recruitment drive. It told of psychological and criminal background checks so lax that psychiatric outpatients had been allowed on the force, and of former drug dealers with felony convictions, now wearing badges, running into their arresting officers at police headquarters.

Although the piece never said so, the requirement that all new officers had to be residents of the District of Columbia—a requirement connected to the goal of increasing the ranks of minority officers—was the chief reason that the department had been forced to lower standards so drastically. Had the applicant pool been open to those outside the District, as is normal in other cities, the number of potential recruits would have been greater and reduced standards less necessary. That this was not mentioned in the *Post*'s coverage of this sordid episode was less surprising than the fact that the *Post* had known two years earlier that the recruitment drive was compromising standards, but had not run a story about it.

According to an account in the *New Republic*, the *Post*'s Metro desk reporter Sari Horowitz had done a story about the D.C. hiring binge, warning of a "disaster in the making." The piece described cops who couldn't read or write, and cops so intellectually unsophisticated that they couldn't understand cause and effect. Although it did not specifically say that most of the problem officers were black, it suggested as much by noting that all new D.C. officers were required to be from within the District. Horowitz's piece quoted both white and black cops denouncing the lowered standards. Nevertheless, it was spiked by the current Metro editor, Milton Coleman.

Coleman insisted that this was because the reporting and editing were inadequate. Others in the newsroom at the time, however, saw it differently. "Milton kept placing obstacles in its way," a *Post* editor insisted to the *New Republic*. "It was the equivalent of placing 100,000 tasks in front of you. 'Well, you haven't proven this. You haven't asked that.' " This was an explosive, fascinating well done series. And his reaction was completely negative and extremely discouraging."

In the wake of the scandal, the *Post* has been much more vigilant about reporting the deleterious impact that concerns for police diversity have had on the department. A mid-1996 report about race-driven promotions blew the whistle on the way the department's "determination to have a representative force" had led to passing grades for officers who had answered fewer than half the questions correctly on one sergeant's/lieutenant's exam.

But the paper was still guilty of sidestepping certain obvious diversity-related dimensions of important stories. The *Post* reported on the huge wave of retirements and resignations that hit the department in 1996—the highest one-year exodus ever, taking the best and brightest out of duty. Yet the paper failed to note the demoralization behind the high retirement rate, which many rank-and-file cops said was the product of the department's heavy-handed racial engineering.

The *New York Times* has also had trouble honestly exploring the downside of programs to recruit and promote more minority officers. Its bias was particularly obvious in the much-publicized 1993 campaign to boost minority police recruitment in New York City.

At the time, blacks accounted for 25 percent and Latinos nearly 24 percent of New York's population. But the nearly 38,000 officers of the NYPD were about 74 percent white, making the department one of the least racially representative forces in the country. The new police commissioner appointed in late 1992, Raymond Kelly, told the press he did not buy into charges of police racism. But he did say that racial imbalance in an increasingly minority city did make the force "less dynamic" and more vulnerable to accusations of racism that, like it or not, take on "a life of their own."

Describing nonwhite recruitment as the "top item" on his agenda, Kelly sent recruiters into black churches around the city and military bases around the country, boosting the applicant pool from 19,000 to 57,000, nearly half of them minorities. He also got approval for a 5-point bonus on the 100-point exam for city residents, a measure clearly calculated to help more minorities pass, and he initiated a review of psychological testing procedures, which up to then had rejected blacks and Latinos at a much higher rate than whites.

Kelly's diversity drive became the subject of glowing profiles in the press. But to insiders with an appreciation for the complexity of the issue—and for the negative impact of earlier diversity efforts elsewhere—Kelly's efforts inspired anxiety.

These fears were vindicated in the spring of 1994, when prosecutors in New York arrested a dozen crooked police officers in Harlem's 30th Precinct. The officers were accused of shaking down drug dealers for more than $400,000 in cash and drugs, of intimidating some witnesses and assaulting others, of tampering with evidence and of selling their shields to protect some dealers and harass their rivals. Protected instead of hounded by the police, drug dealers had multiplied and prices had plunged to the lowest levels in the nation.

The arrests brought swift response from certain quarters, much of it based on the assumption that the officers involved were white, and that the corruption and brutality were a function of their cultural alienation. In a *New York Times* op-ed piece, former *Washington Post* reporter Jill Nelson said the problem was the "ghouls with guns" who were let loose on the Harlem community. Others echoed the same theme, and cited the corruption scandal to make the case that the police force needed to be more representative of the city.

Yet the assumptions driving these reactions turned out to be questionable. Although news reports did not identify police officers in the 30th Precinct by race and ethnicity, photographs and names of the arrested officers splashed across the tabloids indicated that 8 of the 12 were Latino, a fact the department confirmed. One, Patrolman Alfonso Compres, a community affairs officer known on the street as the brutal "Abusador," was from San Francisco de Marcoris, the Dominican Republic's notorious breeding ground for foot soldiers in Upper Manhattan's drug trade. According to authorities, Compres at one point stole coke from a dealer after striking him in the head and then gravely wounded him with a shot to the midsection. Authorities also said that he was making $2000 a week shaking down dealers, and police informants said he had boasted that even if he did go to jail, he would still come out with a lot of money.

I had read about prior scandals in Washington, D.C., and places like Miami, where the rush to boost minority police numbers also resulted in the hiring of cops with problematic backgrounds and low test scores. The Dirty Thirty case, as the Harlem episode became known, gave off the same smell. It only took about a day's reporting for me to confirm the suspicion. According to Michael Julian, then the NYPD chief of personnel, the 30th Precinct was very diversity-conscious; the race and ethnicity of the officers assigned there was carefully matched to the proportions of the predominantly black and Latino population. As a result, more than half the cops were black and almost 40 percent were Latino.

At the time I made my inquiries, authorities had not yet finished sifting through hiring records and files of the Dirty Thirty cops, or any of the others who had come to the attention of the Mollen Commission on Police Misconduct, a high-profile investigation into citywide police corruption. But what they had found up to that point raised troubling questions about the unintended consequences of the department's diversity procedures.

According to the officials I spoke with, many of the indicted officers in the 30th Precinct had rock-bottom scores on hiring exams and would not have been put on the job had the tests not been dumbed down to boost minority pass rates. Investigators had also found that several of the officers had been given approval by background inspectors even though they resided in notorious drug locations and had relatives with multiple felony drug convictions. These were indications, said the officials I contacted, that the officers may have been immersed in the culture of narcotics before they came on the job.

The diversity subtext to the Dirty Thirty case and to other Mollen Commission investigations was also apparent in problems linked to inadequate supervision, which had played a role in the pattern of misconduct. According to the commission, poor leadership had set the stage for rank-and-file corruption; many of the sergeants who were supervising corrupt street cops, investigators found, should never have been promoted, or even hired to begin with. Although the Mollen Commission did not blame the lowered hiring standards associated with diversity for this, the implication was clear: lower the gates for recruits and you'll feel the effects further up the line as well. As Adam Walinsky, the driving force behind the federal police cadet corps plan, noted: "You cannot keep reducing standards for recruiting patrolmen without crippling your capacity to promote sergeants of ability and character."

All of this evidence suggesting a linkage between diversity, lowered standards and police corruption failed to convince the *New York*

*Times*. Despite ample reason to do so, the paper did not bring up the diversity subtext either in its initial reporting or subsequently, when others had made the connection more explicit. The Mollen Commission's formal report, for instance, noted that of the four hundred cops suspended or dismissed since 1988, 24 percent had criminal arrest records prior to coming on the job, and that information "sufficient to question the character" of the officers had been available. The *Times* did not report these conclusions. In fact, about as close as the paper got to admitting the relationship between the diversity drive and corruption was an oblique, euphemistic analysis written by police reporter Clifford Kraus on "The Perils of Police Hiring." In the piece, Kraus said that lowered standards of hiring and training were a symptom of the police department's "rush to hire," and he referred to the racial issue indirectly, citing the "less disciplined pool of high school graduates" who had "exposure to a culture of violence and drugs." Subsequently, the *Times* acknowledged that the vast majority of the problem officers would not have been hired under the new, more demanding screening standards, which were implemented in the wake of the Mollen Commission report. As for the role that diversity played in allowing those officers to become policemen in the first place, the paper said nothing.

The drive for diversity has also been an unacknowledged factor in the disarray and corruption plaguing the New Orleans Police Department as well. With one of the nation's highest rates of violent crime and the country's second-highest homicide rate, New Orleans was a city out of control for most of the 1990s, and the ineffectiveness of its police force at dealing with drug trafficking, burglaries, prostitution, robberies and assaults drew the ire of citizens and federal law enforcement authorities trying to turn the situation around.

Bad police work was undermining prosecutorial effectiveness in almost every case that came through the city's courts. In addition to their legendary ineptitude, New Orleans police were known for their brutality. According to FBI figures, the department has had more brutality complaints filed against it than any other local law enforcement organization in the country. But what made the situation in New Orleans truly remarkable was that in the years between 1993 and 1996, more than fifty officers were indicted for serious felonies ranging from bank robbery and rape to drug trafficking and homicide. Four officers had been charged with first-degree murder; two of them had been convicted and were on Death Row.

Police corruption had long been a major problem in the Big Easy, a result of the low pay and lax ways of supervisors. But the wave of violent criminality among officers was novel, and seemed to be tied to the lowered standards that had been allowed in the drive to bring minority officers onto the force. Of the fifty officers under indictment, a disproportionate number were nonwhite.

Begun in 1987 as a response to a consent decree the city entered with the Department of Justice, the diversity drive in New Orleans was aggressive, and it quickly brought minority representation to 45 percent of the force. Never exacting to begin with, hiring standards were lowered even further, and psychological screening procedures and criminal background checks were relaxed. Officer Antoinette Frank, who killed three people, one of them her ex-partner, in a robbery on a Chinese restaurant, was deemed too unstable to become a police officer when department shrinks first evaluated her. But on the strength of a note from her own physician she was allowed onto the force on appeal. According to testimony at her trial, Frank's incident reports were often unintelligible, and her behavior on the beat so irrational that it was recommended she be returned to the academy for retraining. Later, after her arrest on the robbery/murder charges, a skeleton was found buried beneath her house, raising possibilities of even more violence in her past.

Yet in reporting and analyzing this particular police scandal, both the local and national press studiously avoided the diversity angle. A 1996 series in the *New Orleans Times-Picayune* alluded to "low hiring standards" that had led to sloppy police reports and dumbed-down training courses, but did not connect the dots to the minority recruitment drive. And though it quoted a retired homicide chief as saying "We brought it on ourselves," there was no explicit mention of the diversity programs. Instead, the *Times-Picayune* went with the politically palatable line, blaming "years of neglect, mismanagement and petty politics in every corner of the department."

Mirroring the *Times-Picayune*'s denial were stories on NBC's *Dateline* and CBS's *60 Minutes*, both of which made no mention of the disproportionate number of minorities involved nor the lowered hiring standards that had been allowed for the sake of diversity. While the *New York Times Magazine* did at least acknowledge that many in New Orleans blamed the diversity drive for criminal cops, it quickly covered its flank by saying that dirty officers were merely "following a long entrepreneurial tradition at the department." According to this analysis, there was no difference between the "clean corruption" of white cops shaking down local bars and the "dirty corruption of the lucrative but deadly drug world."

Such logic was repeated in daily *New York Times* dispatches where writer Rick Bragg reported that the hiring of Antoinette Frank and others with similar unsuitable records was simply "a regular practice in a department that in recent years has often had to lower its standards to match pay."

More evidence that enhanced racial diversity did not make for better police-community relations was to be found in the scandal that detonated in the Los Angeles Police Department in 1999 and 2000. The case involved the arrests of more than a dozen plainclothes officers in the department's elite anti-gang squad that operated out of the downtown area of the city known as Ramparts. In the latter part of 1999, Los Angeles district attorney Gil Garcetti announced that these officers had been part of a pattern of drug dealing, violence and murder—revelations which stunned a department that was only beginning to recover from the damage done to its reputation in the Rodney King affair and in the riots of 1992.

It was clear that efforts to boost the diversity of the LAPD were a factor in the Ramparts scandal. The officers involved were disproportionately minorities, and many had been hired at a time when the goal of recruiting more minority officers had compromised screening procedures. Yet the *Los Angeles Times* preferred not to examine these factors. And though it was clear that the case contradicted the logic of police diversity—the high concentration of minority officers in the Ramparts division not only did nothing to stem brutality but actually augmented it—the paper refused to consider the implications of this fact.

The downside of diversity in police hiring may have been swept under the rug, but diversity in higher education has garnered at times active support from the press. According to backers of affirmative action in colleges and universities, the programs are necessary to create a leadership class of minority college graduates who will be serving their respective ethnic and racial communities in an increasingly nonwhite society of the near future. The racial synergy these programs create is also a key ingredient in fostering intellectual excitement on campus.

To critics, though, these campus affirmative action programs represent a paint-by-number approach that asserts a vision of group rights at the expense of fairness to individuals. According to these critics, admissions programs that use race in determining who gets into college and who does not are an institutionalized form of reverse discrimination, shot through with double standards. As such, they amount to a profound breach of constitutional protections with corrosive impact on race relations as a whole.

University admissions officers are very careful about revealing how they operate, and getting information from them about racial handicapping is like pulling teeth. But from time to time they have acknowledged what is going on. According to one admissions official at the University of Virginia, "We are committed to a program of affirmative action and we want to make the university representative of the population of the state as a whole. We take more from groups with weaker credentials and make it harder for those with stronger credentials." Writing about the climate of dishonesty toward race-based admissions decisions in the wake of California's 1996 statewide ban of preferences, the black linguist John McWhorter, author of the *Losing the Race: Self-Sabotage in Black America,* says, "What is alarming is that one can sit through two-hour meetings of concerned Berkeley faculty and administrators without the merest acknowledgment of class, merit or fairness. Instead the agenda is implicitly restricted to speculation on how to reinstate racial preferences in other guises."

Until recently, news organizations have been reluctant to probe these issues very deeply, especially when there is no obvious story like Proposition 209 in California forcing them to do so. Thus have partisans of diversity maintained the fiction that high standards and diversity are not antagonistic, even as evidence has piled up indicating exactly the opposite. Questions related to how the beneficiaries of affirmative action score on standardized tests, their graduation rates compared to others on campus, and other questions key to evaluating university preference systems have largely been left unasked by journalists tackling the subject or by editorial writers promoting the affirmative action cause. Investigative skills used to ferret out information on other tough stories have gone unused in this one.

Substantial racial double standards at Berkeley, for instance, which were the focus of a number of lawsuits in the late 1980s and early 1990s, including one by Asian students, were not pursued by the Bay Area's paper of record, the *San Francisco Chronicle,* even though black students were admitted with average SAT scores 288 points lower than students from other groups, and had a 42 percent undergraduate dropout rate compared with 16 percent for whites. "It would have been taboo for anyone to get up in the newsroom and press that story too hard," a *Chronicle* reporter told me. "People just generally felt it [giving substantial racial preference] was the right thing to do."

The same lack of journalistic enterprise when it came to preferences in admissions was evident in reporting on affirmative action programs at the University of Michigan. University officials took the position that they did not use preferences. But skeptics had long suspected that they were able to boost the numbers of underrepresented minorities only through significant—and largely secret—racial handicapping. Usually in such a case, investigative reporters might be expected to do end runs around such bureaucratic stonewalling, by filing Freedom of Information Requests or by interviewing former admissions officers in the hope they might find one who was bothered by the deception and wanted to talk. Higher education beat reporters in the state did not take these steps, however, and it was left to a Michigan philosophy professor named Carl Cohen to do this legwork himself.

A former member of the national board of the ACLU who calls himself an "active civil libertarian," Cohen was a liberal academic whose work focused on the philosophical relationship between equality and democracy. He had sat on the admissions committees of the University of Michigan undergraduate division and the medical school and had not noticed anything irregular. But in 1995 he read an article in the *Journal of Blacks in Higher Education,* which contained data indicating that the admission rates for blacks applying to college was significantly higher than the admissions rate for whites. Such numbers, Cohen said, broadly suggested that blacks were being given a substantial edge in admissions decisions. Was this going on at Michigan too?

His interest pricked, Cohen asked colleagues close to the admissions process if the university was using preferences. According to Cohen, they told him the information was "confidential." Receiving no cooperation from his own administration, Cohen began submitting Freedom of Information Act (FOIA) requests in late 1995. After initially receiving nothing back, he then began to see a steady stream of documents and records. Among them were the scoring grids that UM admissions officers used to evaluate applicants by race, which Cohen believed were "blatantly discriminatory." (According to one chart, a white or Asian applicant with a GPA between 1090 and 1190 would be automatically deferred while an "underrepresented minority" with the same credentials would be automatically accepted.)

Citing these findings, Cohen wrote a letter of inquiry to the university's board of regents, but got no response. As word leaked out that he had incriminating documents, state legislators asked him to share what he found at a public hearing in Lansing. Preferring to work within appropriate channels, Cohen did not, in fact, reach out to any journalists until *after* he had presented his information to the legislative hearing. But he is still puzzled that no one in the press took the same initiative he did, and that it took so long for the public to be informed about what was going on at a state-supported institution. (The state media finally picked up on the story after a lawsuit, *Gratz v. University of Michigan*, was filed on behalf on one of rejected white applicant—a lawsuit that was initially settled in the university's favor and may go before the Supreme Court.)

"There are a thousands of journalists in Michigan, not to mention the rest of the country," Cohen says. "The state has an obligation to respond to any FOIA request. So why didn't journalists from the *Detroit News*, the *Detroit Free Press*, the *New York Times* or the *Washington Post* send request letters? You can make the case that journalists should have smelled something wrong and made the effort to find out what. So why did they all wait for me? I don't know."

The answer to Cohen's question came in the hostile response that most national news organizations had to the lawsuit against the University of Michigan. The *Washington Post* quoted black students, who said that a little affirmative action was nothing compared with the four hundred years that blacks had been oppressed in America. And while it did good enough reporting the complicated facts, *Time* magazine still signed off with a dig, scolding critics of racial preferences for being "more successful at challenging diversity programs that don't meet with their approval than developing effective ones that do."

Journalists were similarly unwilling to examine the issue of admissions disparities at Georgetown University School of Law in 1991, when one of its third-year students published an analysis of admissions data that showed blacks had been let in with qualifications substantially lower than whites'. According to white student Timothy Maguire who had gotten unauthorized access to the information while performing work-study chores in the admissions office, the average white student accepted to Georgetown had an LSAT score of 43 out of 50 and a GPA of 3.7, while the average black student had a score of 36 and a GPA of 3.2.

Black law students at the school demanded the expulsion of Maguire and the entire editorial board of the school newspaper where this data appeared. Georgetown administrators confiscated every issue of the publication. Law school professors who at first agreed to help represent Maguire fight the expulsion action quickly withdrew their support when students advocated sanctions against them for simply offering assistance.

Notwithstanding its deliberately provocative tone, Maguire's article did call attention to a problem of double standards that Georgetown and many other universities had long refused to confront. But instead of using the incident as a peg to examine law school affirmative action programs, or for that matter to defend a fellow journalist, the media jumped on the anti-Maguire bandwagon. Implying that his revelations were myopic, the *New York Times* editorialized that he "hasn't a clue about the broad purpose of a great law school."

The press responded likewise to an affirmative action controversy that erupted at Rutgers University in New Jersey in 1995, when university president Francis Lawrence made a reference to the "hereditary genetic background" of black students at the school to explain their inability to score as well as whites on standardized achievement tests. In fact, Lawrence was actually arguing that colleges and universities think about moving away from SAT scores to some other kind of measuring system—an increasingly popular liberal opinion. Nevertheless his phraseology unleashed a furor, in the university and in the press. According to *New York Times* columnist Bob Herbert—only one of many black voices condemning Lawrence—the remark represented "an expression of the bedrock concept on which the entire edifice of white racism is built."

The gap in test scores that was at the root of the controversy (the average combined SAT score for blacks at Rutgers was 750, nearly 350 points lower than the average for whites) was important for understanding the story. At no point, though, did the *Times* or any other mainstream news organization report it. The controversy also provided an avenue into another newsworthy aspect of campus affirmative action programs: the intellectual insecurity and frustration such double standards often breed among the recipients of preferences. But journalists did not go there either.

In justifying preferences, university administrators almost always claim that they help universities compensate for the inferior educational opportunities available to poor blacks and Latinos. The implication is that affirmative action benefits the underclass. In truth, however, a large percentage of those admitted under preference programs share the socio-economic profile of their white schoolmates. At some schools, particularly the more prestigious ones, most of the blacks and Latinos admitted come from middle- and professional-class families, and have graduated from integrated, high-achieving, public high schools. Twice as many minority students at Cornell, for instance, come from suburbs as from cities. At Berkeley, 174 out of 257 black freshman admitted in the fall of 1997 came from homes with yearly incomes above $40,000, and the parents of 107 of them made more than $60,000. These statistics and their meaning are for the most part considered taboo by journalists on the affirmative action beat.

The presumably beneficial impact of preferences on the intellectual dynamism of campus life constitutes yet another area of the debate that has gone without adequate scrutiny. The *New York Times,* for instance, has had a decades-long resistance to acknowledging the impact of open admissions policies on City College, part of the larger City University of New York. Leading to gargantuan remediation programs and shockingly low graduation rates, open admissions was a debacle for the school whose formerly stringent standards earned it the nickname of "the Harvard of the Proletariat." Nevertheless, for many years, the *Times* preferred rose-colored accounts that implied that those critical of the effort were alarmist and racially motivated.

By the mid-1990s, though, conditions at the school and in the system as a whole had deteriorated to such a point that this denial was no longer possible. A New York City Comptroller's report disclosed that three-quarters of those admitted to the city system had failed at least one of three basic proficiency exams and required remedial attention. Another study showed that nearly half of all CUNY students dropped out before their junior year and only 22 percent finished their degrees in five years time. Still another disclosed that City University graduates failed New York State teacher certification tests at rates far higher than almost every other institution.

Worse than these statistical studies was the anecdotal testimony that was dribbling in from the front lines. In 1993, while I was researching an investigative piece for the magazine *Lingua Franca,* a remedial English professor at City College told me that only one in five of his students had enough reading ability to comprehend the headline of the student newspaper's sports page: "Student Turnout Nil at Games." In his book *City on a Hill* (1995), James Traub described a place where many students were reading at a third- or fourth-grade level, a place where the excellence of the past had become "the shining exception."

Just where the *New York Times* stood on the issue of declining standards was abundantly clear from a May 1997 piece describing City College's 150th anniversary, written by Joseph Berger, an alumnus of the school. Giving short shrift to the case against open admissions, Berger quoted one college junior who said that City College was still "the Harvard of the poor," but that people just didn't realize it anymore. Closing the piece by exploring the scorn that many in New York now felt toward the school, Berger quoted students who said such feelings represented "subtle racism." According to one student, the school's location—Harlem—"was a buzzword for crime and poverty...not something of quality."

Even more biased journalism came in response to Mayor Giuliani's bid to scale back remediation programs substantially in 1999, which Bob Herbert of the *Times* said was equivalent to "ethnic cleansing." "Who needs remedial classes when you can send students straight to jail?" Herbert asked. Other voices at the *Times* were similarly antagonistic, with Metro columnist David Gonzalez writing about the "CUNY Cure That Lacks a Disease." An editorial under the headline "Assault on Open Admissions" warned that reform would "further whiten New York's professional workforce." Another editorial approvingly quoted one alarmist CUNY trustee who said, "If we were to adopt this [reform] we might as well chisel off Emma Lazarus' welcoming words from the Statue of Liberty."

Attending these hyperventilating broadsides was basic misinformation. According to the *Times'* "Editorial Observer" Brent Staples, "students who need one or two remedial courses are consistently among the system's most distinguished and highest-earning graduates." But in fact, as James Traub has pointed out, the most distinguished and highest-earning graduates of the system are those immigrant kids—mostly white and Asian—entering with no remedial requirements and already speaking English well.

One of the stories that has most flagrantly bared the media bias in favor of campus affirmative action involved recent efforts to roll back racial preference programs in state-supported universities. Although these programs had grown increasingly unpopular by the late 1990s—and in some states have been banned by administrative decision, court rulings, or voter-approved initiatives—the journalistic establishment has clung tenaciously to the old dispensation, filtering news developments through the assumption that all moves against preferences are racially mean-spirited and socially damaging.

The decision by the University of California Board of Regents in 1995 to ban the use of race or ethnicity as a factor in admissions provides a case study. Were there double standards in evaluating different races and ethnic groups for admission throughout the UC system? Did affirmative action enhance the intellectual atmosphere on campus or hurt it? Would minority students be irreparably harmed if they no longer were admitted to the system's flagship schools, Berkeley and UCLA, and had to go to less prestigious campuses in the system?

It was important that the press both frame and provide possible answers to these questions. Instead, reporters let opponents of the ban set the agenda, for the most part simply serving as an echo chamber for the claim that it would be bad social policy for California to have anything other than numerical proportionalism of races and ethnicities on all UC campuses.

Any comprehensive and responsible discussion of the proposal by the University of California Regents to ban preferences in admissions should have conveyed just how determined university officials had been in concealing the inner workings of the preference machine. According to Regent Ward Connerly, when he asked at his first regents' meeting for information on minority preference programs, he was told no such preference programs existed. At one point in the controversy, administrators presented the regents with a report on admissions that was so contradictory and so dishonest that four regents circulated a public letter to their colleagues rebuking the administration, tacitly admitting that they no longer found the UC data credible. Yet university administrators' longstanding culture of resistance surrounding preferences never got the attention it should have received in the press.

News organizations covering the story finally did examine the operational details of the university's preference programs after evidence of its inequities had become too strong to ignore any longer. In May 1995 the *San Francisco Chronicle* reported the wide SAT score disparities among applicants from different ethnic and racial groups—as large as 200 points between blacks and whites. But most other news organizations did not pay much attention to these findings. If they noted them at all they were sure to include comments from affirmative action supporters who—inaccurately—insisted that the tests were culturally biased and were unreliable predictors of academic achievement.

In fact, there was actually far more reportorial sweat—and front-page space—put into exposing the inner workings of the preferences given to children of alumni and the well connected. In defending racial preferences, the pro–affirmative action camp had long cited such forms of favoritism. A multipart series produced by the *Los Angeles Times* just prior to the regents' vote echoed that theme, providing ammunition— in the spirit of two wrongs can make a right—to affirmative action proponents. Although the high rates of minority attrition throughout the UC system suggested that the university was admitting students who were unqualified to handle the work, the coverage tended not to see that angle. Ignoring the SAT disparities and the dropout rate, the *Los Angeles Times* editorialized that "there was no enrollment of unqualified blacks and Latinos in the university system."

Reporters also showed little enthusiasm for scrutinizing claims that the presence of minority students in the university system had enhanced the intellectual climate. Indeed, there had been an increase in *average* test scores and grades at Berkeley over the years, according to statistics, but the average academic achievement levels of minority students were actually *falling* in this period. Yet reporting such a fact would have been off script. Peter Applebome of the *New York Times* said that "grades, test scores and student performance all rose" under affirmative action. ABC News reported that "admissions officers at selective colleges around the country say affirmative action has made campuses intellectually more exciting because it brings in all races."

In late July 1995, after much loud and ugly debate, the UC Board of Regents finally voted in favor of banning the use of racial and ethnic preferences in admissions to graduate school and faculty hiring in 1996, with undergraduate programs to follow the year after.

The ban on preferences at the University of California did have an immediate and sharp impact on the composition of entering classes. At UC's Boalt Hall Law School, for instance, only fourteen blacks were admitted for fall 1996, and all chose other schools. Press accounts said they felt "unwelcome"—largely ignoring the fact that they opted for more prestigious schools or more generous financial aid.

But given the substantial size of the preferences that had been given to minority applicants at these schools, it would have been surprising if the bans had *not* had an impact. As Abigail and Stephan Thernstrom noted, "The magnitude of the drop in minority acceptances will be a good index of the magnitude of preferences that had been given in the past." But instead of exploring this point, the media rang alarm bells about the "resegregation" of American higher education, declaring a full-blown moral and social crisis.

According to a June 1997 *Time* magazine headline, America was moving "Back to the Future," with the termination of affirmative action programs causing minority enrollment to "plummet to 1963 levels." Likewise the tone of a *New York Times* editorial headlined "Segregation Anew," warning of test scores being "fetishized" and of damage to "the social coherence" of states moving away from the preference regime. Almost every network news program, as well as NPR, carried reports echoing this basic theme. A *Los Angeles Times* cartoonist redesigned the University of California official seal from "Let There Be Light" to "Let Truth Be White."

The "resegregation" story line, though, could only be sustained by serious factual misrepresentation. While the numbers of black and Latino students admitted to the Berkeley law school were down, the numbers at the equally prestigious UCLA were not depressed quite so drastically. At some of the University of California's second-tier law schools, such as UC Irvine and UC San Diego, the numbers had even gone up. Yet journalists continued to pursue the resegregation thesis.

There was also considerable disingenuousness in the media insistence that campuses were once again becoming "lily-white." In fact the number of "students of color," as this category was traditionally defined and measured, had gone up, if one counted Asians, whose admissions numbers had soared after the ban on preferences. But reporters, manipulated and misled by university administrators who were no longer counting high-achieving Asians in the "students of color" category, failed to note this—or cynically ignored it.

And having swallowed the line that campus diversity was essential to campus intellectual dynamism, reporters were quick to echo claims that the decline in minority representation meant a decline in the caliber of the educational experience because it would leave students with only the white "point of view." One California law professor was quoted in a 1997 column by Robert Scheer of the *Los Angeles Times:* "How can you teach Brown vs. Board of Education with no African American students in the classroom? Simple. You don't. It is no longer relevant." This vacuous statement cannot withstand even the most rudimentary analysis, yet Scheer treated it like a Socratic insight.

A few months after the resegregation story first began, evidence began to accumulate that minority applications and minority enrollments were not really plummeting at all. While minority admissions to California's law and business schools were down, there was no drop in the university's other graduate programs, and the numbers of minorities applying to undergraduate programs actually rose—a 4.9 percent increase for blacks and a 7 percent increase for Hispanics. In fact, at California's two most selective campuses, Berkeley and UCLA, *overall* minority enrollments had gone *up*. Clearly, predictions of lily-white campuses and a perception of racial inhospitality that would keep nonwhites from even applying were wrong.

And the trend continued to strengthen, with minority enrollments for black, Hispanic and Native American undergraduates at the eight main UC campuses growing to levels above what they were when affirmative action measures were in place (7,336 minority students in the year 2000, up from 7,236 in 1997). As Regent Ward Connerly observed, "The gloom and doom that was being preached by the proponents of preferences was grossly premature."

This was a good-news story, but it was largely ignored or slighted.

Those national news organizations that did report the rise in minority enrollment gave it nowhere near the attention or hype that the original resegregation story got. Often they buried the new information in stories with ambiguous headlines, as in a *New York Times* report in late January 1998: "Some Minority Admissions Drop in California." Black and Latino acceptance and enrollment were in fact down system-wide, but hardly as far as the racial Cassandras had predicted—or perhaps wanted. As in the infamous black church arson story of the year before, news organizations that whipped up the frenzy seemed too embarrassed to correct their initial reporting, and even into mid-1998, commentators continued to refer to campus "white-outs." Nor did they get around to noting that those minorities who did gain admission under the new colorblind rules were far more likely to graduate that those admitted in the past under the affirmative action regime.

Although defenders of affirmative action had previously denied that "preferences" per se existed, when now confronted with undeniable evidence to the contrary, they adopted a fallback position. Affirmative action was indeed based on preferences, the new logic went, but those who benefited from them were just as qualified, and went on to careers just as sound, as those admitted on merit. This 180-degree turnabout itself cried out for journalistic inspection, which never occurred. In fact, the press immediately picked up and supported the research allegedly bolstering these new claims.

Typical was the coverage generated by a study on minority law school graduates produced by Linda Wightman, a sociologist from the University of North Carolina. According to this study, which was published in the *New York University Law Review*, there was "little to no difference" on bar exam passage rates between those admitted to law schools under preference programs and those admitted on merit. But in fact, the gaps were considerable. In California, for instance, 81 percent of whites passed the bar exam the first time around, while only 53 percent of those given preference did. In New York State the differential was even wider, 81 percent to 37.4 percent. Even the sample that Wightman put up for examination showed substantial differences. Despite her stated conclusions, there was, according to those who examined the actual data she was working with, a threefold difference in white versus black bar performance.

Nevertheless, the Wightman study earned a string of uncritical media endorsements from *Time*, *Newsweek*, ABC News and the *New York Times*. According to *Time*, her research proved that affirmative action programs "had incalculable value to the black community as both professional and role models." As Gail Heriot, a professor at the University of California–San Diego Law School later wrote, "Wightman apparently relied on the media not to look too closely at the details of the study. She got her wish."

Another illustration of dubious coverage in this vein centered on a study analyzing the career paths of students admitted to the University of California at Davis Medical School, alma mater of Allan Bakke, whose Supreme Court case in 1978 produced the law governing the use of race in university admissions.

The report, the results of which were published in the *Journal of the American Medical Association*, looked at the after-graduation career paths of students admitted under racial preferences and under other forms of favoritism such as athletic ability and alumni connections. Affirmative action students were less likely to graduate with honors, the study showed. They also performed less well on basic science courses in the first year of medical school. But, the study went on to say, the two groups of students graduated at the same rate and followed parallel career paths, completing residency training at the same rate, selecting specialties in the same percentages and establishing practices with the same racial mixes.

By mixing students preferred for athletic ability and family connections with those preferred simply because of their race, the study willfully compared apples and oranges. Its reliability was also compromised by a failure to take into account the earlier studies reaching the opposite conclusions, among them a 1994 *Journal of the American Medical Association* study which found that preference candidates were three times more likely to flunk out of medical school and eight times more likely to fail Part I of the national medical boards—the section measuring mastery of basic medical and biological sciences. Another study never mentioned was a 1997 Rand Institute analysis of the Davis Medical School class of 1975—the class that turned down Bakke but accepted Doctor Patrick Chavis. According to Rand, only 49 percent of blacks and Hispanics in the class were board certified, compared with 80 percent of whites and Asians.

Nevertheless the career-path study earned front-page treatment by the *New York Times* and by the *Los Angeles Times*, both of which ignored the problems with its methodology. Although the data clearly showed that those students receiving preference had a much higher rate of failure on national medical boards and were not as likely to move into prestigious positions later, the lead of the *Los Angeles Times* story proclaimed that after playing some career catch-up, students given preference "turned out to be just as competent doctors as regularly admitted students."

The entrenched journalistic resistance to rolling back preferences in higher education could also be seen in the resounding acclaim that greeted *The Shape of the River: Long-Term Consequences of Considering Race in College and University Admissions* in 1998. The book was written by two former Ivy League college presidents, Derek Bok of Harvard and William Bowen of Princeton. The authors aimed to study the impact and effectiveness of affirmative action at the nation's top schools, but were just as interested in how affirmative action affected its beneficiaries while they were in school as in how they performed after graduating. When the Supreme Court finally got around to making a definitive decision on affirmative action, the authors said, they hoped that the data in the book would influence them to affirm preferential policies.

Among the central conclusions of *The Shape of the River* were the following: that black students are not admitted under grossly unfair standards and that they do well academically; that black beneficiaries of affirmative action earn advanced degrees at the same or slightly higher rate than whites in law, business and medicine and become more active in civic affairs, becoming in fact, the backbone of the black middle class; that affirmative action fosters broad racial understanding and social harmony, with whites learning much about blacks through friendships that a lack of affirmative action would deprive them of.

These claims were controversial and cried out for rigorous scrutiny of the kind given to more conservative books, such as *The End of Racism* by Dinesh D'Souza, which made the opposite claims. There was much to challenge in the authors' facts and methodological assumptions as well. The average black student at the elite schools that Bok and Bowen studied graduated with a GPA in the bottom quarter of his class, and the black dropout rate was triple that of whites in the same places. This seemed to suggest that black students admitted under racial preference programs were in fact at a disadvantage at these elite schools. Blacks also did far less well on bar exams; over the last twenty years, between 57 and 70 percent of the blacks who took the New York and California bar exams each year failed, as compared with 18 to 27 percent of whites, a disparity that seems to cast doubt on Bok and Bowen's assertion that though given a break on law school admissions, they performed just as well in their careers afterward.

The authors' claim that without affirmative action, black enrollment would decline "most of the way back to early 1960s levels" also cried out for scrutiny. Blacks would not disappear off the college map without preferences, as Abigail Thernstrom observed in the *Wall Street Journal,* but would instead land in schools just below the elite level. There they would have a good chance of doing well in life—as some of the journalists most ardently in favor of racial preferences, such as Bob Herbert and Brent Staples at the *New York Times,* had obviously done after attending just that kind of school.

Yet instead of giving *The Shape of the River* a critical reading, the journalistic establishment for the most part staged a love-in, receiving it as if the cavalry had just ridden to the rescue. Three national newspapers printed excerpts of the book, and many ran special feature and news analysis pieces in addition to the standard book review. The *New York Times* was most responsive, running a Sunday book review, a daily review, a lengthy news feature accompanied by an excerpt, a Week in Review analysis, and a reverent editorial headlined "The Facts about Affirmative Action," declaring that the book represented "striking confirmation of the success of affirmative action in opening opportunities and creating a whole generation of black professionals who are now leaders in their fields and communities." The study was called unprecedented in its "magnitude" and its findings "provide a strong rationale for opposing current efforts to demolish race-sensitive policies in colleges across the country."

The high-water mark of journalistic hostility toward the anti-preference movement, however, was the coverage of Proposition 209, otherwise known as the California Civil Rights Initiative (CCRI). Taking its wording from the language of the 1964 Civil Rights Act, the 1996 initiative asked voters to decide whether the state "shall not discriminate against or grant preferential treatment to any individual or group on the basis of race, sex color ethnicity or national origin in the operation of public employment, public education of public contracting."

To supporters of the measure, the fact that California was the country's most diverse state—made up of dozens of different races, ethnicities and nationalities—argued precisely for a colorblind social ideal. Managing this diversity through color-conscious codes and regulations had sowed confusion, inequity and resentment.

To its opponents, however, Proposition 209 used the language of the Civil Rights Movement in order to betray it and would cast nonwhites back into second-class citizenship by denying them the legal protections they needed to compete on an equal footing. Contrary to those who said mandated diversity was an inappropriate way to enter such a diverse, multiethnic future, opponents of 209 said it was the only way to mediate between so many different groups, and to check the historical privilege of the white power structure and the unconscious racism that still permeated society.

Tapping such deep emotions, the debate over the California Civil Rights Initiative cried out for responsible, sober and honest media attention. The challenge was to acknowledge where the anti-preferences movement had come from and why it became so popular so quickly; to establish baseline facts about what it would do and not do; and to curb the more exaggerated, inappropriate and offensive rhetoric that would no doubt be employed by both sides along the way to election day.

For the most part, however, news organizations reduced Proposition 209 to an expression of "white male anger," ignoring the significant support from women, blacks and other people of color and the reasons why they too backed the initiative. Instead of sponsoring a sober discussion of the initiative's potential impact, reporters typically gave unearned credence and visibility to the opposition's scare tactics, making it seem as though Proposition 209 would cause an apocalyptic change—for the worse—in the way that California did its racial business. The press not only gave a green light to the opposition's violent rhetoric, but also accepted a view that the 209 leadership consisted of bigots engaged in a racist bid to turn back the clock on civil rights.

Looking back on the way his newspaper covered the campaign, *Los Angeles Times* correspondent Ronald Brownstein observed, "There was a reflex in the coverage that started with the assumption that people in it had bad motivations, racial motivations. The basic problem was you were considered either pro civil rights groups or a conservative who wanted to turn back the clock. The idea that you could have a progressive position—one that spurned preferences, but still had concern for minorities—fell on hard ground."

*San Francisco Chronicle* columnist Debra Saunders put it even more bluntly. Interviewed on the eve of the vote, she remarked, "It is the belief [here] that the real job of the paper is to defeat this thing." Discussing the way her colleagues in the press got caught up in the emotions of 209, Saunders said, "It was rare to have a debate over the substance of preferences, rare to have an argument over the actual merits of the issue. Scoring gaps on SAT tests as large as 300 points were meaningless to them. The last thing people wanted to do was debate the issue itself."

Most news reports simply scoffed at the charge that whites suffered reverse discrimination. Instead of looking hard at the operational realities of preferences in state government, journalists laced their reports with snide put-downs that seemed intentionally calculated to ridicule those claiming they had been victimized by the preference regime. "Do you feel that everyone is after your job, and that they might have an unfair advantage? That people can criticize you and its OK? Are you a white American male?" This was the way Jane Pauley, voice dripping with sarcasm, introduced a segment on the CCRI for NBC's *Dateline*.

In some journalistic quarters, the resistance to challenging the racial status quo ran so deep that reporters and editors balked at using the term "preferences," or insisted that it only be used inside quotation marks. According to Dorothy Gilliam, who sat on the National Association of Black Journalists' Media Monitoring Committee, the use of the term interchangeably with affirmative action marked the news media's adoption of "the terminology of the anti–affirmative action forces," and was responsible for "poisoning America's racial well." Gilliam's complaint was echoed by her colleague at the *Washington Post*, ombudsman Geneva Overholser. Dismissing any difference between "recruiting certain classes of people and preferring them," Overholser said that "in the end, 'preference' is not so much an inaccurate term as a loaded one." Affirmative action exists, she concluded, "because there has been a de facto preference for whites and males, remaining in place today, visible to anyone who looks at society's top positions."

To many white Californians, the idea that the immigrants of color pouring into the country at a rate of one million a year, one-third of them into California itself, were automatically entitled to preferences in government employment, higher education and contracting was clearly wrong. Unlike blacks, many Californians reasoned, these new immigrants had suffered from no state-sanctioned system of discrimination, at least in this country. Yet this important part of the CCRI's appeal earned almost no real attention, almost as if raising the subject would only feed nativism. When asked why his paper didn't cover this aspect of the story, *Los Angeles Times* reporter John Balzar told me that it would be "reckless" since "we live in a state where feelings about immigrants boil over so readily."

Inflammatory charges that the California Civil Rights Initiative was racially motivated were perhaps the most important for the media to dissect, but they were also the ones that were handled most irresponsibly. Amplifying the opposition's view that 209 was openly racist—Eleanor Holmes Norton, for instance, called it "a weapon of race war"—news organizations not only refused to look at the more complex reality but indulged in piling on. An editorial cartoon in the *San Francisco Examiner* showed two cackling men with a gas can running away from a burning church marked "Affirmative Action" on the side, and on their shirtsleeves were the letters "CCRI." An editorial in the same paper said the spirit of the initiative was "negative and exclusionary."

The media's acceptance of the slander against Proposition 209 as racist could be seen in the way they reacted to links that the opposition tried to establish between the Ku Klux Klan and the CCRI. During the campaign, *opponents* of 209 paid $4000 for former Ku Klux Klansman David Duke to appear at California State University at Northridge to voice arguments in favor of the proposition. Continuing the dirty tricks, the opposition then circulated a fraudulent letter from Duke to one prominent CCRI leader offering thanks for the "words of encouragement" and for a contribution to his organization which was in fact never made.

Making David Duke into the poster boy for the CCRI was demagoguery of the highest order and should have been revealed for what it was by news organizations. But not a single one of them did so. In fact, an editorial cartoon in the *San Francisco Chronicle* depicted David Duke sitting at a long table in hood and sheet, and alongside him a CCRI leader with head buried under the tablecloth in a way that suggested another hooded sheet. Photo editors were also ready to cement the association, making sure to run large photographs of anti-209 demonstrators carrying signs that read, "The KKK Supports 209. How Could You?"

Proposition 209 did enjoy the majority support of white men, yet during a good portion of the campaign—before the opposition's race-baiting got into high gear—tracking polls showed that it had considerable support from blacks and Latinos as well, the very groups the initiative was said to be biased against. (A June 1996 *Los Angeles Times* poll several months before the vote showed that black support was as high as 56 percent and that 68 percent of Hispanics were behind it.) Such findings were duly noted intermittently in the run-up to the balloting as news organizations tracked the ebb and flow of public opinion. But otherwise, minority and female support for 209 remained off the media radar screen, thus preserving a story line equating 209 with racism and sexism.

By contrast with the disparagement and hostility shown to the pro-209 movement, the press was consistently friendly to the opposition, allowing it to drape itself in the mantle of the 1960s Civil Rights Movement. Typical was the way reporters depicted the so-called California Summer Project, a spurious effort on the part of a small number of college students around the country to place their opposition to 209 on the same plane as the Mississippi Freedom Summer of 1964. An ABC News report implicitly affirmed the linkage with generous amounts of historical footage that draped the students in that august mantle. A *Washington Post* report was even more direct, closing with a statement by a Texas anthropology professor: "I don't mean to sound corny but there is an almost spiritual connection between what we are doing [against 209] and the summer of '64."

Attempts to exaggerate the CCRI's impact on women won similarly supportive and uncritical media responses. According to CCRI opponents, 209 would not only bar the state from favoring women with preferences in hiring and government contracting; it would also (they said in their advertising) strip women of maternity benefits, adversely affect their government pensions, and deprive them of the right to sue for discrimination based on sex as guaranteed under Title IX.

These assertions were absolutely false, and should have been questioned through rigorous reporting and commentary. Instead, reporters took the bait and the campaign began to shift the focus of the initiative to its impact on women, allowing the most blatant falsehoods to pass. Echoing the anti-209 Media Action Kit almost verbatim, for instance, the *Los Angeles Times* editorial page reminded its readers the day before the vote that "6 million women wouldn't have their jobs if it wasn't for affirmative action." Another *Times* editorial used hearsay in telling of a southern California businesswomen who allegedly was told by a male colleague that although her work was good, "It's back to the old boys club; without affirmative action we don't have to use you."

The most serious journalistic deficit in the coverage of the 209 campaign, however, was the failure to take opponents to task for their low-road attacks on the CCRI's leaders. Not only did journalists fail to censure such attacks in the spirit of fair-minded debate, but in some cases they actually added to them. According to *Los Angeles Times* editorial columnist Frank del Olmo, Governor Pete Wilson was "a malevolent little man who doesn't deserve to be governor of California...part of the GOP leadership who don't realize that the future will be painted in colors other than lily white." Piling on, the *New York*

*Times* said Wilson's support for 209 showed that he was "perfectly in tune with the nation's most churlish voters."

The ugliest press attacks, however, were aimed at conservative black businessman Ward Connerly, a member of the University of California Board of Regents who had spearheaded the effort to get the regents to abolish racial preferences in university hiring and admissions in 1995 and then taken on the chairmanship of Proposition 209. Connerly's opposition to racial preferences arose from deep objections to racial classification and from an opposition to having the current generation pay the historical debts incurred long ago. These independent, principled positions infuriated 209 opponents, doubly so because they were coming from a black man who was, in their view, committing race treason. Disparaged by political opponents throughout the anti-209 drive as being a "house nigger" and an "Uncle Tom" who "wanted to be white," Connerly got little better from journalists. One editorial cartoon in the *Oakland Tribune* featured him with a KKK hood and robe hanging nearby. Underneath was the caption "Connerly & Co. Ethnic Cleansers." As the many anti-Connerly hatchet jobs in the state's newspapers showed, reporters let the urge to "to get the goods" on Connerly, as one *San Francisco Chronicle* reporter put it, overshadow the leader's human complexities. "It was considered OK to nail him without considering what he was really saying," one *Chronicle* reporter confessed. "Newsroom culture definitely sent a message that it was OK to go after him."

A proposed meeting between Connerly and *San Francisco Chronicle* reporters to iron out some of these problems never materialized. According to Pamela Burdman, the reporter who tried to arrange it, the idea was dismissed by an editor who called Connerly "an asshole." "Not that I agree with Connerly," Burdman said, describing how disappointed she was in the editor's response, "but I do have the odd sense that we should be telling the truth."

In the campaign's final days, the anti-209 camp ran a series of TV spots featuring a hooded Klansman standing in front of a burning cross with a voice-over narrator warning that David Duke had "come to California to support Proposition 209." George Skelton, a columnist at the *Los Angeles Times,* denounced the ads as "so slimy" that they made ordinary negative ads seem wholesome. Most of the political columnists and editorial writers who had been speaking out against 209 throughout the campaign seemed to have lost their voice, but they recovered when it came time to judge the ads produced by the pro-209 camp, which featured Martin Luther King's famous civil rights speech calling on people to judge each other by the content of their character, not the color of their skin. News reports echoed the anti-209 line that such ads were a sacrilege defaming the memory of King and violating his family's copyright protections.

Virtually every major news organization in the state issued voter recommendations against the proposition. Typifying the alarmism, the *Los Angeles Times* said that voters needed to remember only one thing about Proposition 209: it was "a fraud."

Nevertheless, despite this last rush of invective (or perhaps even because of it, as I will later argue) 209 passed by a wide margin, 54 to 46 percent. Unsurprisingly, support for the initiative was heaviest among white males. But the initiative also received more than half the votes of women and Asian-Americans, 30 percent of votes cast by Hispanics and even 27 percent of those cast by blacks. Moreover, the preference ban was supported by nearly one-third of voters described as liberal—a slap in the face of the press that had portrayed the initiative as a conservative counterrevolution against civil rights.

Still clinging to the insistence that 209 was racist, the bitter-enders in the press ignored the obvious story of female and minority support, and never explained why the initiative resonated so strongly in the electoral cohorts where it was supposed to be anathema. Although they noted the percentages of pro-209 supporters, no major newspaper or network examined the significance of the numbers. Indeed, the *San Francisco Chronicle*'s editorial page scolded its readers and told them to remember that "the results weren't colorblind" and that the vote was carried by "the white majority."

In the aftermath of the defeat, the press continued to echo the mean-spirited, *ad hominem* attacks on the 209 leadership. The worst attacks continued to be aimed at Ward Connerly, who had by now taken the CCRI movement national, founding the American Civil Rights Institute to carry the message to other states. According to *Los Angeles Times* columnist Peter King, Connerly was "the Joe McCarthy of race relations in California," who had made "the golden land of tolerance" into something that looked "quite a little bit like Dixie." Portraying Connerly as a man "infected with a deep anger," King maintained that "some African Americans...question quite frankly whether he is comfortable in his own skin."

Picking up this ball and running with it, *New York Times* reporter Barry Bearak delved into Connerly's complicated family background and the skeletons hidden there in a long front-page piece. Contending that Connerly "has kept a psychic distance from his roots," Bearak described Connerly's grandmother as a self-hating, light-skinned black woman who, according to relatives, called her darker-skinned family members "jigaboo" and "baboon." Bearak also let Connerly's distant and estranged relatives assert that his father did not abandon the family, as Connerly had said, but was driven away by the grandmother. "Maybe that's why Ward has decided to become as much of a white boy as he could," one cousin speculated, tying the alleged racial self-loathing of the grandmother to the political positions of the grandson. "Isn't that what this campaign against affirmative action is all about?" the cousin continued, "So Wardell can bring down black people and forget his own blackness."

Clearly a morality play to advance the idea that true blackness cannot be reconciled with a principled opposition to racial preferences, as Jim Sleeper charged in the *Weekly Standard*, Bearak's effort drew strong criticism from 209 supporters. The *Times*, though, declined to respond. When I asked him about the article, Bearak refused to speak for the record, said that he found my questions "offensive" and then tersely declared, "This conversation is over."

Following on the heels of Proposition 209 in 1998, Initiative 200 sought to ban racial preferences in the state of Washington. The campaign replayed the California 209 script. Supporters saw the battle over I-200 as pivotal in the movement to spread the fight against race preferences. Ward Connerly, who backed this effort too, acknowledged that I-200 could be "the Gettysburg of affirmative action." Opponents and many of their media backers also treated this initiative as a sort of affirmative action apocalypse in the making.

At the local level, every major state newspaper editorialized against the measure. *Seattle Times* publisher Frank Blethen used $275,000 of his company's money to run full-page ads denouncing the I-200. "Let's keep the vision alive. Vote 'No' on Initiative 200. So we can keep moving forward to the future," one ad read. As Ward Connerly wrote in *Creating Equal*, Blethen was heard wandering the halls of the *Seattle Times* building telling subordinates that "we can beat this thing." The paper's news coverage was less obviously one-sided, though clearly biased in favor of those in the opposition camp. Quipped John Carlson, a Seattle radio journalist and political talk show host who became a co-chairman of the I-200 campaign: "Show me a reporter who opposes affirmative action and I'll buy lunch."

I-200 was front-page news throughout the campaign, with a nationwide coalition of proponents of affirmative action, including Vice President Al Gore, cycling through Washington in hopes of defeating the measure. But on election day, when it passed by a large margin, the *New York Times* buried the outcome in an omnibus account of how initiatives around the country had fared. As it did from the beginning of its coverage of I-200, the *Times* had a hard time fitting in news, no matter how consequential, that violated its orthodoxy on racial preferences.

# FIVE

# Immigration

n late June 1999, newspapers and network news broadcasts were filled with accounts of a thirteen-year-old boy who had reportedly left his hurricane-devastated home in Honduras in search of his father in New York City. According to a front-page story in the *New York Times*, which ran under the headline "Seeking Father, Boy Makes a 3200 Mile Odyssey," young Edwin Sabillon had departed from his small Honduran village after his mother and sister had died in the storm, setting out with $24 in his pocket, a bag with a change of clothes, his birth certificate, and three cookies. The story said he had received a letter from his father in America, whom he had never before seen, telling him to meet him near La Guardia Airport in New York City. Hitchhiking his way north, Sabillon had crossed the Guatemalan, Mexican and United States borders before climbing onto a bus in Miami and arriving in New York, where police had put him into protective custody. It had taken him thirty-seven days to make his journey, during which he had charmed "a string of helpful strangers." Among them were a group of "coyotes" in Matamoras, just across from Texas, who had taken him across the border free instead of charging him the usual $5000 fee. The boy's luck held out in Miami too, the story explained, where people inside a Cuban-owned cafeteria took up a collection and gave him $87 for a bus ticket north.

The story was "a Huckleberry Finn tale in reverse," according to the *Times*: "A stubborn boy sets out on the road to join his father, steals across the borders of three countries, gives the slip to lawmen along the way, loses his possessions and is rescued by a succession of good Samaritans." But the *Times* also seemed to be responding to the boy not just because he was plucky, but because he was "a plucky symbol of immigrant virtues," as the paper wrote subsequently.

Reporters from the Associated Press and *Newsday* who went to the boy's Honduran village in search of a good follow-up, however, found that the boy's tale did not wash. The next day, the *Times* was forced to run another story, this one inside in its Metro pages under the headline "Boy's Tale Mostly Fiction, Officials Say." The *Times* explained, "The doe-eyed 13-year-old who captivated the city with his tale of traveling solo in search of his father manufactured much of what he told police and those who helped him." In fact, his mother had not been killed. It was his father who had died, not in a hurricane but from AIDS, which he had contracted in the United States before returning home to die. Emotionally disturbed by his father's passing, the boy had run away from Honduras, landing with relatives near Miami. The *Times* now couched the tale as one of a "resourceful but troubled youngster whose impulsive behavior after his father died made him hard for relatives to handle."

The embarrassment prompted the *Times* to do a postmortem. In general, the editors shrugged off concerns about their own gullibility and the heavy play they had given the story. "I don't see this as major black eye for the media," *Times* editor Joyce Purnick maintained. Perhaps the *Times* should have attributed the account more heavily, Purnick continued, meaning that it should have made it clear whether the police or the boy was making the assertions. But even then, that "wouldn't have changed the tone" of the final article, Purnick concluded. Arthur Browne, the senior managing editor of the *New York Daily News*, which had also given the story banner attention, agreed. "In the end this was not an error that causes any harm. If anything, it's a misdemeanor of the heart," Browne declared.

To the degree that these editors admitted any responsibility at all, they blamed what they called "the crucial obstacles to fact-checking" the story. They admitted that the cynicism that reporters usually cultivate somehow took a back seat on this journalistic ride. "We don't expect children to be as deceptive as this young boy was," Arthur Browne said. "The story was so larger than life, and he had just enough of the brush strokes to make it go."

The story of Edwin Sabillon did little lasting harm. But the easy suspension of disbelief that it revealed on the part of editors and reporters in 1999 seemed to me to be an effect of the same rose-colored glasses through which the journalistic establishment had looked at the subject of immigration over most of the prior decade, when this was one of the most difficult issues in our culture.

Measures designed to enhance diversity in newsroom staffing and coverage have made journalism much more sensitive to the concerns of a huge wave of new, nonwhite Americans and have given the news reporting process greater access to, and sympathy for, these groups than ever before. But sensitivity and access have often been purchased at the expense of rigor, and a thick coat of piety and cant has often obscured plain truths. Too many journalists have been all too ready to celebrate immigration's relationship to America's increasing cultural diversity, even when the facts on the ground don't support such enthusiasm. In the process, they have left important questions unanswered and dismissed legitimate concerns as "nativism." Rather than engage in a full and frank examination of immigration, news organizations have been too ready to follow a romantic script that exaggerates its benefits and ignores its downsides.

There are reasons to be open to an argument about the possible advantages of immigration. The new immigrants have revitalized older, inner-city neighborhoods left for dead, and have brought renewed vigor to the country and its economy. There's also something emotionally gratifying about seeing newcomers of every race and hue follow the footsteps of European newcomers of a century before, with the same hope for a better future. And in a time when patriotism and national pride have gone out of fashion, immigration has rehabilitated the power of the American Dream.

Yet for every reason to be cheerful there are at least as many, if not more, reasons for concern. The influx of new immigrants has put a tremendous strain on schools, social welfare systems, hospitals, prisons and police forces. It has put a strain on our social fabric as well, as Third World immigrants with values and attitudes very different from mainstream American norms pursue the process of assimilation with much less focus—and pressure from the outside—than earlier generations. The huge swell of immigrants, particularly illegal immigrants, has also tended to depress wages in lower-skilled occupations too, and it has allowed a frightening array of criminals and criminal syndicates to set up shop here while no one was really looking.

There are also legitimate grounds for concern over the sheer numbers involved: almost a million legal immigrants annually and another 300,000 to 400,000 illegal immigrants. According to one authoritative report, nearly half of the population of the Dominican Republic said they would emigrate to America if they had the opportunity.

That this immigration is occurring at a time when the disciples of diversity are disparaging the successful formulas and frameworks for absorbing newcomers forged at the turn of the century by Progressive-era reformers and their journalistic allies is perhaps the greatest reason for pessimism. The assimilationist paradigm proved crucial to the successful incorporation of new immigrants then, and has largely spared us the kind of tribal and nationalist frictions that have balkanized many other multiethnic nations around the world. It also became the basis by which immigrants were extended the full "promise of American life," as Progressive-era journalist Herbert Croly described it, shucking off the foreign customs, practices, habits of thinking and values that were—and still are—at odds with "progressive" American ideals of democracy, economic upward mobility, and middle-class life.

The new multicultural paradigm encourages immigrants to maintain a hyphenated sense of self and culture. It tells society it must accommodate new, mostly Third World immigrants as groups or "communities" rather than individuals. It encourages divided loyalties and emotional conflicts of interest. It insists that notions of cultural "uplift" are condescending. And it suggests, as a *New York Times* report on "transnational immigration" did in 1998, that the concept of assimilation is "racist"—ignoring the implications this stance might have for our civic culture.

Many of those espousing multiculturalism, including many journalists, would like to think that the new diversity paradigm is an extension of the old Progressive social ideal, updated to reflect new social, political and cultural realities. Yet nothing could be further from the original Progressive vision than the romantic idealization of ethnic hyphenation. And liberal journalists of the past, who beat back the nativist contention that immigrants weren't capable of assimilating, would find it disorienting to hear their successors argue that assimilation is no longer necessary or even desirable, and that those holding this point of view are guilty of cultural intolerance or nostalgia.

This is not to say that today's journalism should be mindlessly pro-assimilationist, which carries the risk of promoting its own brand of cultural chauvinism. But neither should it proceed from a position that reflexively spurns assimilation, as much journalistic decision making, in thrall to identity politics, seems to do.

One of the areas where news coverage has exhibited a broad indifference to the importance of assimilation—and to salient facts—is in the politics of language, especially where bilingual education is concerned. Unlike Progressive journalists of the last century, who for the most part rejected the idea of teaching immigrants in their native tongue, today's journalists are too ready to bow to bilingual education orthodoxy. The hard questions about bilingual education have often not been posed, and the gap between what its proponents say it is doing and what is actually going on has not been communicated well enough to the public.

When it originated as Title VII of the Education and Secondary School Education Act of 1968, bilingual education was conceived as a limited, short-term means to provide a bridge to immigrant children's eventual mastery of English. In the years since its inception, however, bilingual programs have grown far beyond their original mandate—$7.5 million in 1968 now swollen to more than $10 billion a year spent on approximately five million kids who can't speak English well enough to function in a classroom. And rather than serving as a step toward their eventual mastery of English, bilingual education has become a vehicle for retaining their native tongues and cultures.

While students may find cultural comfort being taught in their native languages, many have been crippled in their search for a meaningful, productive niche in mainstream society. Although the reasons behind the approximately 30 percent Latino high school dropout rate are complicated, those who blame bilingual education cannot be dismissed out of hand; nor can those who link a slowness in learning English to a lack of upward mobility on the part of certain sectors of the Latino immigrant community.

Yet even in the face of ever-mounting evidence that bilingual education may have betrayed its original promise, mainstream news organizations have been very slow to explore the gap between its theory and practice.

Although the dominance of native languages in so-called bilingual classrooms finally became an issue in the late 1990s, abuses of the original intent of bilingual programs remained largely in the shadows for years. Aside from *U.S. News & World Report*, which ran a substantial piece in 1996, few other national publications or major news organization in any city with a high concentration of foreign-speaking students examined this issue with the rigor it demanded.

In late 1991, for example, *New York Times* reporter William Celis wrote about the trend in a piece headlined "Bilingual Teaching: A New Focus on Both Tongues." Although Celis noted objections from critics of bilingual education, the report was clearly positive. "I am luckier than Anglos," one Hispanic grade school girl exclaimed at the end of the piece. "I speak two languages."

More scandalous was the *Los Angeles Times'* indifference to the practice of using inner-city black children in certain California cities to round out bilingual classes for immigrants. According to the *Times,* which reported on the situation only *after* the policy was reversed in 1995, up to six hundred black children were bused into schools with high percentages of Spanish- and Chinese-speaking students in order to fill state bilingualism mandates. The policy reversal was "an attempt to rescue English-speaking students whose academic progress had been sacrificed in the district's efforts to fill empty seats in bilingual classrooms."

The story received little nationwide play even after the policy reversal. Yet according to author and bilingual-education critic Rosalie Pedalino Porter, using black children to fill up so-called two-way immersion classrooms was a practice that was growing nationwide at that time. Some news organizations did the story locally; in 1994, for example, the *Washington Post* ran a front-page story entitled "Plan to Meld Cultures Divides D.C. Schools." But few publications or broadcast news organizations examined it on a national level. And not all of the local stories were as critical as they should have been.

The reluctance of news organizations to draw attention to bilingualism's failures and excesses put them at odds with a culture in which opposition to these programs is swelling, even—and at times especially—among Latinos. A 1996 poll conducted by the Center for Equal Opportunity (CEO) that sampled opinions of six hundred Latino parents in five heavily Hispanic cities found they overwhelmingly desired to have children taught English as quickly as possible and particularly to have all academic subject matter taught in English. Immigrant parents, the survey concluded, think that learning to read, write and speak English is the single most important goal of education. "My children learn Spanish in school so they can become busboys and waiters," parent Ernesto Ortiz wrote in one CEO collection. "I teach them English at home so they can become lawyers and doctors." But statements such as this rarely find their way into the stories pursued by the mainstream media.

Nearly half of the country's three million non-English-speaking students reside in California, where it is estimated that a quarter of the state's five million public school children—more than one million kids—do not speak English well enough to understand what's going on in a classroom. In early 1996, Latino parents in one downtown school district mounted a boycott and pulled their kids out of class in protest over bilingual policies that segregate their children from native English speakers so they can be taught, virtually full-time, in Spanish. They were also angry that this policy had been instituted without their being given the option—as the law provided—of overruling these assignments for their children if they so chose.

Latino parents protesting bilingual instruction for their children should have been prominently covered, at least as a "man bites dog" story. But the *Los Angeles Times* gave it only the most cursory attention, relegating brief reports to the inside pages of its Metro section and ignoring the larger implications of this mounting popular anger. The *Times* did congratulate Latino parents for seizing the initiative. "However," the editorialist insisted, "educators would be derelict of they did not also explain that English only classes are not the best choice for the children." A second editorial on the issue, infused with the same regard for bilingual orthodoxy, advised that dual-language instruction was the best way kids speaking different tongues could learn from one another.

If the media has been skeptical of studies questioning the efficacy of bilingual programs, they have rushed to publicize those that support such instruction. In late 1995, for instance, Virginia Collier, a researcher at George Mason University, released a large study on bilingual education which concluded that the longer a student stayed in bilingual programs, the better this student scored on standardized tests administered in high school. In fact, the highest achievers were children in "two way schools" where English and non-English speakers are mixed together, with half the curriculum taught in English and half in another language.

While many journalists were quick to publicize Collier's conclusions, few had seen her actual data, since she did not release them. That did not stop *Time* from giving her the green light: "While public opinion seems polarized between sink or swim nostalgias and politically correct diversitarians, serious research increasingly points toward a consensus: children learn English faster and are more likely to excel academically of they are given several years of instruction in their native language first."

Those covering the bilingual education beat have often turned a blind eye to the wider impact of these programs on society at large. Yet impartial analyses of the reasons behind white flight from the public schools often cite bilingual programs, which siphon resources away from native-born middle-class children, as a big factor. (In the heyday of bilingual instruction, California spent 65 percent more on "language needs" children than it did on English speakers.) What's more, studies suggest that Latino teens with an inadequate grasp of English are much more susceptible to the lure of criminal gangs. Employers deny dysfunctional English speakers steady work with a future, and college administrators complain that students arriving on their campuses with an inadequate grasp of English must be placed in remedial classes that bear a perverse similarity to the bilingual high school classrooms that failed the students so badly to begin with. Yet these stories, as compelling as they are, don't seem to make their way onto the media radar screen in any meaningful way.

Media resistance to questioning bilingual education was obvious in 1998 with the coverage of Proposition 227, the so-called "Save Our Children" Amendment. Underwritten by conservative computer entrepreneur Ron Unz, Proposition 227 called for severe restrictions on bilingual education in California and represented the first time that controversial bilingual policies were put to the vote. The initiative enjoyed widespread popularity throughout the state, with polls showing huge majorities in its favor, including, much to some journalists' surprise and chagrin, a majority of Latinos.

News organizations might have looked at the referendum as a chance to fill in longstanding gaps in coverage of the realities of classroom bilingualism. They also might have vigorously and evenhandedly investigated the contentions of both the supporters of 227 and their opposition, to help the public sort out the complicated, contradictory pictures they were being bombarded with in campaign advertisements. But with rare exceptions, reporting on both the state and national levels continued to reflect ideological bias, and questions central to establishing what bilingual education was doing to the rising generation of immigrant children were slighted in favor of reporting that alleged "bigotry" as the initiative's driving force.

The *Los Angeles Times*, for example, failed to examine the gap between the theories of dual-language instruction and the realities of "Spanish only" as it affected the fate of students. It also virtually ignored practices that kept kids in bilingual programs well beyond the point—legally and pedagogically—where they were benefiting, and the deeply troubling impact that long-term bilingual education had on the Latino dropout rate and on the job prospects of Latino high school graduates. The issue of teacher incompetence, and the fact that many bilingual teachers were severely limited in their own English skills, also fell through the journalistic cracks. As for the gap between the stated purpose of bilingual programs—steady if slow eventual transition to English—and the true goals in many educators' minds— the retention of Latino cultural heritage and identity in a way that bordered on ethnic nationalism—there was almost no analysis of these issues whatsoever.

Instead of looking at bilingual education in Los Angeles, his own back yard, *Los Angeles Times* reporter Nick Anderson, who had long written supportively of bilingual policies, traveled to Miami and wrote glowingly of a city where dual-language policies were allegedly not only working, but thriving. The implication was clear: Los Angeles should take stock and see that bilingualism could be as good in California as it was in Florida. Anderson's enthusiasm was, of course, news to many familiar with Miami's ethnic and linguistic fractiousness.

The significant ethnic minority support for Proposition 227 was framed in news reports by opponents' implicit charge that it was driven by "false consciousness." During the campaign, polls showed as much as a 60 percent Latino support rate, with Latinos in some areas, such as Orange County, favoring the measure 8 to 1. But the *Los Angeles Times* put the greater emphasis on anti-227 Latino activists with their rhetoric about "ethnic cleansing, California style" and their claims that a generation of Latino youth would drop out of school and run amok on the streets if deprived of bilingual instruction.

Proposition 227 won by more than 20 percentage points—a rebuke to bilingual policies as much as to the groups that had made these policies unquestionable for so long. While Latino support for the proposition's passage was not as heavy as it was in pre–election day polling, it was considerable—almost 40 percent. But instead of examining why this large bloc of Latinos voted for a purportedly nativist initiative, reporters continued to plug the racism script by examining the reasoning of the 60 percent who voted against 227. The *New York Times*, which had called the initiative "a cramped approach to bilingual education," highlighted Latino racial anger and resentment in an analysis that ran under the smug headline "The Reply It Turned out Was Bilingual: No."

Although 227 required California school districts to restrict bilingual policies severely in the months following the election, many in fact ignored it, or interpreted its waiver provisions so broadly as to nullify its impact on students. This was a violation of both the spirit and the letter of the law, about which news organizations should have informed the public. But such analysis as there was of this development bore a strangely approving tone. "Bilingual Education Lives After All" was the headline of one *New York Times* treatment. For Alice Callahan, a left-liberal Episcopal priest working in the Hispanic community who campaigned in favor of the initiative, the inability of journalists to identify with the large minority of Latinos who favored 227 was a revelation: "I have been surprised at how unwilling reporters have been to entertain a view different from their own."

The same orthodoxy that inhibits criticism of language policies also stunts a discussion of other issues linked to the broader subject of cultural difference. Reporting on immigration often ignores or minimizes the extent to which the cultural values, attitudes and customs of new Third World immigrants clash with mainstream American norms. Like their counterparts in academia, pro-diversity journalists tend to celebrate the theory of "difference," but don't like to look too closely at some of the social outcomes these differences cause.

Considering the ease with which discussion of cultural or national traits can degenerate into stereotyping, such reluctance is somewhat understandable. Yet when journalists walk on eggshells as they get close to some of the consequences of cultural difference, they leave a significant gap in our understanding of what the new immigrant communities are all about, what kind of impact they are having on our ideals and institutions, and what we should be doing to help them adjust.

New immigrant groups have historically gone through periods in which they lag behind native-born Americans. Yet the lag experienced by Latinos, particularly Mexicans, who constitute almost two-thirds of all new immigrants, seems to be more persistent. According to Census Bureau statistics, median household income, while on the rise for every other group of Americans, is going down for Latinos. At the turn of the new century, Latinos had a 23 percent poverty rate compared with 8 percent for whites. Hispanic students' high school dropout rate was more than double that of whites. Many social scientists have begun to worry that Latino residents may become trapped as a permanent sub-class of the working poor.

Although discrimination and a lack of English proficiency are factors, there are also cultural issues. This is something that anthropologists, economists and political scientists—mostly liberal Anglos, but some Latinos—have no trouble acknowledging. (Brookings Institution scholar and political scientist Peter Skerry refers to "a cynically anti-achievement ethos"; Latino author Lionel Sosa writes about a web of traditional values promoting humility, pessimism and self-denial that undercuts individual ambition.) Yet aside from some very recent *Los Angeles Times* reports highlighting the role of culture in Latino underachievement, as well as the work of Latino columnist Richard Estrada of the *Dallas Morning News,* who has written anxiously about Latino acculturation to the American mainstream, journalists have given short shrift to the role played by values, attitudes and customs in determining educational and economic outcomes within various Latino communities.

Typical was a piece in which Steven Holmes of the *New York Times,* citing a 1995 study, reported that only 9 percent of Hispanics hold bachelor degrees compared with nearly 25 percent of non-Hispanic Americans. The problem, Holmes wrote, was a function of "endemic poverty, discrimination and lack of recruitment." The human factors that might explain this problem more deeply—most notably what some anthropologists and sociologists call the "lack of a family culture that supports education"—were given no attention.

The high Latino illegitimacy rate, which costs society billions in welfare benefits for families headed by unwed mothers, is just as taboo. Reporters and editorialists have preferred to emphasize the hard-working, family orientation of new Latino immigrants over the very high illegitimacy rates. Even when the latter is acknowledged, journalists still tend to write about it as if it were merely a problem of racial bias and alienation with no cultural issues involved.

In 1993, for example, the *Los Angeles Times* ran a long feature piece by reporter Laurie Becklund, analyzing the booming Latina teen birthrate. According to Becklund, the explosion was responsible for 75 percent of the increase in teenage pregnancy rates in the state of California and one-third of those in the nation as a whole. The piece was uncharacteristically candid. It quoted public school teachers who referred to poor Latina girls as "breeders," and it relayed the teachers' consternation over pupils for whom school seems "merely a waiting room before they go on about the business of childrearing."

Yet when it came to illuminating the reasons for this development, the piece fell back on clichés in which babies are seen as the only life-affirming thing the girls could do in a sea of poverty, drugs, violence and family dissolution—"a cry for love," as the headline suggested. The article mentioned the girls' limited social horizons, yet it gave little sense that they might be a cultural vestige. Nor did it convey any appreciation for the fact that assimilation could help the girls move beyond their roots into a mainstream where female self-assertion was acceptable.

A similarly romantic and highly relativistic approach is frequently taken in reporting on those immigrant cultural practices and customs—

ranging from animal sacrifice to voodoo to arranged marriages and female genital mutilation—that contradict some of our more progressive social ideals. A case in point is the subject of folk healing and traditional folk medicine. A May 1996 *New York Times* piece titled "Mingling Two Worlds of Medicine: Some Doctors Work with Folk Healers in Immigrants' Care," for instance, noted that some doctors who had formerly dismissed the work of these folk healers as "superstitious quackery" were now starting to condone their practices. According to the reporter, Pam Belluck, some doctors say that such practices can encourage patients to follow instructions and improve their attitudes toward illness. Folk remedies also seem to allay psychological and even some physical symptoms. Those who condone the folk practices have to be careful, though. "There are very few people around the hospital around with enough vision [to have this view]," complained one physician. "Most would think this is tantamount to malpractice. It has to be done on the q.t."

While noting some of the problems associated with encouraging folk treatments—an asthmatic patient who suffered an acute reaction after seeing a Chinese herbalist; a diabetic who was given chicken gall bladder twice a day—the piece implied that on the whole, the trend was positive. It was a conclusion contradicted by much other evidence that folk beliefs run profoundly against the grain of Western science and the welfare of patients—an omission that upset some of the doctors interviewed for the report.

According to Dr. Michael Diaz of Mt. Sinai Medical Center, the trend toward sanctioning folk healing represents "politically correct" pandering on the part of administrators and makes little medical sense. "If folk healing practices work so well," Diaz insisted to me, "then why are the morbidity and mortality rates in the countries where they are used so high?" Journalists who write positively about the trend are doing a disservice, he said: "The journalists I've spoken to usually have their minds made up already. They don't allow objective data to override their prejudices."

Consider as well the *Miami Herald's* treatment of animal sacrifice associated with the Afro-Cuban practice of Santeria. In late 1993, the city of Hialejah, Florida, banned the practice of animal sacrifice because it violated laws against cruelty to animals as well as health and sanitation codes. This sparked a controversy that went to the Supreme Court, which ruled that such a ban was a violation of freedom of religion. Practitioners of Santeria were allowed to continue their devotions, within the limits set by city codes.

The case was a complicated one, requiring, as *Miami Herald* columnist Carl Hiaasen put it, that a careful balance be struck between the right "to practice one's religion" and the right "not to live next door to a slaughterhouse." Hiaasen's column aside, the rest of the news coverage was pro-Santeria, careful to screen out the gorier details of a practice dear to many of the paper's Cuban readers.

Most egregious was a *Miami Herald* account that described the ritual slaughter of fifteen animals in a Santeria celebration of the Court's decision. The celebration, organized by a Santeria priest named Rigoberto Zamora, was an effort to dispel the notion that such sacrifices were cruel to animals. By all *other* accounts, the ritual did not have the desired effect. Gory with blood and guts and the bleating of goats and chickens as they died slow, cruel deaths, the scene was ghastly. At one point a goat was stabbed with a rusty knife and decapitated, spraying blood all over.

Yet in *its* account, the *Herald* conspicuously ignored these details, purging the more nauseating sounds and smells. Forgetting the butchered goat, *Herald* reporter Aminda Marques Gonzalez wrote about how reverently "a white rooster was offered to Elequa, its blood squeezed into the basins." The only hint that the event was at all strange came in a description of the arrival of the building owner, who had been alerted by angry neighbors and said he would start eviction proceedings the next day.

Reluctance to discuss the more embarrassing aspects of Third World superstition could also be seen in coverage of revelations in August 1994 that $12,000 in state funds were used to perform an exorcism on a Haitian psychiatric patient at King's County Hospital in New York City. The patient, Alphonse Pecou, had hacked his girlfriend to death and then set her on fire in front of her children. The exorcism was done off premises by the Most Reverend Prophet Alpha Omega Bondu, and was authorized by the hospital's business manager, a member of Bondu's church. According to reports, several high-ranking officials at the hospital were in attendance when Bondu performed his ceremony, which, he claimed, successfully routed four of the seven demons that had gained control of the patient.

King's County Hospital, wracked by favoritism and corruption, had been much in the news in the preceding months, and the incident raised more questions about the administration's competence. "Has the multicultural bug really infected the state bureaucracy to such an extent?" an editorial in the *New York Post* asked. Yet the *New York Times* ignored the exorcism story altogether for three months, and then only acknowledged it in the course of a larger piece detailing a raft of problems afflicting the facility. Buried in a section on expenses run up by the director was a brief and classically euphemistic nod to the $12,000 that officials at the hospital had used to "give religious counseling to a patient who had killed his girlfriend."

Ironically, many times "cultural sensitivity" even trumps feminism in journalism's politically correct hierarchy. The South Asian custom of arranged marriages, for instance, was dealt with in the 1998 *New York Times* series on the new "transnational" immigrants who straddled their new world and the old one they came from. According to the *Times*, many of these new Americans regard assimilation to "a single American norm" as a "dated, even racist concept." In the second installment of the series, *Times* reporter Celia Dugger focused on a community of Jains, an insular, well-to-do caste of Indians who shuttle back and forth between New York City's gem markets and Bombay. The article focused on the practice of arranged marriages, explaining that it is the linchpin of these immigrants' "sense of family and identity."

The piece introduced the reader to an Ivy-educated, New York investment banker who traveled back to India at the behest of his parents to wed a bride they had chosen and then brought her back to New York. The reporter had the candor to describe the new bride's claustrophobic life under the tyranny of the mother-in-law, who wouldn't allow her to leave the house in jeans or travel outside without an escort. Yet the piece rigorously avoided the sort of disapproval that would have informed an article on, say, a patriarch practicing polygamy in some redoubt of the American West.

The subject of arranged marriage was treated deferentially by National Public Radio as well in a June 1999 report headlined "Young Indian-Americans Meld Tradition and Modernism in the Quest for Marriage." The report, by Jacki Lydon, focused on a financial news reporter at the Bloomberg Business News Network in New Jersey. The reporter, a "polished young woman in a smart navy suit and Katie Couric hairdo," was turning thirty, Lydon explained, "in a culture that expected girls to marry before age twenty-five." Choice in such matters is "part and parcel of American life," Lydon noted, yet "one of the most profound schisms between East and West occurs at the marital turning point, when all those western notions of individuality collide with all those Eastern concepts of duty, family, and community."

The piece voiced skepticism about the concept of arranged marriage, echoing the subject's disdain for what her father called just another "business transaction." But it ended with an almost gushy affirmative note, returning to the story of the Bloomsberg reporter who, in the end, had given in to her parents' wishes and was investigating the prospects they had selected for her. Such "parental introductions," Lydon suggested, were a compromise between strict parental arrangement and full-on choice. Instead of questioning the insularity of these Indian-Americans, as would likely have been done in the case of, for example, Hasidic Jews, the piece steered clear of judgments.

The same thing is true about reporting on the African Islamic practice of female circumcision among immigrants to the United States. In 1996, a young West African woman who said she had refused to have the rite performed on her was given political asylum by an immigration court. Although an estimated 150,000 African immigrant girls have been subjected to the same procedure in America by families who insist on maintaining traditional notions of female deference, the media focused only on the practice as it is performed in Africa.

Opponents of the practice, like former congresswoman Pat Schroeder, had, for more than a decade, mounted a crusade to criminalize this disfiguring and life-threatening practice, and a few columnists like Ellen Goodman of the *Boston Globe* and A. M. Rosenthal of the *New York Times* had raised the issue. But there was little of the systematic reporting required to determine the scope and severity of the problem. What reporting was done on the story was freighted with cultural anxiety, clearly subscribing to the idea voiced by one feminist source in a *New York Times* analysis that "the movement against it [genital mutilation] must be led by African activists." Said Linda Burstyn, who finally published a piece on this question in the *Atlantic Monthly* after the idea was rejected at ABC News where she had been a producer, "There was no one who said outright, 'We won't do this because we fear a backlash,' but there was discomfort doing it. Deference to cultural traditions is a very real problem in the press."

Any interest the issue has generated comes only when it casts a bad light on immigration and asylum law. For instance, news organizations devoted a tremendous amount of coverage to the plight of Adelaide Abankwah, a twenty-nine-year-old member of the Nkumssa tribe, who lived in an isolated region of central Ghana before arriving in the United States and seeking political asylum because she faced forced genital mutilation. In the fall of 1996, Abankwah said, her mother— "queen mother" of the tribe—died, and tribal elders decided that she would succeed her. But Abankwah protested, refusing both an arranged marriage and rituals designed to determine if she was a virgin. She had had a boyfriend, she maintained, and if the elders found out about their relationship, they would excise her clitoris. Leaving the tribal homeland, she worked for a while in the Ghanaian capital of Accra before fleeing for New York with a false passport.

The story of a refugee princess seeking asylum to escape genital mutilation was a resonant one, and news organizations gave it considerable attention, often playing it on page one as Abankwah's petition moved through the system. (It was first denied by the U.S. Board of Immigration in April 1999, but was approved on appeal by the U.S. Court of Appeals for the Second Circuit in July.)

In late December 2000, however, the *Washington Post* finally revealed that the Ghanaian woman was telling a very tall tale. According to Immigration and Naturalization Service officials quoted in the *Post* report, Abankwah was not a royal princess but in fact a former Ghanaian hotel cook named Regina Danson who had come into the possession of the real princess's passport when it was lost four and half years earlier. Yet the *New York Times*, which had granted the fraudulent "victim" a prominence she might not otherwise have gained, had a somewhat muted reaction, giving this revelation scant attention in its Metro section.


It is not surprising that many journalists, skittish about acknowledging or addressing the realities of cultural difference, have also been reluctant to explore the impact that high rates of immigration have had on America's general quality of life, which early in the previous century was at the center of the Progressive journalistic agenda. A case in point is the coverage of the underground network of ethnic restaurants and social clubs in and around New York City. Reporters working in the vein of Jacob Riis might have chosen to explore a serious potential health hazard and bribery of health inspectors in this ethnic underground, but the *New York Times* seems more concerned with "cultural integrity."

In 1994 the *Times* printed a story about the underground of illegal Salvadoran immigrants on Long Island. Focusing on Gloria's Cafe in Hempstead, the piece, written by Doreen Carvajal, was headlined "Making Ends Meet in a Nether World." Gloria's Cafe operated on an area zoned for residential use, had no phone listing and did not take credit cards. According to Carvajal, the only sign marking it was the "fragrance of pork-filled tamales and steaming Salvadoran corn tortillas."

Places like Gloria's are often the flashpoint for bitter battles between older residents and immigrant newcomers over garbage, noise, traffic and vermin, along with complaints about tax dollars being spent to clean up after people who aren't even citizens. But Carvajal chose to focus on the way in which Gloria's and places like it function "as a refuge, a comforting place with a familiar feel." Ignored were the restaurant's apparent role as a hub for green card marriages, unlicensed dentistry, and the smuggling of cheap, Third World pharmaceuticals unapproved by the FDA. These crimes were celebrated as a sign of immigrant "ingenuity" rather than a threat to public safety and community norms. It was not until 1998, in fact, that the *Times* awoke to the health risks posed by the illegal sale of prescription drugs in immigrant "pharmacies" like Gloria's. According to public health officials who have been watching the trend for the last ten years, the sale of antibiotics, which are often overprescribed by unlicensed pharmacy operators, has led to an alarming rise in bacterial resistance to these drugs. While these businesses "are often the first place that poor immigrants turn for cheap medical care," the *Times* report said, they are also "endangering those same immigrants' health."

Late in 1999 the *Los Angeles Times* too finally ran a series on underground prescription drug sales to immigrants in that city. The operation of such underground pharmacies had been an open secret in southern California for years, surely something that had been on the radar screen of the paper's reporters with close ethnic ties to the Latino community. Yet despite the obvious ample opportunities for journalistic investigation, it was only when two Mexican immigrant babies had died after receiving injections from unlicensed "clinic" workers in 1999 that the paper paid attention.

Three years earlier, the *New York Times* reported on the effort of Mt. Kisco, New York, to crack down on overcrowded immigrant housing, which town officials said was part of a plan to protect neighbors and residents from the dangers of fire and unsanitary conditions. Three raids netted sixty-five men who were charged with living in space designed and zoned for thirty. The authorities were quickly challenged by Latino advocacy groups, joined by the ACLU. Mt. Kisco, the lawsuit charged, was trying to drive away Hispanic immigrants through selective enforcement of the law. The lawsuit also charged that the town had violated the plaintiffs' freedom of speech and assembly by restricting the area where day laborers could gather, and that police had routinely harassed immigrants congregating on public sidewalks and in the town's public park.

The *Times'* report was clearly written in sympathy with the advocacy groups and the immigrants, described as poor peasants from places where the average wage was forty cents a day. Although reporter Celia Dugger noted longtime residents' complaints about loitering, public drinking and urination, and escalating rates of violent crime, she framed them in a way that made the residents sound cranky and nativist. She made no apparent effort to verify the substance of the complaints themselves by looking at police records, and showed little interest in evaluating the charge of selective enforcement. Quoting the immigrants' landlady, who complained that the town wasn't cracking down equally on Jews, Italians or Irish, Dugger gave the impression that the same kinds of violations were occurring among these groups, when in fact they were not. That the landlady might not be the most objective observer, given her obvious financial interest in packing as many immigrants into the house as she could, passed without notice as well. So did the salient fact that most of the immigrants involved in the controversy—95 percent, according to the Organizacion Hispana, a group participating in the suit—were illegals. This may have had no *legal* bearing on the lawsuit; it certainly had journalistic significance, however.

Since this 1996 report, *New York Times* coverage of immigrant-related quality-of-life issues in suburbia has for the most part continued in the same vein. In 1998 there was a piece about Farmingdale, Long Island, where laborers were wanted, the headline explained, "but Not Living Next Door." In late 1999 it was back to Mt. Kisco, where finicky white residents were raising complaints about a Chinese restaurant where the clientele loitered outside, causing a nuisance. In January 2000 another story with the dateline of Mt. Kisco ran under the headline "For Latino Laborers, Dual Lives." This report's subhead told it all: "Welcomed at Work, but Shunned at Home in Suburbs."


New York City in early 1996 was gripped by the tragic death of Elisa Izquierdo, a six-year-old girl who died at the hands of her mentally unstable mother, Awilda Lopez, originally from Puerto Rico. According to reports, the mother, a believer in Santeria, had beaten the girl for years in order to purge demons she said had possessed her. Officials admitted that social workers had opened a file on the girl, but had not taken any steps to withdraw her from the home despite evidence clearly warranting such intervention.

In its postmortems, the *New York Times* emphasized the institutional dysfunction of the child welfare system at the expense of information that raised other issues. According to a memo from the

Child Welfare Administration's general counsel leaked to the press, for instance, some of the agency's problems were the result of caseworkers who couldn't speak English well enough to perform their tasks, and who came from cultures where corporal punishment was accepted. While the memo made no direct link between the Izquierdo case and these larger institutional and cultural factors, the inference was clear: the hiring of unqualified and unassimilated immigrants at the CWA had played a role in the larger institutional problems that underlay cases like this one.

Yet neither the news story nor the editorial that the *Times* devoted to the memo's disclosure mentioned its references to the inadequate English and different attitudes toward physical punishment in the ranks of CWA caseworkers. Only weeks later, after an embarrassing item ran in the *New York Post* about the *Times'* lapses, did the paper tepidly acknowledge the significant differences in custom that immigrants bring to the issue of punishment, and assert the need for a single standard, while still ignoring the questions of language deficiency and caseworker nonassimilation.

Although various news organizations have raised concerns about the effect of immigration on labor, a tendency to celebrate immigrants' economic dynamism often obscures their impact on native-born workers. A 1996 *New York Times* report on the network of Bangladeshi immigrant contractors that has grown up in New York over the last ten years shows such a bias. Written by Somini Sengupta, a reporter whose ethnicity presumably gave her increased access to New York's burgeoning Asian communities, the piece spotlighted the way this network has been "buoyed by a steady stream of low wage workers from back home and an exclusive network through which skills and resources are passed on." Many of the workers, Sengupta acknowledged, are undocumented, being recruited from the ranks of the thousands of illegal Bangladeshi immigrants who land here every year. The piece also noted that contractors using their labor undercut competitors by half. Yet the link between illegal status, low wages and unfair competition was not made. Instead of also acknowledging the justified anger of native-born contractors and artisans driven out of business by the low-wage, illegal competition, the piece monochromatically celebrated the phenomenon as an illustration of the ways in which "immigrants create niches for themselves in the city's economy."

A more acute failure to take seriously the negative impact that illegal aliens have had on American labor could be seen in an account of the problems associated with diversity in Storm Lake, Iowa. Far from the border towns and barrios that for many define America's immigration policy problem, Storm Lake seemed like an odd place for 1996 presidential candidate Patrick Buchanan to raise one of his trademark stinks about illegal immigrants. But Buchanan's choice wasn't made without some calculation. While still relatively small, the pool of Southeast Asian and Mexican immigrants who had come to Storm Lake in recent years were not an entirely negligible presence. Crime was up, costs for educating immigrant youngsters were taxing the local school system's budget, and a general sense of alienation had begun to erode what for many residents had long been a cozy sense of homogenous isolation. Most significantly, the low wages that the town's largest employer, a meatpacking plant owned by the food conglomerate IBP, was paying its predominantly immigrant work force had led many residents to grumble that American workers were being displaced by those who shouldn't be there in first place.

Steven Holmes, Washington D.C. bureau correspondent for the *New York Times,* heard about the cultural tensions in Storm Lake while preparing to cover the 1996 Iowa Caucuses. He had learned that the town's surrounding area was Iowa's most demographically uniform; people joked to him that in that neck of the woods, even Italians stood out. Holmes arrived in Storm Lake the day Buchanan was to speak, and stayed behind when the rest of the traveling press corps left, talking to a number of people, officials and ordinary citizens alike. His report, which appeared on the front page of the national news section of the *Times* on February 17, 1996, ran under the headline "In Iowa Town, Strains of Diversity." Explaining that the town of 8600 people had only 22 minority residents in 1970, Holmes reported that the place was now almost 10 percent minority. Seeing Storm Lake as a touchstone for something larger, he wrote that the transformation demonstrated "how small towns in the rural heartland are facing the same issues in absorbing immigrants that are confronted by places like New York, Miami and Los Angeles."

Writing about immigration in such a microcosm presented an opportunity for a serious, even-handed assessment of immigration's impact on heartland job markets, which then was shaping up as a key presidential campaign issue. But rather than presenting hard facts and figures in an effort to assess the validity of Buchanan's charges that IBP was using illegal labor that displaced native workers, Holmes made no effort to conduct any "independent investigation" of his own, as he told me in a subsequent interview. Instead, he simply reported that executives of the company "stress they check the relevant documents of job applicants and do not knowingly hire illegal aliens."

One wonders if Holmes would have let a cop accused of brutality against blacks or a corporate executive charged with racial discrimination against minorities off the hook so easily, taking their denials at face value and accepting them as fact.

Holmes' lack of journalistic rigor became even more apparent three months after his story appeared. In May the Immigration and Naturalization Service conducted a raid on the IBP plant and carted away 63 of the 600 workers on the factory floor that night. In fact, according to an IBP spokesman, while company executives in Storm Lake were denying that they "knowingly" hired illegals, others in the corporate hierarchy were cooperating with the INS in planning the raid, afraid the government might make an example of IBP to other employers who had similarly skirted the law.

Given the prominence the *Times* had given Holmes' original "diversity in the heartland" report, the paper should have taken notice of the raid. It did not. Although the downside of immigration was becoming ever more apparent through the election cycle of 1996, the *Times* continued to report on those who questioned current policy as if they were nothing more than nineteenth-century Know-Nothings, fulminating against wholly imaginary demons.


Immigration and crime is an even touchier subject for journalists, even though one out of four federal prisoners is an illegal alien, and foreign felons, abetted by a dysfunctional visa system, have been able to enter and leave the country virtually at will while engaging in an ever-expanding range of organized criminal activities: Nigerians in international car-theft rings; Chinese in extortion, kidnapping and immigrant-smuggling rackets; Dominicans in drug trafficking; and Russians in stock and credit card scams.

To some degree, the immigrant crime is a function of simple alienation; lacking both the opportunities and the skills to find a niche in mainstream America, unassimilated immigrants often find the lures of gang life, and its criminal rewards, the only viable alternative. But for the most part, the journalistic establishment today is skittish about offending the sensitivities of minorities and feeding nativist stereotypes. Of course, stories about immigrant crime get done, but usually only *after* the problem has gotten so bad that it can no longer be ignored and the immigrant criminal organizations have sent down roots that are difficult to attack.

Once again the *New York Times* seems to have even more trouble than most of the elite press with this subject. In case after case, story after story, facts that might suggest a linkage between immigration and crime are airbrushed or minimized.

Throughout most of the 1990s, for example, the *Times* was timid in reporting on the activities of the Dominican gangs that dominated the drug trade in Manhattan's Washington Heights. Given their high unemployment and welfare rates, the American dream has been elusive for most of Washington Heights's 300,000 Dominicans, about a third of whom are estimated to be illegal. But for those working in what has become the nation's largest wholesale and retail markets for cocaine and heroin, Washington Heights was a lucrative place to land. Most of this drug trade was run by young street toughs who called themselves "Dominicanyorks." In their late teens or early twenties, they were usually recruited in their country and came to the States illegally to serve as foot soldiers in the drug trade for several years before returning home, hopefully with enough money to retire. As one wanna-be "Dominicanyork" told the *Wall Street Journal*, "If you are ignorant like me, you can go to New York, sell drugs, get two million pesos, come back home and be somebody."

Violence between rival drug gangs fueled a murder rate in Washington Heights that was the city's highest for years. To launder cash profits and circumvent federal currency controls, drug gangs set up their own illegal wiring facilities, sending tens of millions out of the country illicitly, a flow that beleaguered banking regulators could do little to stop. At one point, death threats by drug dealers stopped uniformed cops from patrolling certain areas, and the INS was so overwhelmed with casework that drug dealers who should have been deported after they finished serving jail time were simply released back onto the streets.

Trying to stem the tide of drugs and killings, the city flooded Washington Heights with plainclothes officers and undercover narcotics agents. Usually young and aggressive, the police officers in these narcotics details saw their buy-and-bust operations as a good way to make detective. One of them was Officer Michael O'Keefe, who arrived in Washington Heights as a nine-year veteran of the NYPD with a reputation for being a tough, hardworking street cop.

On the afternoon of July 3, 1992, working with two partners in an unmarked car, O'Keefe tried to stop a twenty-four-year-old Dominican man named Jose "Kiko" Garcia. O'Keefe was aware of a narcotics operation that was operating along 162nd Street and suspected that Garcia may have been holding drugs for it. He followed Garcia into an apartment building, where his effort to make an arrest turned violent. Within minutes, Garcia lay dying in a pool of blood spreading across the lobby floor.

News reporters generally know that eyewitnesses at crime scenes often hype their stories to get their names in print and their faces on TV—or, if they are family members, to lay the base for profitable lawsuits. They also know that politicians often exploit police-community tensions in such cases to attract publicity and advance their political agendas. Yet in the death of Kiko Garcia (as in the much-publicized death of the West African street peddler Amadou Diallo in 1999), police misconduct of the worst kind was automatically assumed.

Abandoning reportorial skepticism, journalists allowed bogus eyewitness accounts to pass into the news stream with lightning speed, almost unfiltered and unchallenged. According to the *New York Times*, the Garcia case was a vivid demonstration of the pervasive racism, corruption and brutality of the New York Police Department. In this account, a white cop, very likely involved in drug activity himself, had beaten a hapless grocery store clerk with no criminal record to the floor of an apartment lobby, then shot him point blank. With tensions in the area running high, the story helped provoke three nights of rioting that left one man dead, fifty-three police officers in the hospital and a neighborhood gutted by fire. But as a Manhattan grand jury concluded two months later the story was false in nearly every detail.

The *Times'* initial accounts were not as sensational as those of *Newsday*, which ran a headline that screamed "Cop Shooting Victim: He Was Shot in the Back." But the *Times* did emphasize the same details: lobby walls stained with blood; Garcia's sisters wailing and fainting in front of reporters. "People on the street," the *Times* said, described O'Keefe brutally beating Garcia with his police radio before shooting him. Garcia's mother told the *Times* her son died "like a chicken on the floor." The paper quoted Garcia's friends and relatives as denying the police report that he had been armed when he was shot. It also gave prominent attention to the account of Juana Madera, a resident of the building, who along with her sister, Anna Rodriguez, claimed to have witnessed Garcia's killing, saying that it was all the fault of O'Keefe.

*New York Times* reports from the Dominican Republic describing the victim's funeral further reinforced the image of Garcia as a martyr. Highlighting the simple rite attended by grieving relatives, the *Times* dispatch featured Garcia's sister pointing to "her bedroom's naked cement walls" and asking, "If we were involved in drugs, do you think we would be living like this?"

But evidence indicated that Garcia was not the innocent victim that local residents made him out to be. Early in the story's development, *The New York Post,* using information on Garcia's criminal record that was made available by the city shortly after the killing, reported that Garcia was a known associate of Los Cibanos, a well-known drug gang, and that he had pled guilty to felony charges in 1989 after being caught with a packet of cocaine. After that, he had violated his probation, giving a phony address to authorities before dropping out of sight. Authorities also said he was an illegal alien who had slipped into the country four years before. These facts, though, made their way only slowly into the *Times* coverage, well after the city's other papers—with far less power to shape the story and influence the responses of public officials— had reported them. And when the *Times* did make mention of Garcia's illegal status, it was to create sympathy for him by implying that the lack of a green card made employment difficult and drug dealing inevitable.

A week after the shooting, in a front-page Sunday take-out, the *Times* finally noted Garcia's illegal status and his criminal record. But it dismissed as "speculation" reports that he had a continuing involvement with drugs. The article quoted friends and relatives who described Garcia as "timid," a "grown up kid" who "didn't have it in him to deal drugs." The reporters themselves asserted that Garcia "apparently eked out a living peddling clothing on the street." The piece also quoted an acquaintance of Garcia as asking, "Why would he have endured that beating if he was armed?" What went unmentioned was the declaration by the medical examiner's office that there was no forensic evidence for the claim that O'Keefe had beaten Garcia with his radio in the first place.

In contrast with their reluctance to mention Garcia's criminal background, reporters leapt to impugn O'Keefe, mainly through unsubstantiated hearsay. A July 8 *Times* story cited "rumors voiced by elected officials and residents alike that Officer O'Keefe may have been involved in illegal activity." And following up on these rumors in the long Sunday take-out, the paper quoted unsubstantiated allegations from "a former drug dealer" named Andy Hernandez who accused O'Keefe of shaking him down for $2000 in cash and $3000 worth of cocaine. The reporters also quoted a supervisor at the Legal Aid Society, which had represented several defendants arrested by O'Keefe: "He is a cop who was basically thinking he was in the Wild West, and he was making his own rules."

The attack on O'Keefe was part of a larger media script in which the riots were seen "in context" as a tortured cry for justice resulting from a pattern of mistreatment by a police force that was corrupt, brutal and culturally tone deaf. One *Times* article, for instance, examined the link between community resentment and a lack of ethnic diversity in the NYPD under the headline "Suburban Presence in Blue." But while it was true that about a third of the department's ranks lived beyond the city's immediate borders at that point, the 34th Precinct where O'Keefe worked had more minority officers than anywhere else in the city, assigned there specifically to enhance sensitivity to the character of the community.

Discussions of the "context" generally avoided other uncomfortable facts as well. One of them was the huge presence of illegal aliens, whom police estimated were responsible for half of the crimes committed in the neighborhood. Another factor that was ignored was the official laxity that allowed Garcia and many other illegals like him to receive probation rather than deportation for drug convictions and other felonies. The turmoil could also have provided a news peg on which to hang discussion of the problems of witness intimidation and extradition, both of which are complicated by high rates of undocumented immigrants.

It was also quite evident to many observers—some of the tabloids' more street-savvy columnists, for instance—that drug gangs were encouraging the riot in the hope of creating a political problem for the police so they would back off from aggressive street-level anti-narcotics efforts. But the *Times* quoted a Latino community activist calling that claim "totally ridiculous and incendiary," and then pursued the matter no further.

Three days after the shooting, hoping to restore public order in New York on the eve of the 1992 Democratic National Convention, Mayor David Dinkins paid a personal visit to Garcia's family in Washington Heights and invited them the next day to Gracie Mansion, his official residence. He also arranged to have the city pay for Garcia's burial in the Dominican Republic. Many in the city were critical of the mayor. Rudolph Giuliani, then preparing to run against Dinkins the following year, accused him of pandering to the Latino vote and of justifying the rioting by perpetuating "characterizations of Mr. Garcia as an innocent bodega worker victimized by the police." But the *Times* cast Dinkins' actions in an entirely favorable light, crediting him with an "aggressive strategy to restore peace through broad symbolic acts and small administrative gestures."

Two months later, in September of that year, the Manhattan District

Attorney's Office released a report outlining the findings of a grand jury investigation into the Garcia killing. All the evidence corroborated O'Keefe's story that he had shot Garcia in self-defense after Garcia pulled a gun. Physical evidence showed that Garcia had been standing, not lying flat, when he was shot. It indicated that he had been shot twice, not three times as the eyewitnesses had maintained. The grand jury report cited O'Keefe's hysterical radio call for help after the struggle, calling it "hardly the behavior of a cop shooting an innocent man in cold blood." It also claimed that the two sisters whose "eyewitness" accounts were such a prominent feature in early reports of the case could not possibly have seen the killing from where they were standing. And according to the grand jury findings, Garcia was a chronic cocaine user who worked for a drug ring headed by the son of the one of the two sisters, whose apartment was a "safe house" for the operation. Records showed that in March 1992, four months before the incident, police had raided the apartment and seized a videotape showing the son holding bags of cocaine and gloating, "It's legal here." Kiko Garcia also appeared on the tape.

After the grand jury report was made public, the *Times* published an editorial entitled "The Lessons of Washington Heights." The events, the *Times* concluded, taught "the importance of caution and restraint when the next such incident occurs." But the paper of record offered no explanation for why its own reporting had been so wide of the mark, nor an apology to Officer O'Keefe. Neither did it acknowledge the incendiary role its story line of a racist cop killing an innocent immigrant had played in stoking the disorder.

The problem of immigrant criminality has also been a subject draped in oversensitivity and solicitude at the *Los Angeles Times*. The gang capital of America, Los Angeles has nearly 1,250 identifiable street gangs and up to 150,000 gang members—one-quarter of the nation's total, according to 1996 Department of Justice figures. Many of them are illegal Hispanic aliens.

With over seven thousand gang-related homicides in the last ten years, and whole areas of the city now gang-dominated or gang-controlled, the impact of gang violence on the region's quality of life and sense of public safety and order is unmistakable, and is a driving force in wholesale flight—white, black and brown—from the area. Involved in crimes ranging from drug dealing to extortion to contract killing, gangs pose a particular problem for police and for prosecutors due to the systematic way they intimidate or kill witnesses. Throughout the 1990s more than one thousand accused killers, most of them gang members, went free because witnesses were either dead or too scared to cooperate.

Yet despite the urgency of the problem, the *Los Angeles Times'* reporting has lacked the edge required to rally the public behind policy solutions. Slow to acknowledge the problem, particularly the immigrant dimension, when it was burgeoning in the 1980s, the *Times'* reporting has been less than searching, and tends to duck the tougher issues if they challenge the prevailing orthodoxy of diversity or might feed anti-immigrant stereotypes.

These deficits were evident in a multipart series that the paper ran in November 1996 on the 18th Street Gang, the biggest and most insidious in Los Angeles. The result of eight months of investigative work by reporters Rich Connell and Robert J. Lopez, the series examined the gang's history, criminal activities, sociological complexities and impact on residents. It also detailed law enforcement's failures to come to terms with the gang.

The 18th Street Gang had a membership of about twenty thousand, the *Times* reported, far surpassing the much better-known Crips and Bloods. The gang had "literally taken over some parts of the city," the writers explained, quoting a law enforcement source who said 18th Street was "worse than a cancer." The target of two federal law enforcement task forces in recent years—one by the FBI, the other by the Bureau of Alcohol, Tobacco and Firearms—the gang was a hydra-headed monster that was almost unstoppable, making life miserable for families and businesspeople in the areas it controlled.

Citing a confidential 1995 California State Department of Justice report, the series noted the fact that over 60 percent of the 18th Street Gang was composed of illegal Mexican aliens, and that it had strong ties to the state's Mexican Mafia and to criminal enterprises across the border. The series also mentioned that a significant problem among the many budget-strained local, state and federal law enforcement authorities was a lack of communication. Law enforcement agencies, the reporters explained, hadn't adjusted their tactics—by pooling resources or sharing information to meet the challenges posed by the gang's increasing sophistication and its spread across city, state and international borders.

At the series' end, the reporters outlined an action plan: a multi-agency task force with the ability to cross political boundaries; a regional and even national gang intelligence center to help authorities track gang movements and activities; better computer tracking of incarcerated and paroled gang members; and the assignment of parole agents to task forces and to border crossings with Mexico.

But missing from the series was any mention of what many authorities consider to be a significant policy obstacle to fighting the gang effectively—an obstacle inextricably linked to the larger problem of poor coordination between local and federal authorities. The policy, called Special Order 40, specifically prevented the Los Angeles Police Department from asking anyone about their immigration status, checking with the INS, or turning in suspects accused of minor violations, one way of monitoring for more serious offenses. The policy, established in the 1970s in the wake of civil rights complaints, was a controversial one. According to those involved in the fight against gangs, it was one of the primary reasons why the region was having such a hard time coming to terms with the alien gang problem. But the *Times* only got around to mentioning the directive a month after the series, in its coverage of public hearings triggered by the reports, when conservatives on the board of supervisors called for Special Order 40 to be rescinded and ethnic liberals in Los Angeles went into fits denouncing this "racism."

As overdue and as partial as the *Los Angeles Times'* series on the 18th Street Gang was, however, it still proved too much for many in the Latino community and their tribunes at the paper. Editor Frank del Olmo, one of the paper's top Latinos who for years had a total monopoly of immigration-related editorials, tried to balance the series with something more positive. He agreed with many in the Latino community that the 18th Street series trafficked in clichés and stereotypes. (In an interview he said it reminded him of something from a 1950s monster movie.) Consequently the paper's op-ed pages ran a piece by Luis Rodriguez, a former gang member who had done time in prison and now operated a Chicago-based gang rehabilitation organization. Rodriguez said both the size and the dangers of gangs like 18th Street were being exaggerated to fuel public fear and justify the expansion of law enforcement budgets and "repressive" social policy.

The problem of methamphetamine "superlabs" in the Central Valley of California is another major crime story with an immigration subtext that news organizations have had a hard time addressing, as a front-page *New York Times* piece in mid-May 2001 attests. Hundreds if not thousands of such superlabs operate in the agricultural Central Valley, producing what former drug czar Barry McCaffrey has called "the worst drug that has ever hit America." Methamphetamine is highly addictive, often causing violent psychosis in abusers. It is also an environmental disaster: many meth labs employ the severely toxic drug phosphine, which can leave the land and buildings used for lab sites permanently polluted and lab workers with disease that quickly becomes fatal.

The superlab problem, as the article by Evelyn Nieves makes clear, represents a quantum leap from the old days when methamphetamine, also known as "speed" or "crank," was produced on a much smaller scale by white motorcycle gangs such as the Hell's Angels. Today's labs are run by "Mexican crime families" from south of the border who have set up shop in the north in order avoid the hassle of smuggling the drug through the border. These families, the article says, also use their sales network to sell the product nationwide, with drugs produced in California available on the street in Portland, Maine.

But when it came to examining who the lab workers in this labor-intensive industry were, the *Times* reporter seemed to engage in intentional obfuscation.

The Valley's chronic high unemployment rate makes recruiting workers "as easy as selling lemonade on a hot day," Nieves wrote. The crime families consider the work force a "renewable resource," an agent from the Drug Enforcement Agency told her. "When the workers get too sick from all the chemicals they've been ingesting to keep going, they just bring over or recruit others."

In conjunction with the fact that the superlabs are owned by Mexican crime families, and that the workers they hire are considered renewable resources easily replaced by those the crime families "bring over," the article suggests to anyone with a sense of on-the-ground realities in California that the lab workers are probably impoverished Mexican immigrants, a large percentage of whom are undocumented aliens. Indeed, the very sources that Nieves quotes told me, when I contacted them after her piece ran, that the problem definitely had an immigration subtext. "You can't discuss large-scale manufacture [of methamphetamine] without mentioning undocumented illegal Mexican immigrants," said Robert Pennal, a federal agent who heads the Fresno Methamphetamine Task Force and who spent time in the field with Nieves. Carl Faller, the chief assistant U.S. attorney for the Fresno area—whose boss, U.S. attorney John Vincent, was also interviewed by Nieves—roundly agreed. The undocumented status of the workers, he said, "makes them susceptible to exploitation [by drug lab operators] in the same way they've been susceptible to agricultural exploitation for decades."

For touchy-feely relativism in reporting on Latino immigrant gangs, however, nothing could surpass Seth Mydans' 1995 *New York Times* story, "Family Ties Strong for Hispanic Gangs." Fusing a report on the ultra-violence of L.A.'s Latino street gangs with a discourse on their often overlooked sense of family values, the piece reads almost like a parody of culturally sensitive reporting. According to Mydans, the gangs could also be "remarkably warm hearted" with a gallant "respect for motherhood." Hispanic family members were very loyal, he noted, visiting incarcerated relatives in jail. And when young teenage couples bore children out of wedlock, the gang members often stayed at home to look after their offspring, proud and exultant.

News organizations skirt immigration's downside in still another way by accepting the line of columnists such as Anthony Lewis of the *New York Times*, who wrote in April 1996, "In any event, most immigrants, in the classic American story, contribute far more to this country than they cost." Reporters have generally ignored an ever-increasing body of research indicating that the opposite is true.

The costs involved in arresting, providing translators for, prosecuting and incarcerating undocumented immigrant criminals is one subject that news organizations have been very reluctant to acknowledge. In August 1992, Los Angeles County released a report estimating that it cost $75.2 million to arrest, jail and prosecute illegal immigrants in the county's jurisdiction. In the context of southern California's bitter arguments over immigration, both legal and illegal, and its impact on taxpayers, the report was explosive news. It became even more so when the county board of supervisors voted unanimously to endorse the report. Up until that time, there had been no media attention given to the problem, even though it was a subject of heated debate in almost every living room and judge's chambers in the region. Yet instead of building a story around the report in order to better inform the public, the *Los Angeles Times* gave it only 161 words in its news sections—a mere four paragraphs.

Another facet of the immigrant social spending debate where journalists have been less than vigorous in getting to the facts is immigrant welfare dependency. In 1999 the poverty rate for immigrants and their children was 18 percent, while it was 11 percent for native-born Americans and their children. Economist George Borjas has estimated that welfare expenditures on immigrants are between $1 and $3 billion more per year than the immigrant contribution to the welfare system.

During most of the 1990s it was difficult to get conclusive figures on how many immigrants were *on* the welfare rolls, although in 1997 when the reform provisions governing immigrant access to welfare were about to kick in, reporters had no trouble finding estimates to show how many immigrants would be thrown *off* the rolls. This was a sign, according to many observers, of press resistance to admitting facts that might make immigration look like anything other than an unmixed blessing.

A blithe attitude toward welfare dependency among immigrants suffused a February 1995 report in the *New York Times* on one New York immigrant's return to her native Trinidad for the annual Carnival. Following a forty-one-year-old welfare mother of three back to her "roots" among Trinidad's haut bourgeoisie, the reporter explained that in New York she was "a nobody," but "at home" she was "somebody" again— "a young beauty, daughter of…a well known theatre owner who still leads one of the island's most famous carnival bands."

The tale of an upper-middle-class immigrant woman who came to America, bore three children, lived on welfare, and yet still had the resources to return home for Carnival could have raised serious questions of welfare fraud, abuse and corruption. How common was her case? How many other welfare recipients were able to make similar yearly treks? But the *Times*, caught up in the celebratory air, chose to leave these implications of the story unexamined.

Similarly, a walk through any social service office filled with Latino clients would be enough at least to raise questions about the link between high immigration and high rates of child poverty, as would even the most cursory conversation with a caseworker or supervisor. But the media often skirt these relationships. The cost of extending medical services to impoverished immigrants, many of them illegal, is another subject that has gotten short shrift. For most of the 1990s in Los Angeles, for instance, illegal immigrants made up one-quarter of the patients in the overburdened public hospital and clinic system and accounted for two-thirds of the births in Los Angeles County hospitals. Yet a *MacNeil-Lehrer Newshour* report on the L.A. County hospital system's 1995 fiscal crisis typified the willful avoidance that reporters often brought to the subject. Prepared by Jeffrey Kaye, the piece examined the fiscal collapse of the hospital system and the harsh cuts in services that had been planned in response. According to Kaye, the cuts would close 29 out of 39 health care clinics as well as all 6 community health care centers, and cause 6,000 doctors' positions to be eliminated.

Kaye reported that the main reason the county government was in such dire straits was "the decline of the industries [such as aerospace] that once fueled Southern California's economic prosperity." Of course this was an important factor. But so were costs associated with providing free medical care to ever-increasing numbers of (nontaxpaying) illegal immigrants—something Kaye never mentioned. This omission was even more striking given the fact that less than a year before, voters in the state concerned with ballooning state spending on illegal immigrants had cited health care expenditures as a primary reason for backing Proposition 187, the highly controversial ballot initiative that called for barring illegal aliens from most public services.

According to Kaye, however, his avoidance of the illegal immigration factor was not unintentional. Asked about it in an interview, he said that since the issue of providing services to illegal aliens was not a problem *before* the economy went into recession, the segment would be misrepresenting the real source of the trouble if it dwelled on immigration. That it *had* been a problem before, and was now a more acute one, seemed not to enter into his thinking.

There seemed to be a lot of willful denial about the effects of heavy immigration on school spending too. It is hardly surprising that immigration would tax school budgets in a time of increasing public stinginess. Yet journalists, preferring to overlook the strains that record numbers of immigrant children were putting on public education, emphasized the bright side. "Immigrants Jam Schools, Invigorate System," read one *New York Times* headline.

The *Times* has also shown a reluctance to acknowledge immigration as a factor in school overcrowding. As the 1996 school year opened, the New York City public school system discovered that enrollment rates in many of its districts had vastly exceeded estimates. Chaos resulted. In some districts, the *Times* reported, officials had simply no idea how many kids were enrolled or how many were going to show up. Classroom space was carved out of gyms, closets and even lavatories, and officials scrambled to shift kids from overburdened districts to those with lighter enrollments.

The most overcrowded districts were also the ones with the heaviest concentrations of immigrants. Many of the parents who were quoted complaining about the situation in the news media were recent arrivals from Bangladesh, Thailand and other Third World countries. Not long before, the New York Board of Education had issued a report projecting that it would take almost four hundred new schools, at a cost of $10 billion, to accommodate all the new immigrants. Not long after, it released figures showing that immigrant students take longer than most students to graduate, some as much as six or seven years longer, which further contributes to the system's congestion.

In its reporting on the overcrowding crisis, however, the *New York Times* barely mentioned the immigration factor. Instead it chose to blame policy decisions made in the 1970s that closed certain city schools and put a moratorium on new ones, a decision that reflected the declining school-age population of that day. While it was true that long-term policy planning decisions were *part* of the problem, the failure to assign at least some responsibility to the immigration boom came close to being a calculated concealment.


Were it less ideological, the journalistic establishment might acknowledge that public anxiety about the heavy immigration isn't without some foundation. The demographic transformation such immigration has set in motion is unprecedented in America, turning a majority white nation with European cultural roots into a nonwhite plurality with no shared cultural heritage. No other country in history has ever willingly attempted, much less accomplished, a social makeover on this scale. According to polls, most Americans—including most Hispanics—feel uneasy about high rates of immigration and virtually open borders, believing that the harm resulting from such a situation outweighs the gains. Dismayed by the policy dilettantism of political elites, the majority of Americans also resent the fact that they have never been consulted about, much less allowed to debate, the merits of immigration policy with the vigor that the current situation warrants. As Nathan Glazer wrote in the *New Republic,* "When one considers present immigration policies, it seems we have insensibly reverted to mass immigration without ever having made a decision to do so."

Yet for most of the 1980s and early 1990s, journalists helped to chill a much-needed, vigorous debate on immigration and immigration reform. Echoing the activists who made accusations of nativism whenever calls for reform were made, the press helped to establish an embargo on criticism. "A Land of Immigrants Gets Uneasy about Immigration," read one *New York Times* headline, repeating predictions that the country might soon be seeing the bloody ghosts of its anti-immigrant past. Dismissed in one *New York Times* headline as "An Accident of Geography" and in a *Times* op-ed piece as the equivalent of the Berlin Wall, the concept of a border itself was made to seem illegitimate, and those who were calling for beefing up its strength were regularly disparaged as "mean-spirited" chauvinists trying to hold back a human tide that was veritably a force of nature.

In the mid-nineties, with illegal immigrants providing some of the tinder for the Los Angeles riots (almost half of those arrested were undocumented aliens), and with wide holes in the immigration system providing entry for several of the terrorists involved in the World Trade Center bombing, the parameters of acceptable debate widened somewhat. This meant that there was a greater readiness to acknowledge just how much "Chaos at the Gates" there really was, to cite the title of an extensive 1994 *New York Times* series on the porousness of our borders and the disarray in the INS. But the fact that the links between crime and immigration were now being examined in detail did not mean that news organizations were ready to depart from the preconceived pro-immigration script, or were any less reflexive in equating calls for immigration reform with nativism and racism. A 1993 *New York Times* Week in Review story captured the flavor of the antagonism, likening calls for toughening border enforcement to the xenophobia sweeping Germany at the time and to America's own nativist past: "Americans, pinched and worried, say asylum seekers are a burden. They have said so before." Another *New York Times* piece decried what it said was a "rude inhospitality which at other times may have been considered racist or at least xenophobic."

Such knee-jerk conflation of calls for reform with nativism grew loudest in the reporting over Proposition 187, a controversial California ballot initiative that won by a twenty-point margin in November 1994. Driven by the argument that California's generous social benefits had exerted a "magnet effect" on the state's 1.5 to 3 million illegal aliens, the initiative called for an end to nonemergency health care and public schooling for undocumented aliens, and required medical, educational and law enforcement authorities to report them to immigration authorities. Although many of its backers doubted the measure's enforceability, they supported it anyway, hoping it would send a message to Washington that *something* needed to be done about the nation's virtually open border.

There were reasons to be skeptical about the measure. Although most of Proposition 187's supporters were not driven by racism or xenophobia, some clearly were. There were also concerns that Governor Pete Wilson had embraced 187 in order to gain a political advantage over his Democratic challenger, Kathleen Brown. Even the measure's constitutionality was unclear; if it passed, a long series of court challenges were surely ahead.

All of these shortcomings were adequately reported. Largely ignored or minimized, however, were the problems targeted by the proposition. Over half the illegal immigrants in the entire country lived in California, and the state was paying out vast sums of public money because it had lost control of the border. More than 300,000 illegal immigrants had received free public health care the year before—a colossal increase in less than five years. The cost of educating the children of illegal immigrants was estimated at $1.8 billion, and the cost of incarcerating convicted illegals, who made up one-sixth of the state's inmate population, was tabbed at $475 million. True, many illegal aliens were paying taxes; but most of those taxes went to Washington, not Sacramento. At the very least, its supporters hoped, Proposition 187 might trigger a more equitable distribution of such money and a more vigorous debate about illegals.

With sound arguments on both sides, news organizations could have helped the electorate make an informed choice. Instead, they met Proposition 187 with relentless antagonism. According to a *New York Times* editorial, 187 was "meanspirited, impractical and probably unconstitutional." *New York Times* columnist William Safire called it a "nativist abomination" and his colleague on the op-ed page Anthony Lewis saw it as a clear example of "the politics of nativism." On CNN, *Wall Street Journal* columnist Al Hunt called it a "draconian initiative" and said it would "exacerbate xenophobia and racial tensions." Network TV coverage was equally hostile. According to one survey, 75 percent of the nightly stories were predominantly anti-187, with arguments against it outnumbering those in favor by 5 to 1.

The virtual unanimity of the condemnation spoke to the lack of diversity of opinion in the elite national media culture. But at the state level, in the reporting of the *Los Angeles Times*, there was something far more insidious: a case study in journalistic misrepresentation, distortion and bias aimed at beating back the measure. Disproportionately Latino, the *Los Angeles Times* reporting team made itself a vehicle for anti-187 scare tactics, a mission to which the paper's other editorial writers and columnists demonstrated considerable devotion as well.

The coverage showed its bias in its depiction of pro-187 forces— groups that the paper had ignored for years even as their ranks swelled with disaffected citizens. Aside from a single effort to climb inside the heads of Proposition 187 supporters, the *Los Angeles Times* stressed their political ineptitude, paranoia and tendentiousness, along with their wholly incidental links to what the paper said were white supremacist organizations in other parts of the country. The pro-187 group's motto,

S.O.S. (Save Our State), one sarcastic report explained, was coined over dinner at a Mexican restaurant. And the group itself supposedly had little common ground other than "their contempt for immigrants."

The paper's bias was also apparent in its indulgence of the opposition's demagoguery. Mud slinging is a staple of California politics, but the opposition's rhetoric was scandalous even by the state's hardball standards. One Catholic priest said to be "seething with a quiet indignation more often reserved for mortal sin than a ballot initiative" was quoted as saying that the measure was "entirely godless." A Jew quoted in the same piece saw parallels with "Jews being sent back on the ship *St. Louis* during World War II." In another piece, a prominent Latino politician in Orange County who had declared his neutrality was characterized by one Latino civil rights leader as doing "just like the good Germans did when they watched other Germans being marched to the ovens."

During the run-up to the vote, opposition groups mounted a series of marches throughout the region, with Mexican flags often prominently displayed. Students in public high schools—their illegal status identified only in the most indirect way—conducted a series of walkouts in protest, in some cases sparking violence. There were also numerous instances of flag burning, during which Anglos who protested were severely beaten. Yet the *Times* gave these actions only the most cursory attention, avoiding altogether the view that foreign nationals were in some cases violently attempting to sway an American election or were engaging in thuggish, anti-democratic behavior.

The paper also failed to report honestly on how the Mexican government lent support to the opposition. In August, the Mexican government, in a true breach of sovereignty, issued a formal condemnation of the initiative, claiming it would "spur a Latino underclass and spur discrimination." Later, the Mexican government went a step further, offering strategic advice and promising legal assistance should the initiative pass. Such efforts were significant, and were read by many to constitute undesirable meddling in the internal affairs of another country. They also represented profound hypocrisy on the part of Mexican authorities, given their own draconian policies toward the illegal aliens from Central and South America violating *their* borders.

At the time the Mexican government announced its opposition in August, the *Times* duly reported it. But news of its formal assistance to the anti-187 camp did not come until the end of October. Even then, the paper did not say conclusively that the Mexicans were contributing money, although they were. Nor did it treat the question of meddling in the internal affairs of another country with any depth. Only after the balloting did *Times* editorials venture that Mexicans "might be forgiven for a bit of presumption," but no harm was perceived, as a "mature California" could live with "occasional foreign criticism."

The *Los Angeles Times'* most significant lapse, however, was its failure to frame and answer in any definitive and reliable manner the central questions raised by the initiative. Exactly how much of a burden did illegal immigrants pose to the state and how much would the state save by implementing Proposition 187? Did the dire predictions of the opposition—a plague of communicable diseases, rampant juvenile crime by kids being dumped from schools into the streets, and rampant violations of Latino civil rights—have any real validity? At certain points in the campaign, these questions were noted, but rarely in a way that went deeper than the superficial answers supplied by the opposition. The *Times* failed to examine the dramatic decline in the quality of California's public education system over the previous decade—a decline which many observers credibly blamed on the burden of having to educate hundreds of thousands of unassimilated newcomers. (In Los Angeles, nearly half of the city's 700,000 public school students required bilingual instruction.)

The paper did not explore, either, the financial savings for the fiscally burdened public hospital system and the Medi-Cal system that supports it, should they no longer have to service the state's three million undocumented aliens. The state would still have to provide emergency medical care for illegals, the cost of which would still be considerable. (At Los Angeles County Hospital, for instance, 2 out of every 3 births were to undocumented immigrant mothers.) But other medical care would not be compulsory, representing sizeable savings—about which the public was left uninformed.

Instead of doing an honest reckoning of 187 and what its passage might mean, the *Times* maintained its steady drumbeat of incendiary coverage and commentary. Journalists filed stories heavy with hysterical predictions; in one such alarum, an activist was allowed to charge that 187 "could open the door for some racist white supremacist group to attack Latinos." The paper's partisanship was also evident in a string of stories it ran emphasizing the dire impact of the measure's victory upon the immigrant community, many of whom were "Walking in Fear." The proposition's landslide victory, suggested one *Times* writer, was a sign that California "was no longer the land of opportunity."

Editors at the *Los Angeles Times* have officially dismissed the charge that their coverage was biased. But according to a former *Times* writer, many reporters clearly believed their mission was to beat 187. "It never occurred to many of them that this was a complicated issue to be weighed with detachment," he said. "The clear sense was that they were in the middle, fighting the forces of darkness." Eventually, the paper's editors would make oblique admissions of their bias. According to one veteran correspondent, editors planning their coverage of Proposition 209, a 1996 measure to prohibit racial preferences in state institutions, "told us they wanted to be very careful about avoiding the perception of bias this time around. They didn't want what happened during 187 to happen again."

Another recurring story line involves immigrants currently leading upstanding lives who are deported for minor crimes committed in the past. A string of *New York Times* reports in 2000 and 2001, many of them written by *Times* immigration correspondent Chris Hedges, underscored this theme. One of them, which ran under the headline "Condemned Again for Old Crimes," described how the deportation law descended "sternly" and surprisingly on a Filipino man who had been arrested in 1975 on a fairly minor charge of sexual contact with an underage girl and had never been in trouble with the law since. (He was twenty-one at the time; the girl was sixteen years old, and her mother, who disapproved of their boyfriend-girlfriend relationship, had set the arrest in motion.) The motto on the Statue of Liberty should be changed, the man said from a corrections facility, to: "Give me your poor, your tired and your hungry, because we still have empty jail cells."

The *New York Times* could be sympathetic even when the charge was more serious, as shown by the pathos saturating an account of the pain suffered by the family of a Chinese immigrant convicted of smuggling aliens into the country. "Alone and unemployed, she [the man's Chinese wife] worries most now that her husband will be deported," wrote Hedges. Yet somehow the salutary effects of the broader policy changes that allowed the more effective deportation of alien criminals— weakened gangs, safer streets, fewer tax dollars spent arresting, prosecuting and incarcerating foreign-born criminals—did not get the same sympathetic attention as these human interest cases.

An August 1997 two-part story in the *New York Times* dealt with this tougher policy. According to the *Times*, this policy was not as effective as those who had backed it might have liked. Once deported, the felons had an easy time getting back into the States undetected, quickly resuming their criminal activities. "Partly as a result," the *Times* reported, "the effect of the increased deportations are barely perceptible on the streets of the nation's major cities."

But while the effects of the new policy were negligible in the United States, they were "profound," said the *Times,* in some of the countries where alien felons were forcibly returned, such as El Salvador and some of the Caribbean island nations. There, the paper reported, the "unintended side effects" of the new law were troubling, as returning thugs operated with "all the truculence of their parent groups in Los Angeles and other American cities," and exported American gang habits. To underscore that point, the story was illustrated with bold photographs of the repatriated gang members, flaunting their gang signals just as their brethren in Los Angeles were routinely photographed doing.

Such gang activity, said the *Times,* posed a threat to the new-found political stability of Latin American countries that was as bad as the revolutionary violence that had plagued some of them before. According to one police official in El Salvador, "If you keep sending these guys back, we're going to have another civil war on our hands." That such a development would be America's fault was made plain. Keith Mitchell, the president of Grenada, complained about the repatriation of its American immigrant felons: "If they are sending the worst criminals back to us, that is a bit cold, calculating and uncaring, and certainly not the action of a fair and concerned friend."

To frame the story of deported alien criminals in a way that made America a bogeyman for sending the felons to where they originated was a bit of a stretch. And for a news organization that had largely ignored the depredations of gangs operating in our own cities suddenly to manifest concern for their activities in foreign countries was even more dubious.

# SIX

# Reasons Why

Serving a white-bread town in the nation's whitest state, Vermont's *Burlington Free Press* hardly seems the place to look for indications of what the news industry's diversity crusade has done to journalistic candor. But as the wrongful termination trial of former *Free Press* reporter Paul Teetor in 1996 showed, even the doings at a paper in the slow lane of America's fast-changing demographics can be a revelation. In fact, by forcing the *Free Press*'s parent organization, the Gannett Corporation (whose ninety-one newspapers, including *USA Today*, had a daily circulation of 6.5 million at the time) to divulge closely guarded bureaucratic secrets through aggressive moves during the discovery phase of the trial, Teetor's lawyers were able to put the practice of diversity itself on trial. In the process they revealed many of the reasons why well-intentioned efforts to make news organizations more sensitive and inclusive can also make them forbidding places to discuss the sometimes troubling, always morally complex aspects of ethnicity, race and gender.

At issue was whether the *Free Press* acted properly in firing Teetor, a forty-four-year-old white male reporter who had been targeted by Burlington's small but vocal minority community because of an account he wrote about a controversial community forum on racism in March 1993. During that forum, a young, soft-spoken white woman trying to defend native Vermonters against angry accusations of white racism was cut off at the microphone by a black mayoral aide named Rodney Patterson, acting as moderator. Patterson directed that the woman be escorted outside, explaining that the meeting had been "specifically designed for people of color" to describe their "ethnic experiences" of living in Vermont.

Teetor, a hard-charging, often abrasive newshound who had won Vermont's Reporter of the Year award three times, agreed with the woman's perception that the incident constituted "reverse racism."

After interviewing her as well as others in the audience who agreed with her—including several prominent minority citizens—he rushed back to the newsroom. With fifteen minutes to spare before the 11 P.M. deadline, he consulted with the night editor, and then distilled his two hours of notes into a twenty-two-paragraph story. Taking pains to follow the editor's directions not to make the incident with the white woman the lead or even make too much of it, Teetor tucked that event into the middle of the piece.

When his account appeared the next day, minorities charged that the story was "ugly" and "distorted" and that it "inflamed racial tensions." Leading the attack was Rodney Patterson, who, adopting an Al Sharpton mode, threatened to file a lawsuit and march on the paper unless Teetor was fired and an apology published. Later that night, *Free Press* editor Ronald Thornburgh terminated Teetor in a meeting that lasted a minute and a half, without either giving him a chance to defend himself, reviewing a videotape that supported the reporter's account of what had happened, or talking to any officials in attendance who could have confirmed the facts as Teetor reported them. Thornburgh later insisted that he had not caved in to pressure from the minority community, but as Rodney Patterson boasted to another news reporter, "He [Teetor] messed with the wrong person. And I think the *Free Press* was aware that we could rally enough support to cause people to question what they were doing."

When the issue came to trial three years later, in March 1996, the Burlington Superior Court found the *Free Press* and Gannett in the odd position of attacking their own reporter. Attorneys for the chain argued that Teetor's inaccurate and unbalanced account of the race forum "was the last straw, the icing on the cake after a long history of problems." Citing a record of poor performance, unprofessional conduct and a reputation for abrasiveness and recklessness, *Free Press* attorney Robert Rachlin, ignoring all of Teetor's awards, told the *Boston Globe* that the reporter was "a problem employee from day one" who could have been fired much sooner. "If you look at the personnel record you have to ask why the hell they kept him so long. The problem was that Gannett was too kind-hearted."

Teetor argued that the facts and the tone of his story were accurate, and that an incident of reverse racism at a community forum on race was inherently newsworthy. He insisted that his career was being maligned to obscure the fact that he had been "sacrificed on the altar of political correctness" in what his attorney Ritchie Berger told the jury was a "craven" act of "pandering to the minority community" which could have made trouble for *Free Press* editors back at Gannett corporate headquarters. There, Teetor's lawyers argued, sensitivity to minorities has been declared holy writ, and a crush of incriminating internal directives existed to prove it.

Digging into Gannett's corporate diversity records, Teetor's attorneys found documents that shed light on the quota-based system the company used to measure the racial correctness of its editorial products. This was a system, they argued in court, which encouraged hypersensitivity and double standards. It was also an approach that was unnecessary in a setting like Burlington, where minorities represent only about 3 percent of the population.

The documents in question centered on Gannett's "All American Contest," an annual internal review which judged editors on their success at achieving racial balance on their news staffs and their news pages. An important component of this diversity effort was what Gannett called "mainstreaming," a controversial, ill-defined policy of covering the news by racial numbers. Under this regime, reporters had to maintain and consult a minority source list, and had to integrate positive images of minorities into news coverage and photos. After sifting through stacks of coverage and score sheets used by editors to track the amount and quality of the coverage given to minorities, Gannett executives in the Virginia headquarters issued numerically based evaluations and memos praising or scolding editors depending on their performance.

Documents entered into the court record showed that at the time of the Teetor dismissal, the *Free Press* had some of the lowest "All American" scores in the newspaper division and that editor Thornburgh was under extraordinary pressure from Gannett, which ties executive compensation and career security to the contest results, to improve them. This made Thornburgh highly susceptible to Rodney Patterson's threats, Teetor's attorneys argued. If an alienated black community stopped taking calls from his reporters, "mainstreaming" would have been impossible.

To establish just how skittish *Free Press* editors were on the racial front, Teetor's legal team pointed to a July 1993 letter from Thornburgh to his supervisors at Gannett in which he desperately trumpeted the steps the *Free Press* had taken "to strengthen its commitment to diversity." These included the hiring of a Japanese writer and an African-American couple, one of whom would be groomed for management, in keeping with a promise to "seek minority candidates at every editorial opening. " He also emphasized the recruitment of a new managing editor who had formally spearheaded a successful diversity drive at the Gannett-owned *Detroit News*. In addition, the letter crowed about sending a photographer to three minority business forums with the assignment of photographing "every minority face there"; having senior editors meet with the paper's minority committee to review coverage, especially coverage of crime and crime pictures; and making sure that the frequency, size and placement of black crime shots was no more prominent than those of whites. Thornburgh concluded by proudly describing his plans to use the policy of "mainstreaming" in evaluating *all* newsroom professionals at their annual reviews, not just top editors.

In a deposition, Thornburgh admitted he had decreed that one out of six of the faces in a photo series called "Vermont Voices" should be a "person of color." (This feature was discontinued amidst much local ridicule when the scarcity of nonwhite faces in the area required that the same faces of color appear over and over.) A deposition from the paper's star columnist disclosed that Thornburgh had instructed him in a memo that "at least one column in every four should be about a minority or address a diversity issue." In another deposition it was revealed that Gannett executives had told Thornburgh that the proportion of minorities in the Burlington area dictated that one in every ten op-ed pieces be by nonwhites. Court papers also showed that Thornburgh was especially cautious about photographs; a shot the paper ran of a black man raking leaves was a no-no because it might reinforce stereotypes of blacks being suitable for manual labor only. The *Free Press* needed to explode stereotypes that existed around Vermont, Thornburgh wrote in a staff memo—chiefly that blacks are "poor and uneducated."

Teetor also cited two incidents as background for understanding the paper's racial anxieties. One involved the fits of protest triggered in the black community when the paper ran a picture of a snarling, manacled black suspect as he was arraigned in a sensational 1992 murder case. After this incident, a penitent Thornburgh and other editors from the paper met with community leaders, including Rodney Patterson, in a stormy session filled with racial accusation, and promised more "sensitivity." In fact, photos of the defendant did *not* run a year later during the actual trial, which would not have been the case had the defendant been white, Thornburgh conceded in his deposition.

The second background incident that Teetor cited, which occurred two weeks before his dismissal, involved a case of racial trouble elsewhere in the Gannett empire. In February 1993 it was revealed that *USA*

*Today* had run a front-page photo of armed black gang members later found to be staged. With the shots of angry blacks protesting this incident that had made national news still fresh, the *Free Press* was even more nervous than usual, since it was almost guaranteed that a march on the paper, such as the one Rodney Patterson had threatened, would also have made the national AP wire.

The climate of racial solicitude at the *Free Press* was further underscored by the fact that prior to the fateful community meeting, the paper's editors had failed to challenge its ground rules—i.e., that it was exclusively designed for people of color to speak and that those who did not wish to make "public" statements could speak from a "media-free zone" where they would not be identified. These were infringements on First Amendment liberties, Teetor argued, and would have been considered newsworthy in "a normal newsroom." Further discouraging anyone from challenging the ground rules was the understanding that the forum was a good opportunity for the paper to get back into good graces with the minority community and its leaders after the incidents of the year before. According to Teetor, the editors who assigned him to cover the race forum that night had made it very clear he was to "go easy."

Adding to the *Free Press*'s embarrassment at the trial were revelations of the series of missteps that the paper made in addressing the fallout from Teetor's original story and in fighting his legal grievance. A so-called "clarification," which ran the day after Teetor was fired and was clearly intended to appease angry minorities, was itself inaccurate on several critical points, leading a columnist for an alternative weekly to dub the *Free Press* "the gang that couldn't retract straight." The paper was also selective in the letters to the editor it published after the dismissal, censoring those that supported Teetor's account of the forum and criticized his dismissal. In the early stages of the court proceedings, the paper's attorney asked that information relating to personnel records and financial information be impounded under a gag order, a move that was denied by the judge who wryly observed that the *Free Press* was asking him "to prevent newspaper coverage." And while it was not mentioned in court, the psychiatrist Gannett hired to evaluate Teetor declared he had an "anti-authority complex"—an odd charge to use in trying to smear someone in a profession which supposedly regards such as a quality as a job requirement.

As Teetor sat on the witness stand, Gannett's attorneys grilled him about his record of minor suspensions and probations. (Early on at the *Free Press* he had violated rules by using his press pass to gain free entry to a high school basketball game which he was not covering, and had been sanctioned for arguing with an editor over an assignment he said he was not hired to do.) They also pressed him on his dissembling about his age when he first discussed the job, and on his use of Prozac to treat depression. According to one observer, it was an excruciating thing to watch, "like seeing someone get root canal without Novocain."

But the trial proved even more painful for Gannett. Calling several eyewitnesses from the race forum to the stand, Teetor's lawyer Ritchie Berger was able to determine that, in fact, the reporter had accurately described the incident at the race forum. He played a videotape of the meeting, leaving the impression that if anything, Teetor had gone easy, purging his account of the more militant anti-white rhetoric that had singed the room that night.

Turning to Teetor's former colleagues, Berger made them out to be careerist toadies more interested in covering their backsides than in protecting free speech or a colleague's career and reputation. The fact that editor Thornburgh had ultimately been forced to resign from the paper because of his handling of Teetor's firing did not help Gannett's position, nor did the revelation that he had signed a separation agreement with the company in which he had promised not to disparage Gannett in exchange for financial compensation. Berger was also able to make hay out of the inconsistencies between the paper's insistence that Teetor was a problem employee and the congratulatory notes editors were sending him for stories they liked. In addition Berger got Thornburgh to admit that it was standard procedure in any investigation of a reporter's honesty and accuracy to get the reporter's side of the story before making any decisions.

The *coup de grâce* came in Berger's cross-examination of Rodney Patterson, who was forced to concede under oath to having published comments charging that all European-Americans were racists. He also admitted that on the day in question he had a hundred or more protesters—"instant supporters," he called them in an interview with me—ready to march on the *Free Press* if Teetor was not fired. Although Berger could not get Patterson to admit that Gannett's All American plan was a factor in his calculations, he did get him to acknowledge that he was aware of it. When considered in connection with the score sheets, grading charts and other materials from the All American program that were entered into evidence, this neatly tied all the threads of the case together.

By the end of the trial's fourth day, Gannett corporate executives agreed to an out-of-court settlement. This of course made Teetor ecstatic;

after being pilloried by the *Free Press*, he had been blackballed by other news organizations in the state and had been forced into a series of menial jobs for three years while awaiting his day in court. But as a self-described "very left of center liberal" who believed that in fact whites have much to answer for in their treatment of blacks, he was not pleased to have become a poster boy for the excesses of political correctness. And he was still cynical about what his Kafkaesque experience said about the climate of corporate, diversity-obsessed journalism. He had merely done his job—reporting on what had happened to one woman who was denied her First Amendment rights and removed from a public meeting room because of her skin color. Then he had stood up for the rights of journalists. His conclusion from his ordeal? "It is too bad Gannett wants generic stories that don't offend anybody."

Reporters I approached to discuss the specific examples of skewed or politically slanted coverage examined in this book looked at me the way a taxpayer might regard a revenue officer calling from the IRS. Even if they were able to concede that mistakes were made, they were deeply reluctant to acknowledge any link between the effort to enhance diversity within the newsroom and the development of political orthodoxy. Most simply scoffed at the idea of such a connection. In responses that were both passive-aggressive and patronizing, they told me over and over that my line of inquiry smacked of the overheated thinking favored by right-wing conspiratorialists with their dark vision of liberal cabals deliberately distorting the news to suit a left-wing political agenda.

Favoring more benign explanations (and reaching for plausible deniability), these journalists tended to blame the daily exigencies within their various news organizations for whatever problems existed, as well as the often restrictive conventions of the news-gathering process. Stories might sometimes appear as if they were reported through a filter of political correctness, but in fact they simply reflected the pressure of daily deadlines, the limitations of reportorial staff stretched thin by vacations or maternity leave, the inability to get a quote from an opposing voice at the time the story was produced, or the absence of an acceptable "peg" that would make a heterodox story newsworthy or timely.

Yes, some might concede, a single story on any particular day might appear, in hindsight, to take an unbalanced, implicitly or explicitly pro-diversity line. But if I looked at the flow of coverage over time, they insisted, I'd see that there was no ideological slant. Most of those I spoke with also took considerable pains to remind me that I should-n't think there ever was a "golden age" of objective reporting. Some, implicitly acknowledging political skewing even as they explicitly denied it, suggested that given how bad things were in the white-dom-inated newsrooms of the past, mistakes like the ones I was pointing to represented a long overdue "balancing of the books" we could all live with.

Of course, the vast majority of news organizations do not have diversity programs as highly codified and rigid as Gannett's, and the notion of die-hard liberals standing around in the corners of newsrooms plotting to infuse news reporting with left-wing bias is a caricature. In fact, the problem is both more subtle and more insidious. What really undercuts the worthy goal of enhancing diversity is the overall climate these diversity efforts create in the newsroom—a climate often directly at odds with the very kind of free and open exchange of competing cultural viewpoints that true diversity should exalt.

In theory, diversity is supposed to be a matter of reporters from all different ethnicities, races, genders and sexual orientations doing their work as searchingly as possible on a wide variety of subjects, and func-tioning as a sort of equivalent of a representative democracy. But in practice, the regime that diversity has created does not work like this. Certain unfashionable or disfavored voices are overlooked or muted for a variety of reasons, and certain groups feel more empowered in the journalistic shouting match than others.

Although efforts to expand representation by ethnicity, race and gender have succeeded at increasing the numbers of minority staff members and raising the profile of minority issues, the actual intellec-tual or ideological diversity of news organizations has contracted. For all the talk of multiculturalism, newsrooms have become more "mono-cultural," defined by diversity that is in fact only skin deep. As Art Carey of the *Philadelphia Inquirer* says, what results is "phony diversity, a cosmetic, Benetton advertisement vision of diversity," a diversity of skin color and sex organs and ethnicity, but not a genuine diversity of intellects and ideas."

If a publisher was interested in real diversity rather than diver-sity on the cheap, he would hire, for instance, a female reporter who opposes abortion, or a born-again Christian, or for that matter, a Repub-lican. I don't necessarily endorse the viewpoints of any of these groups, yet researching this book has convinced me that these viewpoints, and others considered retrograde, are systematically excluded from today's newsroom. In fact, by targeting women and minorities (who are traditionally more liberal than white males), diversity efforts have actually accentuated the newsroom's longstanding liberal cast. According to a 1996 Freedom Forum survey of national journalists in Washington, D.C., only 9 percent of those surveyed self-identified as conservative, while 61 percent described themselves as liberals. The same study found that only 4 percent identified themselves as Republicans, while 50 percent said they were Democrat. Another survey, this one by Times-Mirror, found a similar, substantial imbalance, with liberals overwhelming conservatives in broadcasting by a factor of three to one and in print by a factor of four to one. Bias, wrote columnist James Glassman in response to the Freedom Forum results, "is the shameful open secret of American journalism."

According to Michael Barone, senior writer for *U.S. News & World Report*,

> As managers seek a more superficial facial diversity of women, blacks, Hispanics, Asians, Native Americans, etc....rather than a true variety of viewpoints, newsroom cultures move farther left every year. On any suburban street in America you will find plenty of people who vote for Republicans and Democrats and are happy to tell you why. But in most newsrooms those few who vote Republican tend to keep their mouths shut, while those who vote Democratic smugly continue to assume that every decent, thinking person does the same.

At some news organizations, particularly those with the greatest commitment to diversity, having liberal values has almost become a condition for employment, and a kind of ideological self-selection process winnows out those who won't "fit in"—the very code words that had long excluded nonwhite minorities. "The filter is invisible," complained Linda Seebach, editorial writer for the *Rocky Mountain News*, "but it is definitely there."

Even when reporters and editors who don't subscribe to the liberal worldview manage to get hired, they find that their perspectives and experience aren't always valued, particularly those with strong religious or moral beliefs. In fact, many put considerable effort into keeping their opinions and beliefs hidden, much like homosexuals did in decades past. According to former *Los Angeles Times* reporter Jill Stewart, "There is a real anti-religious bigotry going on here. It is not cool to say you go to church or synagogue, or say you have religious or moral objections to abortion. You have to be secular."

In recent years, some news organizations have deliberately tried to hire conservatives, much in the same way that some news outfits once had their token minorities. The profession would be better off if they hired journalists who possessed skepticism, a regard for hard truth and an impatience with the "smelly little orthodoxies," as Orwell described them. This recruitment of token conservatives hardly makes a dent in the organizational culture of the newsroom, since most are hired as columnists or commentators and have little impact on the setting of the news agenda. And the majority of the nation's top news organizations still have the same kind of massive ideological and cultural imbalances as the editorial page of the *New York Times*, which has been scrupulous in hiring editorial writers who are gay, black, Latino and female, but has left it at that in the matter of diversity.

The kind of journalists who are attracted to writing and reporting on special "diversity" teams—or those that managers allow to be assigned to such teams—work against ideological balance, indeed, against diversity itself in the truest sense of the word. "There's a certain kind of person who is motivated to want to be on the race-and-demographics team," an editor who was in charge of such a team at the *San Jose Mercury News* told me recently. "The impulse of these reporters is to build [minorities] up."

Although the "gritty" days of the old *Front Page* journalism are fogged with nostalgia, it is true that in that era, journalists did have roots in working-class communities, which gave them a good understanding of the public's political and cultural center of gravity. But today's journalists, whatever their color, gender or background, are largely brought up and educated in an insular, upper-middle-class universe. They have all attended the same universities and all been exposed to the same politically correct pieties. Contrary to the image of journalists as people capable of moving fluidly among many different classes of people—as capable of bellying up to the bar with dockworkers as of discussing the complexities of health care policy with doctors—reporters today tend to be an inbred bunch, uneasy away from their own kind. (Increasingly they are even marrying each other too, further compounding the problem of caste insularity.) Some seem painfully narrow in their real-life experience, and are reluctant to move beyond the comfortable orbit of the already known. Former *Washington Post* ombudsman Richard Harwood said it well:

> Diversity may have brought attitudes, perspectives, political values, and interpretations of reality that challenged or diluted the predominant worldview of white males, but newsroom diversity has done little to change its dominant social and political values.... Journalists for the most

part are children of the professional and managerial classes and attend
colleges and universities staffed by leftist intellectuals.... The best and
brightest move on to the most influential newspapers, all of them located
in metropolitan centers dominated by the urban liberal bourgeoisie.

The increasing liberalism of the newsroom combined with more
parochialism amplifies a disconnect from the rest of mainstream society,
particularly on divisive cultural and racial issues. According to various surveys comparing opinions and attitudes of reporters and editors
with those of the population at large, journalists are overwhelmingly
in favor of affirmative action (81 percent, compared with 51 percent of
the general public) and abortion on demand (51 percent versus 33 percent). They are also largely pro-immigration and overwhelmingly
supportive of gay and lesbian issues. (According to a 1995 *Los Angeles
Times* poll, only 41 percent of the public thought homosexuality morally
acceptable, while 83 percent of the media thought so.)

Without counterbalancing influences, the worldview and prejudices of the liberal-leaning newsroom majority manufacture what
become philosophical "givens." In addition to limiting the scope of the
questions that get raised in newsroom debates among reporters and
editors, these givens can also foster blind spots in the setting of the
news agenda, and affect what is considered newsworthy or what issues
get priority. As John Leo has noted in the *U.S. News & World Report*,
right-wingers who propound liberal conspiracies that slant the news
"don't understand how journalism really works." Nobody sets out to
propagandize readers and viewers, says Leo; "the bias is usually an
unconscious byproduct of an elite newsroom culture." While large
majorities of Americans oppose such things as partial birth abortion
and affirmative action, "in the newsroom the lopsided majorities go
the opposite way."

This is most certainly the case in the coverage of affirmative
action, at least prior to 1995 when the dam of public outrage finally
burst in a series of populist initiatives to curtail racial preferences. As a
*New York Times* reporter told me, "No one wants to do a story on
affirmative action because they just don't see anything wrong with it."
Says former *Philadelphia Inquirer* editor Don Kimmelman, "You would-
n't expect *Inquirer* people to go after stories about race-norming in
testing with the same zeal as other issues, for example; it neither out-
rages or interests them."

The philosophical givens affect coverage of the other issues too.
Lacking experience in the armed forces, for instance, many of those
assigned to cover the integration of gays and women into the military

have shown an inability to appreciate the realities of service life and the uniqueness of the military culture. And largely lacking religious belief themselves, it has been too easy for journalists to dismiss evangelical Christians, in the words of a *Washington Post* reporter, as "largely poor, uneducated and easy to command." Conservative author David Frum was correct when he wrote, "Most reporters covering the rise of the religious right can make no human connection with these people. They see them as dangerous." Indeed, as *Post* editor Leonard Downie was embarrassed to admit after his paper failed to cover the massive anti-abortion March for Life in 1990, not only were few of the *Post* staff pro-life, but "few had spent much time with anyone who was."

While reporters and editors are attentive and deferential to liberal groups, particularly liberal civil rights organizations, conservative groups have had a hard time winning equal time. "There are just as many special interest groups on the right [as on the left]," says Jill Stewart, a former reporter at the *Los Angeles Times*. "But they are often invisible in the debate. The people on the right are often aggressively trying to get into the paper and they simply can't."

The regime of diversity has also laid a cloud of anxiety and intimidation over the contemporary newsroom, making those with misgivings or questions constantly worried about the reaction of peers and fearful for their jobs and careers. "I deplore the fact that the issue is so sensitive that reporters don't want to talk by name," one Washington bureau chief told me during a discussion of diversity. Then he hastened to add, " I don't want to contribute to that but I would rather not be quoted by name either."

After unloading a number of criticisms about diversity at his paper and its adverse effects on ethnic and racial coverage, an editor at the *San Francisco Chronicle* was quick to beat a retreat in a fax he sent me. He had offered some fairly outspoken opinions on the cynicism of managers tasked with implementing diversity, and was particularly trenchant in his comments on the paper's racial and ethnic color-coded assignment policies. But in the fax he insisted that everything needed to be seen "in context," and, he claimed, "affirmative action is an art not a science." The fax reeked of anxiety, and seemed more an exercise in covering the backside than in clarification. I got the sense he had thought about what he told me and panicked, fearful that being quoted might make him an enemy of the state.

And it is not only those at lower rungs of the newsroom ladder who feel inhibited about speaking their minds. At the 1994 convention of the American Society of Newspaper Editors, Bob Haiman, director of the Poynter Institute, asked members if political correctness was a problem, defining it as "a rigid orthodoxy, usually of a doctrinaire liberal tilt, which precludes the acceptability of a contrary viewpoint and allows those who insist on raising a contrary view to be ridiculed, shunned, denounced, attacked or silenced." Out of 41 editors polled, 38 answered yes, political correctness had indeed led to a tilt or spin in their paper's coverage and had cut down or inhibited vigorous, candid and open debate and dissent. But of those 38, only 2 said they would allow Haiman to use their names in a panel discussion conducted during the convention. In fact, many pled with him not to use their names. "Whatever happened to courage in our business?" asked Gene Cryer, one of the two member-editors who allowed himself to be identified.

With publishers like Arthur Sulzberger Jr. making diversity such a public crusade—calling it "our cause," vetting new hires, and warning managers that they can either get with the program or find their career options "dramatically narrowed"—it is little wonder that career-conscious reporters and editors are reluctant to speak out. Explained one *New York Times* reporter:

> Of course the paper is not a centrally controlled, Leninist organization. But there is a party line, particularly on race and gays. You don't get orders from on high, but it [pronouncements like Sulzberger's] does affect the atmosphere. The sense is "The Chairman has spoken. Now it is up to us to implement it." That is bound to affect people's vision. You are not going to get ahead at this newspaper by going up to someone like Arthur and saying, "We've gone too far; we've lost credibility." Arthur is certainly not going to race down to the newsroom and embrace you.

It should be noted here that in the course of this book I have been hard on the *New York Times*—some might say too hard. But as America's newspaper of record, which sets the news agenda for so many other print and broadcast organizations around the country and also takes the lead in newsroom policies and practices that other organizations eventually embrace, the *Times* is a looming fact in our national and intellectual life. Like it or not—and the *Times* obviously likes it—the paper is a metaphor for American journalism.

In many ways, news organizations have become the same kind of petty, dysfunctional cultures as college campuses, where transgressions against the dominant line of thought can result in ideological blackballing and ostracism. No matter how much journalistic malpractice it may involve, those who toe the line earn rewards: better assignments, promotions, jobs at better news organizations. Those who refuse, or insist on asking the hard questions, run the risk of punishment, excommunication, or banishment to career Siberias. Like academics, journalists spend far more time in distractedly assessing the ideological bona fides of critics than in assessing the soundness of their complaints. And like university administrators, newsroom managers allow aggrieved minorities incredible latitude in registering their accusations. As in the academy, critics learn to survive by biting their tongues. A dinner party remark from a *New York Times* writer to whom I had described this book proved the point: "So, you aren't planning to stay in journalism after the book's out, are you?" she chuckled.

Even the ideal of objectivity itself has come under increasing attack. Some, like *Newsweek*'s Ellis Cose, ask, "Is objectivity (or even fairness) possible when dealing with people from different racial groups and backgrounds? Can any of us be trusted to make sense of lives essentially alien to our own?" But there are also many who dismiss the notion of objectivity outright, such as ABC News's Farai Chideya, who calls it "a shield for ignorance"; or the *Philadelphia Inquirer*'s Acel Moore, who calls it "a cop out" that betrays one's racial heritage; or the *Los Angeles Times*' Sam Fulwood, who calls objectivity, along with the ideal of even-handedness, "one of the many lies we tell about journalism."

The problem, says Tom Rosensteil of the Pew Center's Project for Excellence in Journalism, is that traditional notions of objectivity have been wrongly tarred as "White Guy Objectivity." In many newsrooms today, Rosensteil maintains, "If you started talking about objectivity being the holy grail of journalism, you'd be laughed at as a retrograde thinker, part of the old guard." Many of the new minority journalists recruited under the aegis of diversity reject the thinking of their predecessors in the 1970s and 1980s who said they wanted to be journalists pure and simple, not ethnic journalists. Instead, they see themselves emphatically as "members of a community" whose job is to celebrate and never criticize. Rosensteil explains, "They are not as invested in the core values of the newspaper—not as loyal to the institution. There just is not as much agreement anymore on the basics."

The growing disdain for objectivity results from a convergence of several intellectual fads, some with roots in the multicultural university, saturated as it is with the deconstructionist ethos. To be sure, today's journalists may not themselves have read Jacques Derrida or Michel Foucault, but they have been educated in an ambiance where ideas hostile to objectivity have become the white noise of the academic endeavor, and where "race-class-gender" has become a brain-numbing intellectual mantra.

One of the academic clichés that has penetrated journalism to its detriment holds that "reality" is merely a set of power relationships in which those who are in control—i.e. white people—impose their vision of the social order on people of color, who in turn must defend themselves by creating "competing narratives."

Even more a problem is the spread of cultural relativism. Now so ubiquitous in the thinking of almost everyone educated in American universities that it is seldom examined, this relativism discourages journalists from making the kinds of judgments necessary to see, frame and pursue stories that might question the values and attitudes of minority communities—or to consider whether rejecting the assimilationist ideal is a good thing.

Yet another intellectual fad that has moved from academia to the newsroom is concern over the "contextualization" of facts and imagery and a preoccupation with the problem of minority stereotyping. Echoing the deconstructionist belief that language controls social reality, those concerned with contextualization place an excessive importance on the need to purge news coverage of stereotypes harmful to the public image of minority groups—even if this purging comes at the expense of facts.

Convinced that the media is part of an establishment that has systematically worked to damage black, Latino and gay groups' sense of self-worth even as it cements supremacist attitudes in the white majority, many reporters see their jobs as less a matter of reporting reality than of reducing stereotypes which may "armor our enemies," as one speaker at a National Lesbian and Gay Journalists Association meeting put it. This is an inversion of journalistic responsibility undermining the spirit of curiosity and candor central to the profession. Yet listening to many reporters and editors talk about why certain stories were not done—such as underclass illegitimacy, benefit fraud among illegal immigrants, or gay promiscuity as a factor in the spread of AIDS—one repeatedly hears a concern for validating stereotypes that might "feed a conservative backlash."

One newsroom where concerns for stereotypes have been particularly vexing is the *Washington Post*. In October 1997, the *Post* ran a front-page piece about teenage welfare mothers, illustrating it with a large photograph of fifteen-year-old Kyisha Whittico sucking her thumb as she cradled one of her two children and watched TV. Minority staffers at the *Post*, outraged at what they considered an unflattering image that misrepresented the true face of welfare, protested the story. Siding with them, *Post* ombudsman Geneva Overholser wrote a shrill, scolding column charging that the picture "plays into the most virulently persistent narrow-minded notions: that the face of welfare is black and female."

In order to avoid this kind of situation, many national news organizations now routinely assign reporting beats and editing responsibilities by race, gender or ethnicity—although many news executives deny they do so. Clearly, race-conscious assignments can earn news organizations access in certain communities where distrust or language barriers have posed historical challenges. But combined with the assault on objectivity, the practice of making certain beats color-coded can often give rise to boosterism and overprotectiveness. Forsaking detachment for solidarity, many minority reporters assigned to cover the sensitive issues of race, immigration or gender have often fallen into the trap of identifying too strongly with sources and subjects and allowing political agendas or concerns for community self-esteem to undermine professional detachment.

"I've definitely seen reporters punt on stories because they felt they would reflect badly on their communities," said one *San Francisco Chronicle* editor, mentioning specifically a Latina reporter who refused to join an investigative team on a story about immigration fraud among California migrant workers because she thought the story, which had been brought to the paper by an immigration reform group thought to be "right wing," would confirm stereotypes and feed an anti-immigration backlash.

As Michele Malkin (who dislikes being identified as a "Filipino-American journalist") wrote in a *Seattle Times* column published just after the UNITY '99 convention, "Reporters hired because of racial preferences wind up reinforcing each other, leading to groupthink" and an "unspoken mandate of strict political conformity. If you don't accept the left-leaning agenda of advocacy, you're enabling racism. If you don't support the pursuit of racial hiring goals as a primary journalistic goal, you're selling out."

As I have suggested, the tensions between partisan cheerleading and professional detachment have been especially sharp among gay journalists. Caught between objective reporting and advocacy, between being "a traitor or a faggot," as *New Republic* editor Andrew Sullivan described it, gay journalists have had a hard time balancing pressure from their community for positive imagery, with the obligation to report facts regardless of their political impact. *New York Times* reporter

Frank Bruni has observed that gay reporters covering the AIDS beat "were members of a community with a clear political line on AIDS. They crossed that line at the peril to their social standing. They toed that line at peril to their professionalism."

Illustrations of this loss of professional detachment are not hard to find. During the controversy over the "outing" of Peter Williams, Pentagon spokesman during the first Bush administration, it was gay reporter Victor Zonana and other members of the *Los Angeles Times* gay caucus who made an issue of Williams' sexual orientation. According to one reporter in the newsroom at the time, the efforts represented "out and out flacking" for the gay lobby, antagonistic to the idea of a presumably conservative gay man working for a Republican administration. At the 1992 convention of the National Lesbian and Gay Journalists Association, the late Randy Shilts, whose work exposing health risks of gay promiscuity was central to helping American society come to terms with AIDS, was denounced as "the Dan Quayle of journalism." (In response, Shilts decried what he called "lavender fascism.") At the 1993 NLGJA convention, public television's Robert MacNeil was loudly booed for noting that "There are a large number of Americans who for religious or other reasons think of homosexuality as wrong. And they are as entitled to their opinion as those who think homosexuality is right."

The activist impulse was even more strikingly underlined at the 1995 NLGJA convention during a panel discussion concerning the issue of gay marriage, gay adoption and benefits for domestic partnerships. During this session, gay reporters and activists strategized together on how to put the best "spin" on the issue so that "a majority of people come out in favor of gay marriage," as Philadelphia lawyer and gay political activist Andrew Park explained. The collusion between reporters and activists that occurred during this session represented an obvious conflict of interest. But the session contained an even more startling moment when one panel attendee who identified herself as working at ABC News—a lesbian currently embroiled in a child custody case—stood up and brazenly vowed to use her position in a punitive manner. "I have kept it out of the media so far, but all I can say is that if the judge does not award me custody, she is going to make the news," the ABC staffer told the audience, to great applause.

An increasing number of newsroom feminists have also shown that they no longer think reportorial detachment is an important value. In July 1998, for example, former *Time* reporter Nina Burleigh got her allotted fifteen minutes of fame when she wrote a piece for *Mirabella* magazine describing the physical attraction she felt toward President Clinton while covering the White House in the mid-1990s. She was "quite willing to let myself be ravished" by Clinton, Burleigh wrote, describing her feelings after the president brushed against her legs while playing hearts aboard Air Force One. Later, when asked by the *Washington Post* whether she could be objective about Clinton given such feelings, Burleigh scoffed. "I would be happy to give him a blowjob just to thank him for keeping abortion legal," she told the *Post*. "I think American women should be lining up with their Presidential kneepads on to show their gratitude for keeping the theocracy off our backs." Continuing the flippant tone, Burleigh later wrote that she believed objectivity to be a "Platonic ideal" and insisted that reporters who said they were capable of such "android-like unbiased observational qualities" were being pious and unrealistic.

It is in the ranks of black journalists, however, that one hears the sharpest partisan notes. In her memoir *Voluntary Slavery*, former *Washington Post* reporter Jill Nelson wrote that she functioned not only as a reporter, but also as an "ambassador" from the "mythical monolithic black community." Being hired at the *Post*, for her, was not only a matter of getting a great job but also of legitimizing herself as "a spokeswoman for the race." At a Columbia School of Journalism seminar in 1997, another prominent black journalist, *Time* columnist Jack White, said he was both a good journalist and a "loyal brother" who originally entered the profession "to advance the liberation of an oppressed people."

Of course, many black journalists don't feel obligated to enlist as soldiers for the cause, but the guilt-tripping can be hard to deal with. As the *Washington Post*'s Nathan McCall admitted in his memoir, the experience of being tongue-lashed by a famous civil rights activist for being part of the white media left him deflated and anxious. "It was one of the several times since I had become a journalist that I had the frustrating experience of being cited by other blacks as one of the enemy, as a part of the establishment that worked methodically and consistently to cripple their lives."

The attitude of racial solidarity sometimes manifests as obstructionism by mid-level minority editors intent on suppressing any challenge to their sensitivities. "I have not seen a situation where a truly brilliant piece did not get in the paper," one *Washington Post* reporter told me, "but the resistance and rancor you encounter on certain controversial stories is real." Another *Post* reporter described minority colleagues doing end runs around white editors who challenged them for violating standards of neutrality and fairness or for projecting a simplistic, racially accusatory tone. Still another member of the *Post* staff said to me, "When white editors put up resistance to these kinds of pieces, black reporters often just go over their heads to black editors further up the line, who'll pass it through the system without a problem."

Outside the newsroom, the sharpened partisan edge often turns into outright political involvement. In 1994 Paula Walker Madison, a former Nation of Islam member and now general manager and president of KNBC in Los Angeles, said before an audience of minority journalists, "A lot of us who are gathered in this room have friends who are elected officials or want to be elected officials and frankly in our down time we sometimes coach them in the language of the news media: how to get over and not get caught [in a gaffe]."

White reporters, concerned with violating unspoken ideological work rules laid down by minority colleagues and with being labeled racist, are not in a position to speak out. As *New Yorker* writer Jeffrey Toobin told an audience during a 1997 seminar at the Freedom Forum, "What is at work in the media is not racism but a certain paralysis about race.... There is a fear of being called racist that has a tremendous effect on people."

Meanwhile, black reporters who don't toe the party line have it even worse, exposing themselves to accusations of being racial traitors, Uncle Toms, or sellouts. A case in point was the reaction that black reporter Juan Williams got from some of his peers at the *Washington Post*. Vilifying him for his criticism of black politicians and his unsparing view of the black underclass, self-identified "race woman" Jill Nelson called him an "Uncle Neocon SOB—the perfect Negro at least in the eyes of the white folks because most of the time he writes and apparently believes what Caucasians think black folks should feel and think." As Williams has said of the heat he has taken for holding local black politicians in D.C. to account for their failings, "You are not supposed to go in there and skewer politicians who are self-serving and egotistical and even corrupt. Instead you are supposed to be somehow sympathetic, because they are black." Not that all of the pressure comes from fellow blacks. As Williams has explained, his efforts while an editorial writer at the *Post* to expose malfeasance and corruption of black officials in Washington were met with disdain from white colleagues too, who felt that black politics were in their infancy and that it was unfair to hold black officials to the same standard as whites. Told he was going too hard on Marion Barry, he grew "isolated" and became known as "tainted material."

Even journalists working at less liberal papers can have the rug pulled out from under them. In 1997, Scott McConnell, the editorial page editor at the *New York Post*, set off a firestorm of protest from the local Puerto Rican community over an editorial that raised reservations about statehood for Puerto Rico and urged that Congress move slowly on this issue. At a luncheon meeting that McConnell likened to a show trial, about thirty Puerto Rican politicians, university officials and others took turns denouncing the editorial, saying it was riddled with stereotypes. Refusing to apologize for what he had written, McConnell was called into the publisher's office and told that he had no right to speak for the paper on the issue of Puerto Rican statehood. A few weeks later he was fired.

Describing his ordeal in the journal *Heterodoxy*, McConnell wrote, "I think the collision between me and my bosses was due to deeper shifts in American society. If the traditional duty of the press is to inform and to provoke, the unspoken but ever more enforced imperative of multiculturalism, even for a conservative paper like the *Post*, is 'Do Not Give Offense.' These aims clash, and as I found out, people like myself who commit an unwitting sin against 'diversity,' have to pay the price."


Not to be ignored in assessing the impact of the diversity agenda is the notion that it is the spiritual successor to the Civil Rights Movement of the 1960s. This has allowed civil rights professionals to define the parameters of acceptable discourse on such issues as racism and affirmative action. As Ronald Brownstein of the *Los Angeles Times* says, "Either you accept the civil rights groups' agenda or you are pandering to the right."

Co-opting the aura of the Civil Rights Movement has coated the diversity principle with an overly righteous, even messianic tone that fosters self-stroking and confuses moral imperatives (or what are perceived as such) with professional duty. At the 1999 UNITY convention, presidential candidate Al Gore got a rousing ovation when he demagogically denounced Washington State's Initiative 200, a ban on racial preferences, which had passed the previous year. "How in God's name do some people in our nation get the impression that one generation after *Brown v. Board*, one generation after civil rights laws, all of a sudden we have a colorblind society?"

Such self-righteousness tends to reduce the issues to a matter of "an enlightened us and an unenlightened them—those who need to be shown the light and be battled," as the *Philadelphia Inquirer*'s Art Carey describes it. This is not good news for the cause of nuance and complexity. Complains former *Los Angeles Times* reporter Jill Stewart, "The whole debate gets lowered to a grade school level of oversimplification: good versus evil," with little effort made on the part of the diversity crusaders to see the other side. "They are really quite smug," Stewart maintains. "They are not questioning themselves anymore. The impulse and sensibility that used to enjoy puncturing the platitudes and orthodoxies has been socialized out."

Echoing the revivalist certitude at the 1992 ASNE meeting, the *Times'* new young publisher, Arthur Sulzberger Jr., arrogantly brushed away complaints of political correctness at a panel discussion at the UNITY convention in 1994: "If being labeled PC is the burden we must carry for offering readers a broader, more complete and therefore more accurate picture of the diverse world around us, it is one I bear proudly." On another occasion he said, "If white men were not complaining, it would be an indication we weren't succeeding and making the inroads that we are."

If the consequences for journalism and the society that depends on it were not so serious, this fatuous self-regard and absence of healthy self-criticism could be amusing.

# SEVEN

# Consequences

**B**ill Clinton envisioned his much-ballyhooed 1997–98 Presidential Race Initiative as an important national endeavor that would help cement his legacy in American history. Placing it rhetorically alongside such memorable achievements as the freeing of the slaves and the Civil Rights Movement, he said it represented a chance to "take a comprehensive look at what it will mean when we are truly a multi-ethnic society in a way we have never been before."

According to a White House planning brief described in *U.S. News & World Report,* aides working on the initiative had given high priority to "working with the media to encourage positive depictions of diversity." They saw an important role for the media in other ways too, making Clinton available for exclusive interviews and encouraging him to speak about the Initiative at the annual convention of the National Association of Black Journalists in Chicago that July.

Journalists covering the initiative gave it prominent, earnest and supportive attention. No major news organization drew attention to the fact that the seven-member national advisory panel included no critics of racial preferences (a term now increasingly used to describe affirmative action), a fact that would hardly encourage a free and frank dialogue on the country's most contentious racial issue. Instead, there were glowing profiles of the panel members—all of them strong advocates of affirmative action—extolling their "diversity" and praising their credentials and experience.

The coverage also took a decidedly uncritical stance toward the animating assumption of the president's panel: that the days of the old race-neutral melting pot were over and a new, more explicitly race-conscious "Diversity America" had dawned. In other words, the Race Initiative's guiding premises were controversial and had far-reaching implications that journalists with an understanding of history and racial politics might have paused to question. But the media treated these premises as it had consistently treated the whole concept of multiculturalism right from the beginning: as a fait accompli, which only reactionaries would balk at. Congratulating Clinton for leading the way to a new definition of nationhood in which diversity is "a strength not a weakness," a *New York Times* editorial declared that the Race Initiative might be remembered as a "turning point" for Clinton and for the country. The audience at the National Association of Black Journalists was similarly enthusiastic, applauding vigorously when the president told them that "the paradigm is shifting" and that efforts banning affirmative action in state-funded higher education were "moving the country in exactly the wrong direction."

Despite being launched with such high hopes and grand expectations, the Race Initiative quickly foundered. Instead of encouraging a racial dialogue, it encouraged a monologue from which dissident voices and perspectives were eliminated. Not surprisingly, within six months the one-sided nature of the initiative had earned it public ridicule. Even White House aides admitted that "things had gotten out of hand" and that the inclusion of some conservatives on the panel might have given the project the chemistry it obviously lacked.

Clinton's Presidential Race Initiative soon sank from view. But it left behind a question: Would it have been intellectually more dynamic and politically effective had the press been more skeptical when it was first announced? Might a more rigorous and challenging response to the steering panel have prompted the White House to add at least one prominent opponent of affirmative action when the effort was first announced, thereby giving the panel at least some semblance of ideological balance? While those running the show in the White House were happy to be the object of such sympathetic attention, in hindsight a little more rigor might have helped the initiative make a real contribution to racial understanding instead of becoming just another failed public-relations gesture.

We joke about newspapers being good for wrapping fish or lining hamster cages. But news organizations have always played a crucial role in our democratic political culture, raising important questions and supplying factual information in order that policymakers and the public at large can make sound choices about the kind of society we want to live in. This function is doubly important today as we proceed through a crossroads moment of profound ethnic, racial and cultural change. The country has never been more in need of clear, candid discussion and debate—a service that only a frank, free and forthright press can provide.

But an ideological orthodoxy, very much the product of the crusade to enhance diversity, has made it harder than it should be for the press to spur needed debate. This deprives policymakers and the public of the basic facts and guidance they need in the search for sound, well-informed answers to difficult national questions. Journalism is potentially a kind of map whose accuracy becomes even more important as the nation's social and cultural topography shifts beneath our feet. But when it comes to reporting on the complicated issue of diversity, the press today is an unreliable guide; the map it offers is sketchy in some places, and full of outright misinformation in others. It can lead us in the wrong direction.

Ironically, the ideologically driven pro-diversity coverage has had unintended consequences that undercut the very aims it is meant to bolster. By enhancing sensitivity to the plight of minority groups chaffing at norms defined by the dominant culture, media diversity was supposed to help immigrants, blacks, gays and women. Diversity was also supposed to help the media itself, boosting its credibility—and salability—among groups it had long ignored or long alienated. But the one-sided reporting that has attended this effort has actually been bad for these minority groups, and in many ways has helped to feed a reactionary dynamic. As for helping to make the news industry stronger as a business and as a profession, diversity has often had the opposite effect, turning off many of its consumers and undermining the credibility and authority of the media as a public institution.

But the larger damage has been to the nation's civic culture as a whole and its ability to respond to the changes that unprecedented demographic change has brought and will further bring. As one thoughtful reporter at the *San Francisco Chronicle* reflected, "The ultimate goal is a society with as much racial and ethnic fairness and harmony as possible, and we can't get there unless we in the press are ready to talk about it in full."


In addition to having a questionable effect on public attitudes toward the group whose agenda it means to favor. The increasingly diversity-obsessed and overly sensitive media have also had undesirable effects on American liberalism and its institutional embodiment, the Democratic Party. While conservatives often rail about the unfair disadvantage they labor under because of the press's automatic identification with liberal ideas, values and politics, the truth is that such sympathy has not been an unmixed blessing. In fact, it has contributed to liberalism's political dysfunction by feeding its insularity and arrogance, and abetting its intellectual stagnation. Why engage in self-criticism when the media keeps saying you're right?

Knowing that the press is a sort of echo chamber for its principles has made it hard for liberals to "look skeptically or critically at their own values and assumptions," as liberal historian Alan Brinkley has said. It has also deprived liberalism of a vital source of feedback needed to calculate the effect of its theoretical worldview on the real world. Of course, the press is hardly the sole source of liberalism's intellectual crisis. But the codependency has made it hard for unfashionable ideas on colorblindness and race-neutrality to pierce the shell of reflexive liberal dismissal and suspicion. It has also limited the influence of those inside the liberal camp who have tried to promote a reevaluation of the cult of race, ethnicity and gender.

In fact, there are plenty of liberals who eschew the left's celebration of racial and ethnic group differences and its insistence that narrow group identity should be the organizing principle of our society. According to these thinkers, a society that parcels out opportunities on the basis of race, ethnicity and gender will always be a society full of resentments. As Jim Sleeper, author of *Liberal Racism*, maintains, it is precisely because we are becoming more diverse as a nation that we should reject self-conscious diversity efforts that "work overtime" to heighten the importance of race in American public life. Rather than affirming the centrality of race and subculture, we need to revive popular faith in the ideals of assimilation and integration which have always been at the core of the progressive civic faith.

The transformation of liberalism from a race-neutral to a race-central philosophy was a complicated historical process. But the press, because it put up so little institutional resistance to the growth and spread of this racial essentialism, bears considerable responsibility for the traction it has gained in our culture. The press has been much too ready to side with those of the left who, in a McCarthyesque way, dismiss race-neutral liberals as closet conservatives or cranks. This has made it hard for people like Jim Sleeper to get a fair hearing and, more importantly, for their ideas to get the consideration they deserve.

If the press's reflexive, pro-diversity bias has proved damaging for liberalism in general, it has been exceptionally damaging in the fight to save American liberalism's most cherished cause: racial preferences. Had the media establishment been more aggressive in challenging racial preferences, it would have been difficult for liberal supporters of such policies to ignore their unfairness and the resentment they were generating.

The media preoccupation with race, ethnicity and gender has also obscured the importance of class in American life and the threat posed by the widening inequities of a competitive international economy. At the beginning of the new millennium it often seems as if the press now has only one way of talking about disadvantage, which is in terms of racial and ethnic discrimination. In the process, the wider "moral, social and economic ascendancy of the affluent," as political writer Tom Edsall has described it, has been given short shrift.

By siding so openly with the cultural left on controversial diversity issues, the press has compounded the estrangement and anger of much of the electorate, unintentionally feeding the cultural and political backlash against that agenda. *Atlantic* editor Michael Kelly summed up this dynamic most perceptively during the 1996 presidential campaign. Voters, said Kelly, then writing for the *New Yorker*, "are attracted to ideas that the fourth estate regards as beyond the fringe.

> They want illegal immigration stopped…. They regard affirmative action as reverse discrimination and the welfare system as immoral…. They are distressed by gay marriage, strongly oppose out of wedlock births and would like to see at least some limits on abortion. They believe that these positions are legitimate regardless of whether they violate party orthodoxies or the mainstream media's sense of propriety. They are angry that their views have been ignored and derided.

The press's uncritical acceptance of multiculturalist assumptions may have propelled an anti-diversity backlash in more subtle psychological ways as well. A press that defends affirmative action by insisting that blacks should not have to meet the same meritocratic standards as whites may have encouraged many whites to think that blacks are simply not capable of doing so. A press that refuses to identify crime suspects by race in order to protect the sensitivities of the black middle class might just be supporting the impression that all criminal suspects are minorities.

In telling the public that new immigrants should not have to adapt to the values, practices and language of their new society, the press may, in fact, be saying that they can't, which only reinforces prejudice against them. Feeding the public a steady diet of stories in which immigrants are made to appear as luckless victims of an inhospitable Anglo main-stream could persuade that mainstream to decide that immigrants are too problematic, and that maintaining high volumes of newcomers may not be worth the trouble, especially if we enter a cyclic recession. Immigration sociologist David Hayes Bautista has noted that the more the advocates of Latino victimization press their case, the more fodder they provide for arguments to curtail Latino immigration. What comes across more than anything else, Bautista maintains, is the portrait of "an essentially passive and fatalistic people largely incapable of making it in a modern society."

So too the boomerang effect of images of unrelenting black victimization. As Michael Lind noted in the *New Republic,* "The liberal strategy of de-emphasizing genuine progress made by blacks for fear of promoting [political] complacency has backfired, creating a distorted image of generic black degeneration, like something out the racist tracts of the 1900's in the minds of frightened whites."

The diversity crusade has had another set of unintended, anti-progressive consequences as well that affect the media itself. The obsession with diversity has contributed to a significant decline in morale in the media and induced an attrition of journalistic talent. Although it was not the sole factor that convinced many longtime staffers at the *Los Angeles Times* to take a 1995 buyout offer, disenchantment with the paper's diversity-related excesses were certainly a part of why so many talented veterans left when management made its offer. As one of them told the *Washington Post,* "There is a factionalism at work at this paper which I think is extremely counterproductive. Shelby [Shelby Coffey, then editor in chief] has alienated many of us who are not regarded as minorities."

Others find the intellectual pieties that surround the discussions of race, ethnicity and gender to be confining, amounting to what some have called "ideological work rules." "There is a socialization process at the *LA Times,*" says Jill Stewart, a former reporter for the paper who describes a kind of Gresham's Law whereby the bad drives out the good: "People who care about complexity leave the paper and people who want simplistic answers stay." Adds a reporter who covers race and immigration for the *San Francisco Chronicle,* "I'm really thinking about getting out of journalism. There's too much oversimplification. Everything has to be black and white and people have to demonized for what they think. There's a real lack of subtleties and nuances and polit-ical correctness is a big part of that." Still others leave because even liberal hell-raising just isn't fun anymore. "There are so many people out there who are terminally earnest—they've taken the life out of it," the *Philadelphia Inquirer*'s Art Carey complains.

The diversity drive has also had unintended consequences on the news business's bottom line. Publishers and editors concerned about declining readership and broadcasters worried about a decline in viewers initially imagined that diversity would help news organizations find new minority markets. Arthur Sulzberger Jr. was wrong when he told that 1992 summit conference, "Diversity not only makes good moral sense, it makes good business sense too." In fact, the effort has not become the "cornerstone of growth" that people like Dorothy Gilliam, former *Washington Post* columnist and former NABJ president, predicted. Indeed, according to some analysts, news organizations have staked far too much on what is essentially a myth of the minority news consumer. Research has shown that the minority readership gap was not in fact as big as was originally described, and that most minority consumers want just what everyone else wants: timely information and analysis produced with professional detachment and objectivity, to help them sort through complicated issues. Candor, yes; pandering, no.

The failure of the diversity campaign to deliver on its promise of profitable new minority markets was underscored by the demise of *New York Newsday*. A paper that attempted to position itself as "a thinking man's tabloid," *Newsday* very deliberately tried to appeal to New York's burgeoning minority middle class. Producing some of the most aggressive affirmative action in the news business, it assembled a staff that was demographically correct in terms of race, ethnicity and gender. Very obviously edited with the political sensitivities and concerns of a nonwhite market in mind, it devoted a great deal of attention to race, immigration and gay issues, and hired ethnocentric columnists who very self-consciously presented themselves as representatives of their various "communities."

On its good days, *Newsday* offered windows onto a fast-changing New York, opening the minds of readers to sights and sounds of new immigrant communities and black neighborhoods long neglected by the city's other papers. But more often than not, the paper had what *Village Voice* writer Ellen Willis called, "a self parodying subservience to the worst aspects of identity politics. Overly concerned for minority sensitivities, it patronizingly airbrushed unflattering realities from its racial and ethnic coverage and editorially championed virtually every multicultural nostrum around, often with a clucking, holier-than-thou attitude."

The diversity formula made the paper popular among New York

liberals, particularly those in the media, but it did not translate into a solid readership base. In the spring of 1995, *Newsday*'s parent company, Times-Mirror, closed it down, the paper having lost a significant percentage of the readers it began with in the mid-1980s. In the end, as former *Newsday* editorial writer Jim Sleeper observed, it became the product of a company that "panders to identity in a drive for elusive market shares."

Perhaps more important than the failure to attract new minority consumers is the impact of the diversity agenda on mainstream white news consumers who represent the bulk of the news market. According to surveys, increasing numbers in this group are alienated by diversity-skewed reporting. Much of the American public has the sense that news organizations have a view of reality at odds with their own and that their reporting and commentary come from some kind of parallel universe. Research has also shown that readers find the sanctimonious tone of the press off-putting too. Notes the *Philadelphia Inquirer*'s Art Carey, "The arrogance and the smugness—the sense that we know how people should live and exist—the hectoring and lecturing tone of the paper. These are some of the reasons we're on the slide, why we are losing readers all the time. People are offended. People are alienated."

One of the things this alienation has done is to boost the stock of Rush Limbaugh, Matt Drudge and others in the conservative talk radio and Internet circuit. Talk radio's surge in popularity is one of diversity's most unintended consequences. While it may not always have its facts nailed down, this populist, largely conservative medium does get out the news that mainstream journalists have long ignored or suppressed. It also gives voice to ideas and perspectives that have been shunned or derided by traditional news outlets where diversity-driven orthodoxy has crimped the parameters of acceptable discourse. As Robert Bartley, editor of the *Wall Street Journal*'s editorial page, observed, "If it finds the mainstream press lacking, the public will simply find its own sources of information—as declining readership and network news ratings suggest is already happening." The surging popularity of Fox News Network is a clear manifestation of Bartley's prediction, as viewers abandon what they see as biased traditional networks in favor of an upstart with a broader sense of "fair and balanced."

The most serious consequence of diversity-obsessed journalism is the deepening credibility crisis of the entire news profession. Letting its own preconceived view of the world interfere with its reporting, the press has simply gotten the story wrong too many times—gays in the military, the Kelly Flinn affair, the burning of black churches, and the so-called "resegregation" of higher education—to retain its claim on public respect and authority, and to play the special role it always has in our civic life. "Every story we get wrong causes us to lose more of our credibility and integrity," explains *San Francisco Chronicle* columnist Debra Saunders.

Once the most vital force in America's political life, news organizations have forfeited their leadership role. Today, many of them—even as they crow about "getting right with the future," as *Miami Herald* publisher David Lawrence puts it—seem stuck behind the ideological curve, wedded to a rigid view of diversity that the general citizenry finds both irrelevant and suspect. Far from being a progressive source of new ideas, in many instances the press represents a tired bulwark of liberal dogma and reaction, enforcing a PC conventional wisdom. What progressive reform there is occurs without or despite it, such as reforms in California's bilingual education programs and New York City's quality-of-life initiatives. As *Los Angeles Times* journalist Ronald Brownstein says, "The public is moving beyond the choices we have set up for it and we in the press are often the last to acknowledge that."


In the end, though, the press's diversity crusade has performed its greatest disservice in the damage it has inflicted on the country's broader civic culture. At this complicated historical juncture, with the nation facing the crucial task of absorbing people from different cultures and reapportioning power and rights among various competing groups, the press should be trying to sharpen what the progressive social philosopher John Dewey called the "vital habits of democracy." According to Dewey, these vital habits are: the ability to follow an argument; to grasp another's point of view; to expand the boundaries of understanding; and to debate the alternative purposes of what might be pursued. In addition, a press that was really trying to help society negotiate this tricky historical moment should also be trying to encourage a spirit of public cooperation and public trust that inspires people to rise beyond their own narrow group interest, to feel a sense of shared fate, and to take the steps necessary to build a common future.

In theory, newsroom diversity is supposed to encourage all this. Through the self-conscious inclusion of groups previously marginalized by the dominant white media culture, diversity was supposed to widen and deepen the radar screen on which society sees itself. This would, its champions assured, enrich the mix of images, information and perspectives we consume, putting our collective sense of ourselves in sync with the complexities of our fast-changing society. But in practice, as shown by the coverage I have examined in the course of this book, the media's diversity crusade has proven a failure.

Instead of raising the tone of public discourse and making it more intellectually sophisticated, the diversity ethos has dumbed it down, blunting the public's faculties for reasoned argument just when the edge has never had to be sharper. Instead of expanding the "boundaries of understanding," it has narrowed them; instead of presenting "alternative pursuits," it has conveyed a restricted sense of the available policy options. A sound public debate about such complex issues as affirmative action, immigration, gay rights and race requires intellectual rigor and an appreciation for nuance, not the mind-washing pro-diversity incantations and clichés that the press has tended to favor. A sound public discourse requires candor and frankness, not a scrim of false piety and euphemism that conceals unpalatable truths. A sound public discourse requires the press to be an enemy of political demagoguery, not a vehicle for it.

In the end, the realization of a workable multiethnic and multiracial civic future requires ample reserves of public trust. But an ideological press whose reporting and analysis is distorted by double standards, intellectual dishonesty and fashionable cant favoring certain groups over others only poisons the national well. If the United States is ever to find a framework for handling its ever-increasing multiplicity, it will need: 1) sound policy guidance from journalists capable of producing reporting and analysis uncolored by political dogma; 2) a public confident that it is not being sold an ideological bill of goods that runs counter to the realities it sees in its eyes and feels in its bones; 3) a revival of a civic ideal that transcends narrow subcultural identities. To the extent that the diversity agenda encourages none of these, the task of building a progressive, multiethnic and multiracial society has been made more daunting than it inherently is.

In 1832, Alexis de Tocqueville said that newspapers in young America were necessary in order to unite the many "wandering minds" and individual points of view he encountered in his travels. "The newspaper brought them together," he wrote, "and the newspaper is still necessary to keep them united." Tocqueville's observation seems even more important today, when we face unprecedented ethnic, racial and cultural change, and the expanding diversity of our population makes public consensus more elusive than ever before. Although its legitimacy is under a cloud of its own creating, the news media still plays a critical role in the civic life of the country. As the primary shaper of our civic culture, it sets the terms through which we relate to each other both as individuals and as groups, and provides the mirror by which we understand ourselves as a collective entity. It is important that it tell the full story, and not just the part that fits a preconceived script or affirms a narrow orthodoxy. The mirror the press holds up to our nature, in other words, must show the whole picture.

# Acknowledgments

T hanks to Adam Bellow for launching this ship and exceptional thanks to Peter Collier and Glen Hartley for helping me bring it to shore. Thanks also to Jeff Paul at the Social Philosophy and Policy Center and Larry Mone at the Manhattan Institute, as well as the Bradley, John M. Olin and Earhart Foundations. Special thanks to Liza Featherstone, Jeryl Brunner, Sam Goldman and Jennifer Keiser for research assistance and to Eric Wybanga for astute editorial feedback. I am also grateful to the friends and colleagues who gave me encouragement along the way, especially Fred Siegel, Erich Eichman, Jim Sleeper, James Taranto, Andrew Hazlett, Lindsay Young, Michael Barone, Dan Schechter, Donna Brodie, David Seaman, Bob Moss, Adrian Benepe, Suzan Sherman, Juliet Heeg and Noelle Mills. Finally, I am grateful to my late parents, to my brothers and sisters, and to members of my extended family. As always, their unconditional suppport was key.

# Notes

## Abbreviations

## Preface

1–2 Nicholas Lemann, "What Happened to the Case for Affirmative Action?" *NYT Magazine*, 6/11/95.

3–4 Chavis misconduct and suspension: *BGlobe*, 8/14/97; *LAT*, 6/6/97.

4 *LA Times* on Chavis suspension: *LAT*, 6/20/97.

4 Chavis once affirmative action exemplar: *LAT*, 9/2/97.

4 Chavis no "cautionary tale": *WaPost*, 9/26/97.

6 "I was born into a tribe …": Kara Briggs, NPR, 7/14/99; see also McGowan in *WSJ*, 7/16/99.

8 "armed neutrality in the face of doctrines …": see review of Linda Simon, *Genuine Reality: A Life of William James* (Harcourt, Brace & Co., 1998), in *NYT*, 2/16/98.

## Chapter One: Overview

10 "religious belief in absolutely nothing …": Richard Cohen, *WaPost*, 5/19/98.

10 "the way we view each other …": Arthur Sulzberger Jr., *NYT*, 7/29/94.

11 Pearlstine decree on bonuses: *Columbia Journalism Review*, May–June 1998.

12 "voodoo is a religion …": Dan Seligman, "The Voodoo Style of the New York Times," *NYPost*, 12/7/99.

12 "change pod" at *San Jose Mercury News*: "Rethinking the Race Beat," *Columbia Journalism Review*, July–Aug. 1999.

13 foundation grants for minority journalists: *NYT*, 4/17/2000.

14 proportion of minority journalists: American Society of Newspaper Editors, Year 2001 figures.

15 Barry's support for death penalty: Vanessa Williams, *WaPost*, 4/28/97.
15 1996 study, white view of standards: *Columbia Journalism Review*, May–June 1998.
16 "a shell of its former self": "Living the Crazy Life of an Urban Newspaper," *NYT*, 11/15/99.
16 Lawrence, "how you work it out": *New Yorker*, 6/7/99; also *MacNeil-Lehrer Newshour*, 4/19/95.
16 Dugger, "Will the *Herald* pander …": *New Yorker*, 6/7/99.
16–17 *Miami Herald* on Elián González: see *New Republic*, 5/15/00.
17 "mainstreaming" at *USA Today:* Christopher Caldwell, "Affirmative Sourcing," *Forbes Media Critic* I, no. 1 (1993); McGowan, "Reporting by the Numbers," *WSJ*, 3/18/96.
17–18 *LA Times* buyout: *NYT*, 2/1/93; *WaPost*, 2/1/93.
18–19 Willes' diversity plan: *WaPost*, 5/21/98.
19 Baker, "manipulative, market-driven …": *WaPost*, 5/21/98.
19 del Olmo, "to try to get us …": *NYT*, 10/19/98.
19 Sulzberger, "the single most important issue": *WaPost*, 11/27/93.
19 Sulzberger, "We can no longer …": *NYT*, 9/10/93.
19 Sulzberger, "you can't merely bring …": *Columbia Journalism Review*, Nov.–Dec. 1993.
19 Frankel, "own little quota plan": *New Yorker*, 6/28/93.
20 on Angela Dodson: *NYPost*, 12/21/95; 2/14/96.
20–21 on Patricia Smith: *Brill's Content*, Sept. 1998.
20 Storin on Smith's fabrication: *BGlobe*, 6/21/98.
21 "An honorable commitment …": Ellen McNamara, *BGlobe*, 6/27/98.
21 Hispanic reporter, "a racist institution": *WaPost*, 8/25/98.
21 Raines, "a white guy with …": *NYT* editorial, 8/13/98.
22 Bradlee, "It's been a terrible time …": *WaPost*, 8/25/98.
22 *Post* hiring standards: *New Republic*, 10/2/95.
22 Amity Shlaes controversy: *Investor's Business Daily*, 3/13/95.
22 "The circulation of newsroom petitions …": Scott McConnell, "Who Was Crying Wolf," *NYPost*, 5/6/94.
23 "We have rules …": *Philadelphia City Paper*, 4/28/95.
23 EEOC complaint on *Globe* internships: *WaPost*, 3/17/97.
24 "We couldn't get past …": *NYT*, 11/8/98.
26 Salins, "What are we going to become? …": *WaPost*, 2/22/98.
27 "a dated, even racist concept": *NYT*, 7/19/98.
28 "blindspots" on Crown Heights riot: *NYT*, 7/22/93.
29 "chilling effect": Jeff Jacoby, *BGlobe*, 11/3/97; original column: 10/23/97.
32 "we are still in a racist nation": *WaPost*, 7/28/94.
32 "All someone has to do …": *Esquire*, March 1993.
33 Sulzberger, "First you have to …": *Newsweek*, 10/4/93.
33 Graham, "Looking for a …": *New Republic*, 10/16/95.
33 "unhealthy and unhelpful": see McGowan, *City Journal*, Summer 1993; "just pathetic" and "drivel": *San Francisco Examiner*, 1/23/94.
34 Rotello, "It has gotten to the point …": National Lesbian and Gay Journalists Association Convention, 1995.

## Chapter Two: Race Issues

36–38 Mary Anigbo vs. Susan Ferrechio: *New Republic*, 12/30/96; *WaPost*, 12/16/96.

36 D.C.'s first Afrocentric program: *WaPost*, 8/14/93.

37 *Post's* 560-word item: *WaPost*, 8/14/96.

37 Ferrechio on Anigbo's plan: *Washington Times*, 8/14/96.

37–38 Anigbo vs. Ferrechio: *Washington Times*, 12/4/96.

38 Anigbo conviction: *WaPost*, 8/9/97.

39 *Washington Times* on Anigbo incident: 12/11, 12/12, 12/13/96.

39 "the alleged assault": Colbert King, *WaPost*, 12/14/96.

39 activists who rallied to Anigbo: *WaPost*, 12/7/96.

39 Anigbo's legal and financial troubles: *Washington Times*, 12/11/96.

40 "an incident undeserving ...": Courtland Milloy, *WaPost*, 12/18/96.

40 response to Milloy column: Geneva Overholser, "Inciting or Insightful," *WaPost*, 12/22/96.

41 "potential, pathological ...": Jill Nelson, *Volunteer Slavery: My Authentic Negro Experience* (Noble Press, 1993), p. 62.

41 "American journalism is often misleading ...": Farai Chideya, *Don't Believe the Hype: Fighting Cultural Misinformation about African-Americans* (Plume, 1995), p. 3.

41 "city room of many colors": *Newsweek*, 10/4/93.

41–42 Jacoby, "Blacks and whites think ...": see *New Republic*, 6/22/98.

42 Reviews of D'Souza, *The End of Racism*: Sean Wilenz, *New Yorker*, 10/2/95; Jack White, *Time*, 12/2/95.

42 welfare mothers and "insistent, if unconscious racism": Rosemary Bray, *NYT Magazine*, 11/8/92.

43 "the most maligned moms ...": Les Payne, *Newsday*, 5/12/96.

43–44 Norplant controversy: Howard Kurtz, *Media Circus* (Randon House, 1994), ch. 5; and Richard Bernstein, *Dictatorship of Virtue* (Knopf, 1994), pp. 15–19.

43 "misguided and wrongheaded ...": *WaPost* editorial, 1/20/91.

44 King, "most aggressive" quota plan: Howard Kurtz, "Inquirer Quotas Divide Staff," *WaPost*, 2/26/91.

44 Boldt, "I'm aware how much easier ...": *WaPost*, 1/20/91.

44 Sandra Evans on child protection system: *New Republic*, 10/2/95.

45 Downie, "solution" stories: *New Republic*, 10/2/95.

45 "juvenalization of violence": Leon Dash, *WaPost*, 11/29/98.

45 "What was the point ...": William Raspberry, *WaPost*, 12/14/98.

46–48 Controversy over Richards, *Cocaine True*: McGowan, *WSJ*, 4/14/94.

47 Brent Staples review of *Cocaine True: NYT Book Review*, 2/6/94; Richards' reply: 3/6/94.

48 Moore, "the demonization of black men": *WaPost*, 7/29/94.

49 other papers ran racial identifier: eg. *NYPost*, 5/27/93.

49 *Times* on rape case of Sept. 1996: see Evan Gahr, "Pressnotes," *NYPost*, 10/6/96.

50 first *Times* report on Rolland: *NYT*, 3/1/2000; see also Kay Hymowitz, *WSJ*, 3/3/2000.

50 "A Life of Guns, ...": *NYT*, 3/2/2000.

51   Lynn Hirshberg, "The Godfather of Rap: Suge Knight," *NYT Magazine*, 1/14/96.

52   "damned by some, deified by others …": *WaPost*, 2/28/97.

52   Johnson profile: Jon Jeter, "Facing Life's Trials after Half a Life in Prison," *WaPost*, 2/1/96.

52   Johnson robbery and suicide: *WaPost*, 2/29/97.

52   "There are still hundreds …": Dorothy Gilliam, *WaPost*, 3/1/97.

52   "Terence Johnson died before …": Patrice Gaines, *WaPost*, 3/9/97.

52–53   "Black people always seemed …": William Raspberry, *WaPost*, 3/3/97.

53   "The major sentiment …": David Barstow, "Anti-Drug Tactics Exact a Price," *NYT*, 4/1/2000.

54   Barry's drug habits: Harry Jaffe and Tom Sherwood, *Dream City: Race, Power and the Decline of Washington, D.C.* (Simon & Shuster, 1994), p. 134; see also *New Republic*, 10/2/95.

54   Williams, "black politics were in their infancy …": Kurtz, *Media Circus*, p. 112.

54   "Did your white editor …": *WaPost*, 4/6/94.

55   *Post* tailing Barry on vacation: Jaffe and Sherwood, *Dream City*, p. 198.

55   "white self-satisfied contentment": Nelson, *Volunteer Slavery: My Authentic Negro Experience* (Noble Press, 1993), p. 199.

55–56   Nelson, "Backlash over Barry Case," *WaPost*, 6/9/90.

56   "sullen disgruntled Mau-Mau"; "about the vindication of a reality …": Nelson, *Volunteer Slavery*, p. 213.

56   "Barry Win Transcends City's Barrier," *WaPost*, 9/15/94.

57   "war against the city"; " … its last plantation": Dorothy Gilliam, *WaPost*, 5/24/97.

57   "… a historic figure": Kevin Merida, *WaPost*, 5/22/98.

57–58   Clay's slander of Franks: *WSJ* editorial, 12/2/97; see also Eric Breindel, "Black Conservatives Fair Game for Slander," *NYPost*, 3/5/97; and *NYPost*, 11/24/96.

58   Jackson, "This is no time …": *NYT*, 1/19/01.

58   "insider" journalist story line: *NYPost* Media Watch, 1/23/01.

59   "Hatred by the powerful …": Anna Quindlen, *NYT*, 6/28/92.

59   Lena Williams, "It's the Little Things," *NYT*, 12/14/97.

60   "clash of two cultures": *WaPost*, 1/16/94.

60   blacks more likely to commit hate crimes: *NYT Magazine*, 9/26/99.

60   "We made an agreement …": Mike McAlary, *Daily News*, 3/28/94.

60   "white bitch" etc.: *Staten Island Advance*, 4/8/97; 4/22/97.

61   Breindel, "If this was a long-term boycott …": McGowan, *City Journal*, Summer 1993.

61–62   Crown Heights riot: see McGowan in *City Journal*, Summer 1993.

62–63   *LA Times* coverage of Los Angeles riots: Scott Shuger, *WSJ*, 6/16/92.

63   "reluctance to view those nights …": Itabari Njeri, *LAT Magazine*, 5/31/92.

63–64   Koppel on riots: ABC *Nightline*, 5/1/92, 5/2/92.

64   Korean vs. black deaths: *Sacramento Bee*, 5/5/96.

64   Smith, "It's on now!": *NYT*, 12/9/95.

65   "cracker lover": *NYT*, 12/12/95.

65   "Don't buy from crackers": *NYT*, 12/11/95.

65    "with 20 niggers ...": *Daily News*, 12/9/95.

65    "damn Jew": *NYPost*, 12/11/95; *NYT*, 12/12/95.

65    "a simple morality tale ...": *NYT*, 12/10/95.

65    "the work of a madman": Carey Goldberg, *NYT*, 12/10/95.

65    on Roland Smith: *NYT*, 12/12/95; 12/18/95.

65    Powell as a "social arsonist": Mike McAlary, "Vendor Sows Hate and Reaps Death," *Daily News*, 12/13/95.

65–66    Powell as "an elder statesman": *NYT*, 12/18/95.

66    "Freddy's dead": *Daily News*, 12/9/95; *NYT*, 12/11/95.

66    Slave Theatre rally: *Daily News*, 12/15/95.

66    Purdy profile of Fred Harari: *NYT*, 12/16/95.

67    "The Reformation of a Street Preacher," *NYT Magazine*, 1/24/93.

67    "a sin and a shame ...": *NYPost*, 12/13/95.

67    racially inflammatory statements: *NYT*, 12/11/95; *Daily News*, 12/14/95.

67    Charisse Jones, "Sharpton Bouyant in a Storm," *NYT*, 12/26/95.

67–68    Ronald Taylor coverage: Associate Press, 3/3/2000.

68    Taylor story on inside pages: *NYT*, 3/2/2000.

68    "What took so long? ...": salon.com, 3/3/2000.

68–69    Chinese takeout killing in Queens: *NYT*, 9/9/2000.

69–70    Don Terry on Farrakhan, *NYT*, 3/3/94.

70    Steven Holmes on Farrakhan, *NYT*, 3/4/94.

70    Michel Marriott on Farrakhan, *NYT*, 3/5/95. For material not included in *NYT* see *Chicago Tibune*, 3/12/95–3/15/95.

70    "a smokescreen to conceal ...": Nathan McCall, *WaPost* Outlook, 10/15/95; see also *New Republic*, 11/13/95; Linton Weeks, "Wheel a Farrakhan Deal," *WaPost*, 10/28/95.

70    "belongs to the people ...": Don Terry, *NYT* Week in Review, 12/15/95.

70–71    Michel Marriott, "A Bus to the Black March," *NYT*, 10/16/95.

71    "created the sheltering atmosphere ...": *WaPost*, 10/17/95.

71    "liberating and inspiring ...": Dorothy Gilliam, *WaPost*, 10/21/95.

71    "conspiracy theory and numerology": *NYT*, 10/17/95; see also *WaPost* Style section, 10/17/95.

71    television coverage of Farrakhan speech: ABC, NBC, CBS, CNN, all 10/17/95.

71    "a searing demand ...": Fulwood and Lacey, *LAT*, 10/17/95.

71    "Music expands my breast ...": NPR, 5/30/96.

72    "World Friendship Tour": *WaPost*, 2/12/96.

72    correspondent in Sudan: *NYT*, 2/13/96; see also Hilton Kramer, "A Case of Benign Neglect," *NYPost*, 2/20/96.

72    Farrakhan, "The Jews put the Romans ...": *NYT*, 2/21/96.

72    standing ovation: NABJ convention, July 1996.

73    "grab her by the throat ...": Sam Fulwood III, *Waking from the Dream: My Life in the Black Middle Class* (Anchor Books, 1996), p. 212.

73    Nathan McCall, *Makes Me Wanna Holler: A Young Black Man in America* (Vintage, 1994), 375.

73    Gumbel softballs: Brent Bozell, "Gumbel: Goodbye and Good Riddance," *NYPost*, 1/6/97.

74   "How Race Is Lived in America," *NYT*, 6/4/00–7/16/00.

74   " 'Free at last ...' ": E. R. Shipp, *Daily News*, 5/18/94.

74   Gay Talese in Selma: Jim Sleeper, *Liberal Racism* (Penguin, 1998), pp. 67–69.

74   "black life is still not ...": Rick Bragg, *NYT*, 7/11/97.

75   "concentration camps": Courtland Milloy, *WaPost*, 10/15/95.

75   "Three Strikes" law and African-Americans: *WaPost*, 3/5/96.

75   trafficking offenses, not mere possession: John J. Dilulio Jr., "No Angels Fill Those Cells," *WaPost*, 3/17/96.

75   Center for Equal Opportunity Report: *WSJ*, 12/4/96.

75   race and mandatory sentencing: *WaPost*, 10/9/96.

75   racial disparity in homicide investigations: *LAT*, 12/3/96.

76   Latif shooting: *NYPost*, 1/13/94; *New York Newsday*, 1/13/94.

76   Latif profile: Felicia Lee, "Slain Youth Is Called Nonviolent," *NYT*, 1/13/94.

77   "A picture began to emerge ...": David Firestone, *NYT*, 1/14/94.

78   Michele McQueen on Campbell: *Nightline*, 4/15/97.

78   AP report on Campbell: 4/3/98.

78   Michael Fletcher on Campbell: *WaPost*, 5/23/97.

79–80   James Fyfe on Diallo shooting: *WSJ*, 2/28/2000.

80   "taking on the sinister ...": Bob Herbert, "Going to Extremes," *NYT*, 3/28/99.

80   Bronx DA's statement: Eric Fettman, *NYPost*, 2/1/2000.

80   "Black New Yorkers are in a fury ...": Bob Herbert, *NYT*, 2/11/99.

80–81   police department statistics: Heather MacDonald, *City Journal*, Summer 1999 (also for other aspects of Diallo case).

81   "exchanged the fear of crime ...": *NYT* editorial, 4/2/99.

81   "In Two Minority Neighborhoods ...": *NYT*, 3/29/99.

81   "In a Quest for Peace ...": *NYT*, 2/6/99.

81   "Killing Heightens the Unease ...": *NYT*, 2/14/99.

82   "the large amount of balanced press ...": "The Wrong Venue," *NYT* editorial, 12/18/99.

82   "... a Year of Scorn and Isolation": *NYT*, 1/29/2000.

82   "Defense Wants Diallo Jurors ...": *NYT*, 1/30/2000.

82   "blue wall of solidarity": *NYT*, 2/22/2000.

82   "were understandably outraged ...": "The Message of the Diallo Protests," *NYT* editorial, 2/27/2000.

82   "The hope here is that the cops ...": Bob Herbert, "At the Heart of the Diallo Case," *NYT*, 2/28/2000.

82–83   Reginald Bannerman case: *NYT*, 10/2/99; 11/19/99.

83–84   "Groups Say Crime Reports Affect Hiring," *USA Today*, 8/22/95.

84–85   Fort Bragg swastika incident: *NYT*, 9/20/96 (first report); 12/11/96 (second report); see also *WSJ*, 9/18/96.

85   Good Ole Boys Roundup: NPR *Weekend Edition*, 7/23/95, 7/17/95; *NYT*, 7/20/95.

85   *Times* admits photos were bogus: *NYT*, 8/27/95.

86   black leaders suspicious of ATF: Pierre Thomas, "ATF Troubled by Allegations of Racism," *WaPost*, 6/21/96.

86   *Times* front-page Texaco story: Kurt Eichenwald, *NYT*, 11/4/96.

86    Henderson, "functional equivalent ...": Malcolm Gladwell, *New Yorker*, 11/25/95.

86    "the only thing unusual ...": Bob Herbert, *NYT*, 11/10/96.

86–87   "rare and revealing glimpse ...": Jack White, *Time*, 11/18/96.

87    "that says all the right things ...": Kurt Eichenwald, *NYT*, 11/10/96.

87    front-page correction, epithets never uttered: *NYT*, 11/11/96.

87    *Time* correction only in some editions: *New Republic*, 12/9/96.

87–88   Geddes, "so did the court": see "Texaco Ransoms Image for $170 Million," *WSJ*, 11/12/96.

88    plaintiff's attorney tactics: Holman Jenkins, *WSJ*, 8/12/97.

88    "a leader in the struggle ...": "Texaco's Turnaround," *NYT*, 12/22/96.

88    "racial McCarthyism": Richard Cohen, "The Texaco Story (Cont.)," *WaPost*, 11/12/96.

89    civil rights paradigm: Michael Kelly, *New Yorker*, 7/15/96.

89–94   1996 church fires: see analysis by Michael Kelly, *New Yorker*, 7/15/96; and *Forbes Media Critic*, Fall 1996.

90–91   database search: Michael Fumento, *WSJ*, 7/8/96.

91    not only "disgraceful, it is disgusting": A. M. Rosenthal, *NYT*, 6/11/96.

92    "a myth, probably a deliberate hoax": Fumento, *WSJ*, 7/8/96.

92    truth behind "epidemic of terror": Michael Kelly, *New Yorker*, 7/15/96.

93    "a matter of pervasive racism": see *Forbes Media Critic*, Fall 1996.

93    "an effort to turn back the clock ...": Melissa Faye Green, *WaPost*, 7/1/96.

93    "the social and political climate": Dorothy Gilliam, *WaPost*, 7/6/96.

93    "no evidence of a single pattern ...": Fox Butterfield, *NYT*, 7/21/96.

93    Patrick applauded by NABJ: *LAT*, 9/2/96.

94    National Church Arson Task Force: report issued 6/8/97; see also *WaPost*, 6/9/97; *WSJ*, 6/16/97.

94    "Panel Says Churches Are Still Targets," *NYT*, 6/9/97.

## Chapter Three: Gay and Feminist Issues

95    Jennifer Egan, "Uniforms in the Closet," *NYT Magazine*, 6/18/98.

96    Rich Merritt's porno career: *Advocate*, 2/16/99.

96    *Times'* clarification of magazine story: *NYT*, 2/4/99.

96–97   *60 Minutes* on Kelly Flinn, 5/11/97.

98    Alwood, *Straight News*: *WaPost*, 6/3/96.

98    "Homo Nest Raided ...": *WaPost*, 6/3/96.

98    Jeffrey Schmaltz on coming out: *WaPost*, 9/12/93.

98    more and better coverage boast: *NYT*, 9/10/93.

99    "What remains as certain ...": Frank Rich, "The Family Research Charade," *NYT*, 12/5/98.

100   explanations for ignoring Dirkhising: *WaTimes*, 3/3/01; see also "Hideous Murder Still Not Covered," *NYPost* Media Watch, 3/27/01.

100   Andrew Sullivan on Shepard vs. Dirkhising: *New Republic*, 4/2/01.

101   Elinor Burkett, *The Gravest Show on Earth: America in the Age of AIDS* (Houghton Mifflin, 1995), pp. 11, 13.

101–2   Fumento, *The Myth of Heterosexual Aids*: see *Forbes Media Critic*, Fall 1996; *Washington Monthly*, March 1993.

102   black and Latino AIDS rates: "The Homecoming," *New Republic*, 6/5/95; also, "The White Cloud," *New Republic*, 6/5/95.

102   on denial of the black community: *NYT*, 6/29/98.

103   CDC campaign: *WSJ*, 5/1/96.

104   Act Up "a quagmire of backbiting ...": Burkett, *Gravest Show*, p. 336.

104–5   "Why We Don't Get the Truth about AIDS": NLGJA convention, 10/21/95; see also Burkett, *Gravest Show*.

105   Bruni, "But I never pursued it ...": Burkett, *Gravest Show*.

105–6   Brownstein on Clinton's pledge: see *Forbes Media Critic* I, no. 1 (1993).

106   "This most fascinating ...": Carl Cannon, "The Story in the Closet," *Forbes Media Critic* I, no. 1 (1993).

106   "Fashions in bigotry ...": Anna Quindlen, *NYT*, 1/31/93.

106   "...demonstrable humbug—and bigotry": Anthony Lewis, *NYT*, 1/29/93.

106–7   *Times* on Joint Chiefs and Nunn: *Columbia Journalism Review*, Nov.–Dec. 1993.

107   Jeffrey Schmaltz on Steffan and Peck, see *Columbia Journalism Review*, Nov.–Dec. 1993.

107   "their own reaction...": Catherine Manegold, *NYT* Week in Review, 4/18/93.

107   Existing rules would work; rape statistics: *Columbia Journalism Review*, Nov.–Dec. 1993.

108   Elizabeth Kolbert, "The People Are Heard ...": *NYT*, 1/29/93.

108   "the outbreak of phonathon democracy ...": Anna Quindlen, *NYT*, 1/31/93.

108   "Tomorrow's march can be helpful ...": *NYT* editorial, 4/24/93.

108   Schmaltz, "remarkably restrained": *Columbia Journalism Review*, Nov.–Dec. 1993.

108   *Times*, "the people next door": *Columbia Journalism Review*, Nov.–Dec. 1993.

108   Howard Kurtz on self-censorship: *WaPost*, 5/9/93.

109   "a benighted retreat ...": *NYT* editorial, 9/19/93.

109   "the archaic and homophobic ...": *NYT* editorial, 12/24/93.

109   increase in discharges and attrition: *NYT*, 4/7/98.

109   Timothy Wiener on McVeigh, *NYT*, 4/7/98.

110   "BOYSRCH" e-mail: "McVeigh's Navy," *NYPost*, 5/23/98.

110   "Reggie and Billy": *Newsweek*, 3/20/2000.

111   "Irish and Roman Catholic": *NYT*, 3/14/92.

111   Abrams, "powerful First Amendment right ...": *NYT*, 3/15/92.

111   Siegel on right of association: *WaPost*, 3/15/92.

112   "an embarrassment to the traditions ...": "A Sad Day for the Irish," *NYT* editorial, 3/17/92.

112   "parading bigotry": *NYT* editorial, 1/25/92.

112   "stinks of the stereotype ...": Anna Quindlen, "Erin Go Brawl," *NYT*, 3/14/91.

112   "writ-ensconced and wary ...": Francis Clines, "Gays and Greens and Gulf in Between," *NYT*, 3/13/94.

112   "face of American racism": Orlando Patterson, *NYT*, 3/15/93.

112   "One thing to remember ...": *NYT*, 3/17/93.

113 "What is clear about ILGO ...": Anne Maguire, *NYPost*, 3/12/96.

114 gay marriage in context of Civil Rights: "The Freedom to Marry," *NYT* editorial, 4/7/96; see also Anna Quindlen, *NYT*, 7/5/92.

114 ABC News on Hawaii case, *Day One*, 6/13/94.

114 ABC News, "For Better or Worse: Same-Sex Marriage," *Turning Point*, 11/7/96.

115 hope "is that my students ...": Carey Goldberg, "A Kaleidoscope Look at Gay Marriage," *NYT*, 2/6/2000.

115 "He knew and we know ...": Carey Goldberg, "Vermont Moves Step Closer to Same-Sex Civil Unions," *NYT*, 4/19/2000.

115 "What I don't understand ...": Evelyn Nieves, "Ballot Initiative That Would Thwart Gay Marriage Is Embroiling California," *NYT*, 2/25/2000.

115 profile of Chief Justice Amestoy: Carey Goldberg, "How Vermont Top Judge Shaped Law on Civil Unions," *NYT*, 2/27/2000.

115 "a breakthrough for fairness": "Vermont's Momentous Ruling," *NYT* editorial, 11/22/99.

115 "motivated by blind prejudice": *Seattle Times* editorial, 2/16/95.

115 "What are we afraid of?" William Raspberry, *WaPost*, 1/27/97.

115–16 homosexuals raising children in suburbia: *NYT*, 5/16/96.

116 "there's no studies ...": "For Better or Worse: Same-Sex Marriage," ABC *Turning Point*, 11/7/96.

116 "quality of the parents ...": *Newsweek*, 11/4/96.

116 "have become increasingly broad ...": Carey Goldberg, *NYT*, 12/5/96.

116 "Two Kids and Two Moms," Newsweek, 3/20/2000.

116 "The technical flaws ...": Maggie Gallagher, "The Gay Parenting Science," *NYPost*, 3/30/2000.

116 "In the 70s adults suddenly ...": Maggie Gallagher, "Are You a Homophobe?" *NYPost*, 4/7/2000.

116–18 Stacey and Biblarz study on gay parenting: Erica Goode, *NYT*, 7/17/01.

119 New Jersey Supreme Court ruling, *NYT*, 8/5/99.

119 "As a group with an important role ...": "Bigotry in the Boy Scouts," *NYT* editorial, 8/5/99.

119–20 "loss of support": Kate Zernike, *NYT*, 8/29/2000.

120 five-paragraph correction: *NYT*, 9/6/2000.

120 more mistakes in *NYT* report: *WSJ* editorial, 9/11/2000.

120 parents endorse Scouts policy: Michael Kelly, *NYPost*, 8/30/2000.

120 "How many errors ...": Nicholas Von Hoffman, *New York Observer*, 10/16/2000.

120 " ...*Gays in the News"*: Richard Brookhiser, *New York Observer*, 9/11/2000.

121–22 Jeff Jacoby vs. *Globe* gay lobby: see *U.S. News*, 11/17/97. See also Jacoby, *BGlobe*, 10/23/97.

122n. Kate Millett as "an unsmiling thick-eyebrowed sphinx ...": *Time*, 8/31/70.

123–24 David Shaw on abortion coverage: *LAT*, 7/1–7/4/90.

124 Michelman, "sensationalize": Gerry Gray, *NYT*, 6/19/95.

124–25 *NYT* editorials on partial birth abortion: 4/11/96; 9/26/96.

125  Frank Rich, "Partial Truth Abortion," *NYT*, 3/9/97.

125  Ed Bradley, CBS *60 Minutes*, 6/2/96.

125  Ruth Padawar on partial birth abortion: *Bergen (NJ) Record*, 9/15/96.

125  David Brown, "Late Term Abortions: Who Gets Them and Why," *WaPost*, 9/17/96.

126  *WSJ* on partial birth abortion: editorial page, 9/26/96.

126  "The bill banning the procedure ...": *NYT* editorial, 9/26/96.

126  Fitzsimmons, "... spouted they party line": David Brown, *WaPost*, 2/17/97.

126  unhealthy mothers or unhealthy babies: NPR, 2/26/97.

126  "begins the end run process ...": Frank Rich, *NYT*, 5/11/97.

127  "... a certain kind of suture": Deborah Sontag, *NYT*, 3/21/97.

127  "If anti-abortion activists ...": John Leo, *U.S. News*, 5/10/96.

127  "Journalists are more disproportionately ...": Jonathan Alter, NPR *Media Matters with Terry Eastland*, 1/24/97.

127–28  women in the military: see Stephanie Guttman, "Sex and the Soldier," *New Republic*, 2/24/97; see also Dana Priest in *WaPost*, 9/13/97.

128  "Master of the Sword": *WaTimes*, 6/25/97; *NYT Magazine*, 10/12/97.

129  Martha Radditz on service academy anniversary: NPR, 7/9/96.

129  "a gender neutral tragedy": *NYT* editorial, 3/2/95.

129  Mishap Investigation Report vs. public statements: *San Diego Union-Tribune*, 3/26/95.

130  survey of Gulf War veterans: Eric Schmidt, "War Is Hell; So Is Regulating Sex," *NYT*, 11/17/96; see also *NYPost*, 9/15/97.

130  *Stars and Stripes* reports: Stephanie Guttman, *The Kinder, Gentler Military: Can America's Gender Neutral Fighting Forces Still Win Wars?* (New York: Scribner, 2000), p. 195.

131  USS *Eisenhower* first co-ed cruise: *Time*, 4/17/95; see also David Evans, "The Navy's Blues," *NYT* op-ed, 6/8/96.

131  *Stars and Stripes* on pregnancy in Bosnia: see *Austin Herald Statesman*, 7/23/96; also Suzanne Fields, "Time to Rethink Co-ed Soldiering," *NYPost*, 3/16/97.

132  Aberdeen Training Grounds scandals: "Sleeping with the Enemy," *New Republic*, 6/23/97.

132  "If I didn't feel like cleaning ...": *WaPost*, 5/15/97.

132–33  "the most politically correct institution ...": Richard Cohen, "Duty, Gender, Country," *WaPost*, 4/24/97.

133  John McQwethy on trial of Delmar Simpson: ABC News, 4/17/97.

134  Martha Radditz on female soldiers in Bosnia: NPR, 5/14/97.

134  10 percent evacuation rate: *WaPost*, 12/30/97.

134  Dana Priest on women in Bosnia: *WaPost*, 3/3/97.

134–35  female trainees in "the crucible": NBC *Dateline*, 3/16/97.

136  five retired aviators on Lohrenz: *San Diego Union-Tribune*, 5/14/95.

136  need to enforce a single standard: Robert Caldwell, *San Diego Union-Tribune*, 3/26/95.

136–37  Gary Matsumoto on Lohrenz: NBC *Dateline*, 7/3/96.

137  Martha Radditz on Lohrenz: NPR, 5/13/97.

137  *Newsweek* report on Lohrenz: 3/17/97.

137–38   Admiral Lyle Bien report: see *WSJ*, 2/21/97; see also Robert Caldwell, *Las Vegas Review Journal*, 3/4/97.

138   "these women will make it ...": CMR Notes, Center for Military Readiness, October 1997.

138   "Grounded Pilot Returned to Flight," *WaPost*, 6/21/97.

139   "consistent with those who broke military law ...": *LAT*, 5/22/97.

139   debunking the feminist spin: *Time*, 6/2/97.

140   Tamara Jones on Flinn: *WaPost*, 4/28/97.

140   "underscores the unevenness ...": Elaine Sciolino, "From a Love Affair to Court-Martial," *NYT*, 5/11/97.

140–41   Morley Safer on Flinn: *60 Minutes*, 5/11/97.

140   "She was the poster pilot ...": *American Journalism Review*, Oct. 1997.

141   "a return to Puritanism": Robert Scheer, "Scarlet *A* Stands for Absurdity," *LAT*, 5/20/97.

141   "But what else do high-ranking white guys ...": *American Spectator*, July 1997.

141   Fogelman, "this fact thing": *WSJ*, 7/29/97.

141–42   Lott, "this so-called question of fraternization": *WSJ*, 5/22/97.

142   "a scapegoat deserving of mercy ...": "Trent Lott's Military Mind," *NYT* editorial, 5/21/97.

142   like *The Scarlet Letter:* Maureen Dowd, "Sex, Lies and Bombs," *NYT*, 5/21/97.

142   "blackening" Flinn's reputation: *NYT* editorial, 5/23/97.

142   Gayla Zigo letter: *WaPost*, 7/22/97; *NYT*, 7/22/97.

142   Snowe, "the wing commander ...": Maureen Dowd, *NYT*, 6/7/97.

142   "the absurdity of the military's strictures ...": *NYT* editorial, 6/6/97.

143   "Now that the Air Force ...": "Double Standards, Double Talk," *NYT* editorial, 6/6/97. On Ralston vs. Flinn see also Richard Cohen, *WaPost*, 7/10/97; Thomas Friedman, *NYT*, 6/12/97.

143   "a litmus test ...": James Webb, *Weekly Standard*, 1/20/97.

## Chapter Four: Reporting by the Numbers

144   Houston Proposition A ballot language: "Clarity in Houston," *WSJ*, 6/30/98.

144   "Houston's voters had put a surprising brake ...": *NYT*, 11/6/97.

144–45   Texas judge's reversal: *NYT*, 11/6/97.

145   "Given its exhaustive coverage ...": Michele Malkin, *Seattle Times*, 7/7/98; see also *U.S. News & World Report*, 8/10/98.

145   Michael Fancher reply: "Times Gave Story on Houston Ballot Measure Short Shrift," *Seattle Times*, 7/26/98.

146   Krock, "a senior partner with private business": Paul Craig Roberts and Lawrence M. Stratton, *The New Color Line: How Quotas and Privilege Destroy Democracy* (Regnery, 1995), p. 82.

147   "If they don't like integration ...": J. Anthony Lukas, *Common Ground: A Turbulent Decade in the Lives of Three Families* (Vintage, 1986), p. 504.

147   "The mass media has created ...": Frederick Lynch, *Invisible Victims: White Males and the Crisis of Affirmative Action* (Prager, 1991).

149   "cultural illiterates" could pass: Heritage Foundation, *Policy Review*, Winter 1993.

149 "was only a test": *Chicago Tribune* editorial, 7/27/94.

150 *Buffalo News* and officers' photos: *Columbia Journalism Review,* July–Aug. 1990.

150–52 For a discussion of coverage of the police corruption scandal, see McGowan, "The Corrupt Influence of Diversity Hiring," *WSJ,* 6/20/94.

150 "a third-grader could pass": *Policy Review,* Winter 1993.

151 three hundred officers not allowed to testify: *New Republic,* 1/19/98.

151 113 cops indicted for felonies: see Jaffe and Sherwood, *Dream City,* p. 310.

151 Keith Harriston, "City Paying Dearly for Its 1989–90 Rush to Hire": *WaPost,* 12/16/93; see also *New Republic,* 10/2/95.

151 Horowitz, "disaster in the making": see *New Republic,* 10/2/95.

152 Kelly, "less dynamic ... a life of their own": see McGowan in the *Forward,* 6/25/93.

153 Nelson, "ghouls with guns": see *WSJ,* 6/20/94.

154 Walinsky, "You cannot keep reducing standards ...": *NYPost,* 12/86.

155 24 percent had criminal arrest records: Mollen Commission Report, p. 113.

155 Clifford Kraus, "The Perils of Police Hiring," *NTY,* 9/18/94.

155 *Times* on new screening standards: *NYT Magazine,* 2/9/97.

155–56 New Orleans Police Department: see *NYT,* 5/13/95; 8/18/95; *New Orleans Times-Picayune,* 5/26/96; 5/28/96.

156 Frank's incident reports: *NYT,* 5/13/95.

156 skeleton beneath her house: *NYT,* 11/9/95.

156 series in the *New Orleans Times-Picayune:* 5/26/96; 5/28/96.

157 "following a long entrepreneurial tradition ...": *NYT Magazine,* 3/31/96.

157 "a regular practice ...": Rick Bragg, *NYT,* 7/13/95.

158 "We are committed to a program ...": see Michael Lind, *The Next American Nation* (Free Press, 1995), p. 167.

158 "What is alarming ...": John McWhorter, *WSJ,* 4/15/98.

158 black students admitted with lower SAT scores: *San Francisco Chronicle,* 5/16/95.

159–60 affirmative action at University of Michigan: *New Republic,* 11/22/97.

160 nothing compared with four hundred years: *WaPost,* 12/5/97.

160 "more successful at challenging ...": *Time,* 11/10/97.

160 Georgetown law school admissions: Timothy Maguire, *Commentary,* April 1991.

161 "hasn't a clue ...": "A Numbers Game at Georgetown," *NYT* editorial, 4/18/91.

161 "an expression of the bedrock concept ...": Bob Herbert, *NYT,* 4/18/95.

161–62 socio-economic profile of minority students: Lind, *The Next American Nation,* p. 168.

162–63 declining standards at City College: McGowan, *Lingua Franca,* January/February 1993; James Traub, *City on a Hill: Testing the American Dream at City College* (Addison Wesley, 1994), p. 343.

162 City College's 150th anniversary: Joseph Berger, *NYT,* 5/8/97.

163  "ethnic cleansing": Bob Herbert, *NYT,* 5/28/99.

163  David Gonzalez, "CUNY Cure That Lacks a Disease": *NYT,* 5/13/98.

163  "Assault on Open Admissions": *NYT* editorial, 3/19/98.

163  "If we were to adopt ...": *NYT* editorial, 5/9/99.

163  "students who need ... remedial courses ...": Brent Staples, "Blocking Promising Students from City University," *NYT,* 5/26/98.

164  Connerly requests information; regents doubt administration report: *NYPost,* 9/6/96.

164  wide SAT score disparities: *San Francisco Chronicle,* 5/16/95.

164  preferences to children of alumni: *LAT,* 3/21/96.

165  test scores and grades at Berkeley: Stephan Thernstrom, *The End of Preferences: Behind the UC Admissions Controversy* (Center for Equal Opportunity, 1997).

165  "grades, text scores ...": Peter Applebome, *NYT,* 3/22/96.

165  "admissions officers at selective colleges ...": ABC News, 7/20/95.

165  blacks felt "unwelcome" at Boalt Hall: *LAT,* 3/24/97.

165  "The magnitude of the drop ...": Thernstrom, *The End of Preferences.*

165  "Back to the Future": *Time,* 6/2/97.

165  "Segregation Anew": *NYT* editorial, 6/1/97.

165  "Let Truth Be White": see *U.S. News,* 4/27/98.

166  UC second-tier law schools: *U.S. News,* 12/29/97; see also *U.S. News,* 4/27/98; *NYT Magazine,* 5/2/99.

166  "students of color" vs. Asians: Thernstrom, *The End of Preferences.*

166  "How can you teach Brown ...": Robert Scheer, *LAT,* 9/2/97.

166  overall minority enrollments at Berkeley and UCLA: "The New Segregation," *WSJ* editorial, 5/9/97; see also *U.S. News,* 1/5/98; *LAT,* 7/12/97; 1/29/98.

166  minority enrollments at eight UC campuses: *NYT,* 4/5/2000.

166  Connerly, "The gloom and doom ...": *NYT,* 4/3/2000.

167  "Some Minority Admissions Drop in California": *NYT,* 1/14/98.

167  "white-outs": *U.S. News,* 4/27/98.

167  "little to no difference": *Time,* 6/2/97; see also *U.S. News,* 11/24/97.

167  "had incalculable value ...": *Time,* 6/2/97; see also ABC News, 6/12/97.

167–68  "Wightman apparently relied ...": Gail Heriot, *Weekly Standard,* 7/21/97.

168  career paths of UC Davis medical students: *LAT,* 10/8/97; *NYT,* 10/12/97; 11/8/97; *National Review,* 10/13/97.

168  Rand Institute analysis: Thernstrom, *The End of Preferences,* footnotes.

168  career-path study on front page: *NYT,* 10/12/97; 11/8/97; *LAT,* 10/8/97.

169  Derek Bok and William Bowen, *The Shape of the River: The Long-Term Consequences of Considering Race in College and University Admissions* (Princeton University Press, 1998); see also Stephan Thernstrom, *WaPost* op-ed, 12/14/98; Stephan and Abigail Thernstrom, *Commentary,* Feb. 1999.

169–70  Abigail Thernstrom: *WSJ* op-ed, 10/2/98.

170  *NYT* on *Shape of the River:* Alan Wolfe in Book Review, 10/25/98; news feature and excerpt, 9/9/98; Week in Review analysis and editorial, 9/14/98.

172   "Do you feel …": Jane Pauley, NBC *Dateline*, 1/23/96.

172   "poisoning America's racial well": Dorothy Gilliam, *WaPost*, 5/22/95.

172   "in the end, 'preference' …": Geneva Overholser, *WaPost*, 8/13/95.

172–73   editorial cartoon on CCRI: *San Francisco Examiner*, 6/16/96; see also *LAT*, 9/2/96.

173   "negative and exclusionary": *San Francisco Examiner* editorial, 9/15/96.

173   "words of encouragement": *WaPost*, 10/92/96; see also "The Political Education of Ward Connerly," *San Francisco Chronicle* editorial, 9/7/96.

173   cartoon of Duke in hood and sheet: *San Francisco Chronicle*, 9/6/96.

173   photographs of anti-209 demonstrators: *San Francisco Chronicle*, 11/7/96.

173   *LA Times* poll: 11/6/96.

173–74   California Summer Project: ABC News, 8/16/96; *WaPost*, 6/19/95.

174   CCRI impact on women: NPR *All Things Considered*, 2/4/95; see also NPR, 2/21/96; 2/23/96.

174   "6 million women …": *LAT* editorial, 11/1/96.

174   "It's back to the old boys club …": *LAT* editorial, 7/21/96.

174   "a malevolent little man …": Frank del Olmo, *LAT*, 12/15/96.

174   "perfectly in tune …": "The California Factor," *NYT* editorial, 3/26/95.

175   cartoon of Connerly with KKK robe: *Oakland Tribune*, 9/30/96.

175   "so slimy": George Skelton, *LAT*, 9/31/96.

176   209 as "a fraud": *LAT* editorial, 11/1/96.

176   analysis of votes for 209: *USA Today*, 11/12/96.

176   "the results weren't colorblind": *San Francisco Chronicle*, 11/7/96.

176   "the Joe McCarthy of race relations …": Peter King, *LAT*, 3/16/97.

176–77   "has kept a psychic distance …": Barry Bearak, *NYT*, 7/27/97.

177   Jim Sleeper on Bearak: *Weekly Standard*, 8/11/97.

177   "the Gettysburg …": Ward Connerly, Creating Equal: *My Fight Against Race Preferences* (Encounter Books, 2000), p. 219.

177   "Let's keep the vision …": *Seattle Times*, 9/1/98.

177   "we can beat this thing": Connerly, *Creating Equal*, p. 228.

177   "Show me a reporter …": *Seattle Times*, 10/9/98.

178   *Times* omnibus account: *NYT*, 11/4/98.

## Chapter Five: Immigration

179   on Edwin Sabillon: "Seeking Father, Boy Makes a 3200 Mile Odyssey," *NYT*, 6/29/99.

180   "Boy's Tale Mostly Fiction, Officials Say": *NYT*, 6/30/99.

180   *TImes* postmortem: *NYT*, 7/5/99.

181   nearly half of the Dominican Republic: *NYT*, 11/28/99.

182   "transnational immigration": *NYT*, 7/19/98.

183   *U.S. News* on bilingual education: 9/25/95; see also *WSJ*, 5/14/96.

183   William Celis, "Bilingual Teaching: A New Focus on Both Tongues": *NYT*, 11/27/91.

184   black children used to fill bilingual mandates: *LAT*, 6/1/95.

184   "Plan to Meld Cultures Divides D.C. Schools," *WaPost*, 10/26/94.

184   CEO poll: *The Failure of Bilingual Education* (Center for Equal Opportunity, 1996).

184   "My children learn Spanish in school ...": *The Failure of Bilingual Education.*

185   cursory attention to Latino boycott: *LAT*, 2/13/96.

185   editorials on boycott: *LAT*, 2/26/96; 2/18/96.

185   "While public opinion ...": *Time*, 10/9/95.

186   Latino dropout rate: Alice Callahan, "Desperate to Learn English," *NYT* op-ed, 8/15/97; see also *New Republic*, 6/22/98.

187   Nick Anderson on Miami bilingual education: *LAT*, 5/28/98.

187   polls showed 60 percent Latino support: *WSJ*, 6/4/98; *LAT*, 2/10/98; 4/13/98.

187   "Bilingual Education Lives After All," *NYT*, 10/3/98.

188   Latino poverty and dropout rates: Center for Immigration Studies, Washington, D.C., 1999.

188   "cynically anti-achievement ethos": *WaPost*, 5/10/97.

188   Sosa on traditional values: Lawrence Harrison, *WSJ*, 7/13/99.

188   *LA Times* on Latino culture: 5/18/99.

189   Richard Estrada: *WaPost*, 8/24/99; 8/26/97.

189   "endemic poverty ...": Steven Holmes, *NYT*, 7/26/95.

189   Latina teen birthrate: Laurie Becklund, *LAT*, 3/15/93.

190   "Mingling Two World of Medicine": *NYT*, 5/9/96.

191   Carl Hiaasen column: *Miami Herald*, 7/4/93.

191   Santeria ritual slaughter: Aminda Marquez Gonzalez, *Miami Herald*, 6/11/95.

191   exorcism at King's County Hospital: *NYPost*, 8/16/94.

191   "Has the multicultural bug ...": *NYPost* editorial, 8/25/94.

192   "give religious counseling ...": *NYT*, 11/25/94.

192   "transnational" immigrants and arranged marriages: *NYT*, 7/20/98.

192   Jacki Lydon, "Young Indian-Americans Meld Tradition and Modernism," NPR *Weekend All Things Considered*, 6/19/99.

193   columns on female genital mutilation: Ellen Goodman, *BGlobe*, 10/19/95; 4/7/96; 3/27/97; A. M. Rosenthal, *NYT*, 7/27/93; 6/13/95.

193   "There was no one who said outright ...": Linda Burstyn, *Atlantic Monthly*, Oct. 1995.

194   Ghanaian woman's tall tale: *WaPost*, 12/20/2000; see also *NYPost*, 12/21/2000.

194   Metro section report: *NYT*, 12/21/2000; see also front-page story by Celia Dugger, "U.S. Grants Asylum to Woman Facing General Mutilation Rite," *NYT*, 6/14/96.

194–95   Gloria's Cafe: Doreen Carvajal, "Making Ends Meet in a Nether World," *NYT*, 12/13/94.

195   illegal sale of prescription drugs: *NYT*, 2/2/98; 3/29/99.

195   *LA Times* on underground prescription drug sales: 2/27/99; 5/24/99.

195–96   Mt. Kisco and overcrowded housing: *NYT*, 12/1/96.

196   "But Not Living Next Door": *NYT*, 11/28/99.

196   Chinese restaurant loitering controversy: *NYT*, 11/8/99.

196   "For Latino Laborers, Dual Lives": *NYT*, 1/5/2000.

196    report on Elisa Izquierdo death: *NYPost*, 4/10/96; see also "The Blame for Child Abuse," *NYPost* editorial, 4/10.96.

196–97    memo from CWA counsel: *NYT*, 11/24/95.

197    *Times'* lapses on Elisa: Hilton Kramer, "Cover-Up Journalism," *NYPost*, 12/12/95.

197    *TImes* on different customs of punishment: *NYT*, 2/29/96.

197    Bangladeshi immigrant contractors: Somini Sengupta, *NYT*, 7/6/96.

197–99    Storm Lake, Iowa: Steven Holmes, "In Iowa Town, Strains of Diversity," *NYT*, 2/17/96; see also IBP press release, 5/10/96.

200    "If you are ignorant like me …": Jose De Cordoba, *WSJ*, 7/29/92.

200–4    coverage of Washington Heights, O'Keefe, Garcia: see McGowan, "Race and Reporting," *City Journal*, Summer 1993.

205–6    18th Street Gang, *LAT*, 11/17; 11/18; 11/19; 11/21; 11/27; 12/11, all 1996.

206    *Times* mentions Special Order 40: *NYT*, 12/17/96; see also 12/20/96.

206    Luis Rodriguez op-ed: *LAT*, 2/9/97.

206–8    methamphetamine "superlabs": *NYT*, 5/13/01.

208    Seth Mydans, "Family Ties Strong for Hispanic Gangs," *NYT*, 9/11/95.

208    "In any event, most immigrants …": Anthony Lewis, *NYT*, 4/26/96.

208    161 words on costs of immigrant criminals: *LAT*, 8/12/92.

208    poverty rate for immigrants: Center for Immigration Studies Year 2000 Report.

209    return to Trinidad for Carnival: *NYT*, 2/28/95.

209    immigration and child poverty: see *LAT*, 12/11/96.

209–10    fiscal collapse in L.A. County hospitals: Jeffrey Kaye, *MacNeil-Lehrer Newshour*, 8/2/95.

210    "Immigrants Jam Schools, Invigorate System": *NYT*, 4/26/92.

210–11    New York school overcrowding: *NYT*, 9/8/96.

211    "When one considers …": Nathan Glazer, *New Republic*, 12/27/93.

211    "A Land of Immigrants Gets Uneasy about Immigration": *NYT* Week in Review, 10/14/90.

211    "An Accident of Geography": Seth Mydans, *NYT*, 11/13/90.

211    equivalent of the Berlin Wall: *NYT* op-ed, 12/18/89.

212    almost half of those arrested: Scott Shuger, *WSJ*, 6/16/92.

212    "Chaos at the Gates": *NYT*, 9/11/94–9/15/94.

212    "Americans, pinched and worried …": *NYT* Week in Review, 6/13/93.

212    "rude inhospitality …": *NYT*, 12/13/92.

213    "mean-spirited, impractical …": "Indecent Proposition in California," *NYT*, 10/25/94.

213    Safire, "nativist abomination": see *LAT*, 10/26/94.

213    "the politics of nativism": Anthony Lewis, *NYT*, 1/14/94.

213    "draconian initiative": Al Hunt, *WSJ*, 4/7/94.

213    network TV survey: *Media Watch*, Media Research Center, December 1994.

214    S.O.S. motto, "contempt for immigrants": *LAT*, 9/4/94.

214    Catholic priest "seething with a quiet indignation …": 10/26/94.

214    "Jews being sent back …": *LAT*, 10/3/94.

214    "just like the good Germans …": *LAT*, 10/21/94.

214  Mexican government support to opposition: *LAT*, 8/15/94; see also *LAT*, 11/10/94.
215  Mexicans "might be forgiven …": *LAT*, 8/16/94.
215  L.A. County hospital births: *LAT*, 7/10/94.
215  187 "could open the door …": *LAT*, 12/31/94.
215  "Walking in Fear": *LAT*, 11/20/94.
215  "no longer the land of opportunity": *LAT*, 11/10/94.
216  Chris Hedges, "Condemned Again for Old Crimes": *NYT*, 8/3/2000.
216  Chinese immigrant smuggler: Chris Hedges, *NYT*, 1/10/01.
216–217  *Times* two-part story on deportation policy: *NYT*, 8/10/97; 8/11/97.

**Chapter Six: Reasons Why**
218–24  Teetor vs. Gannett: see McGowan, *WSJ*, 6/18/96.
226  1996 Freedom Forum survey: see Ben Wattenberg, *NYPost*, 4/26/96; "Poll Takes Liberal View of Press," *WaPost*, 5/27/96.
226  "the shameful open secret …": James Glassman, *WaPost*, 5/7/96.
226  "As managers seek …": Michael Barone, *American Enterprise Magazine*, March-April 1996.
227  "There's a certain kind of person …": *Columbia Journalism Review*, July–Aug. 1999.
227–28  "Diversity may have brought attitudes …": Richard Harwood, *WaPost*, 12/16/97. On journalism and class see *WaPost*, 6/23/96; *Columbia Journalism Review*, July 1992; May 1994.
228  journalist opinion on affirmative action, abortion, etc.: *NYPost*, 9/14/2000; on religion see *WaPost*, 5/22/95.
228  "don't understand how journalism …": John Leo, *U.S. News*, 4/20/98.
229  "largely poor, uneducated …": *WaPost*, 2/6/93.
229  "Most reporters covering …": David Frum, *Business Week*, 5/8/95.
229  Downie, "few had spent": quoted in *Business Week*, 5/8/95.
230  Sulzberger, "our cause": *New York Magazine*, 9/30/91.
230  "dramatically narrowed": *New York Daily News*, 3/7/95.
231  Cose, "Is objectivity (or even fairness) …": "Race: America's Rawest Nerve," *Freedom Forum Media Studies Journal*, Summer 1994.
231  Chideya, "a shield for ignorance," *New Yorker*, 9/9/96.
231  Moore, "a cop out": *Philadelphia Inquirer*, 7/27/95.
231  "one of the many lies …": Sam Fulwood III, *Waking from the Dream: My Life in the Black Middle Class* (Anchor Books, 1996), p. 228.
232  "armor our enemies": Andrew Park, NLGJA Convention, 1995.
232  teenage welfare mothers: *WaPost*, 10/19/97.
232–33  "plays into the most virulently persistent …": Geneva Overholser, *WaPost*, 10/26/97; see also *New Republic*, 11/17/97.
233  "Reporters hired because of racial preferences …": Michele Malkin, *Seattle Times*, 7/13/99.
233  Sullivan, "a traitor or a faggot": Frank Rich, *New Republic*, 4/17/96.
233–34  Bruni, "members of a community …": Elinor Burkett, *The Gravest Show on Earth: America in the Age of AIDS* (Houghton Mifflin, 1995), p. 7.
234  "the Dan Quayle of journalism": Burkett, *Gravest Show*, p. 295.
234  Shilts, "lavender fascism": Burkett, *Gravest Show*, p. 295.
235  Nina Burleigh, "I would be happy to give him …": *WaPost*, 7/6/98.

235   White, "loyal brother": Columbia School of Journalism seminar, June 1997.

235   "It was one of the several times ...": Nathan McCall, *Makes Me Wanna Holler: A Young Black Man in America* (Vintage, 1994), p. 306.

236   Walker, "A lot of us who are gathered ...": UNITY Convention, July 1994.

236   Toobin, "What is at work ...": Freedom Forum, 3/25/97.

236   "Uncle Neocon SOB ...": Jill Nelson, *Volunteer Slavery: My Authentic Negro Experience* (Noble Press, 1993).

236   Williams, "You are not supposed to ...": Tucker Carlson, "The Post's Other Op-Ed Page," *Forbes Media Critic,* Summer 1996.

236   Williams on disdain from white colleagues: Howard Kurtz, *Media Circus* (Random House, 1994), p. 112.

237   McConnell, "I think the collision ...": cited in *New York Observer,* 11/17/97.

238   Sulzberger, "If being labeled PC ...": "Myths and Stereotypes," UNITY Convention, July 1994.

238   "If white men were not complaining ...": *New York Daily News,* 3/7/93.

**Chapter Seven: Consequences**

239   Presidential Race Initiative: *U.S. News,* 6/23/97.

240   "turning point" for Clinton: *NYT,* 6/16/97.

240   "the paradigm is shifting": NABJ Convention, 7/17/97.

240   "things had gotten out of hand": Richard Blow, *George,* March 1998; see also *Time,* 12/22/97.

242   Brinkley, "look skeptically or critically ...": E. J. Dionne, *WaPost,* 3/27/98.

242   reject efforts that "work overtime": Jim Sleeper, *Chicago Tribune,* 10/12/93; see also Sleeper, *Liberal Racism* (Viking, 1997).

243   "are attracted to ideas ...": Michael Kelly, *New Yorker,* 3/12/96.

244   Bautista, "an essentially passive ...": *LAT,* 12/29/96.

244   "The liberal strategy ...": Michael Lind, *New Republic,* 6/19/95.

244   "There is a factionalism ...": *WaPost,* 2/1/93.

245   Gilliam, "cornerstone of growth": *Columbia Journalism Review,* Jan.–Feb. 1994.

245   myth of the minority news consumer: *Columbia Journalism Review,* Jan.–Feb. 1994.

245–46   demise of *New York Newsday:* Jim Sleeper, *New Republic,* 8/21/95.

246   "If it finds the mainstream press lacking ...": Robert Bartley, *WSJ* editorial, 11/27/96.

247   Lawrence, "getting right with the future": *MacNeil-Lehrer Newshour,* 4/19/95.

247   Dewey, "vital habits of democracy": Bill Moyers, *Baltimore Evening Sun,* 3/24/92.

248   Tocqueville, "The newspaper brought them ...": *NYT,* 12/29/97.

# Index

Abankwah, Adelaide, 193-194
ABC, 6-7, 63, 92, 100, 116; News, 15, 41, 72, 114, 133-134, 165, 167, 174, 193, 231, 234; *World News Tonight*, 92
Abortion, 29, 123-127, 225, 229, 236
Abrams, Floyd, 111
Act Up, 104, 112
*Advocate*, 95-96
Affirmative action, 1-5, 6-7, 29, 228-229, 239-240; and higher education, 157-170; and police departments, 148-157
Afrocentrism, 36, 71
AIDS, 28, 34, 97, 101-105, 107-108, 180, 231, 233-234
Al-Khadafy, Muammar, 72
Alter, Jonathan, 127
Alwood, Edward, *Straight News: Gays, Lesbians and the News Media*, 98
American Civil Liberties Union (ACLU), 49, 159, 195
American Civil Rights Institute, 176
*American Journalism Review*, 140
American Society of Newspaper Editors (ASNE), 9, 13-14, 20, 23, 229, 238
*American Sociological Review*, 116
Amestoy, David, 115
*Amsterdam News*, 47, 67
Annapolis, *see* U.S. Naval Academy
Ancient Order of the Hibernians, 111-113
Anderson, Nick, 187

Anigbo, Mary, 36-40
Applebome, Peter, 165
Arson, *see* Black church burnings
Aryan Brotherhood, 89
Asian American Journalists Association, 12
Associated Press (AP), 68, 78, 91, 93-94, 100, 145, 180, 222
*Atlantic Monthly*, 59, 193, 243

Bakke, Allan, 2, 4, 168
Balmaseda, Liz, 16-17
*Baltimore Sun*, 11, 106
Balzar, John, 172
Bank of America, 2
Bannerman, Reginald, 82-83
Bargain World, 66
Barnes, Edward, 46
Barnicle, Mike, 21-22
Barone, Michael, 226
Barry, Marion, 15, 54-57, 236
Barstow, David, 53
Bartley, Robert, 246
Bautista, David Hayes, 244
Bayles, Fred, 91
Bearak, Barry, 176-177
Becklund, Laurie, 189
Belluck, Pam, 190
*Bergen (New Jersey) Record*, 125
Berger, Joseph, 162-163
Berger, Ritchie, 219, 223
Biblarz, Timothy, 117
Bien, Lyle, 137
Bilingual education, 25, 27, 33, 183-188, 215, 247